SURVIVING
IN
SYMBOLS

Surviving
in
Symbols

A Visit to the
Pictish Nation

Martin Carver

BIRLINN LTD
with
HISTORIC  SCOTLAND

THE MAKING OF SCOTLAND

Titles Available

WILD HARVESTERS: The First People in Scotland

FARMERS, TEMPLES AND TOMBS
Scotland in the Neolithic and Early Bronze Age

SETTLEMENT AND SACRIFICE
The Later Prehistoric People of Scotland

A GATHERING OF EAGLES: Scenes from Roman Scotland

SURVIVING IN SYMBOLS: A Visit to the Pictish Nation

SAINTS AND SEA-KINGS: The First Kingdom of the Scots

ANGELS, FOOLS AND TYRANTS: Britons and Anglo-Saxons
in Southern Scotland (AD 450-750)

THE SEA ROAD: A Viking Voyage through Scotland

ALBA: The Gaelic Kingdom of Scotland AD 800-1124

BURGESS, MERCHANT AND PRIEST: Burgh Life in
The Scottish Medieval Town

PUIR LABOURERS AND BUSY HUSBANDMEN
The Countryside of Lowland Scotland in the Middle Ages

THE AGE OF THE CLANS
The Highlands from Somerled to the Clearances

First published in 1999 by Canongate Books Ltd.
This edition published in 2005 by Birlinn Ltd,
10 Newington Road, Edinburgh EH9 1QS

www.birlinn.co.uk

ISBN 1 84158 381 2

Series Design: James Hutcheson

Design: Alistair Hodge

Printed and bound by GraphyCems

Previous page
A panorama of Nechtansmere, scene of a crucial battle in 685,
when the Pictish forces defeated those of Northumbria
and put an end to Anglian expansion northwards.

Contents

A Preliminary Gallop   7

Out of Prehistory   10

According to the Neighbours . . .   13

Imprinted on the Land   18

Thinking Christian   40

Open Air Archive – Windows on Pictish Life
and Thought   53

People and Politics   57

How Will We Find out More?   60

Sites Around Scotland   62

Further Reading   63

Acknowledgements   64

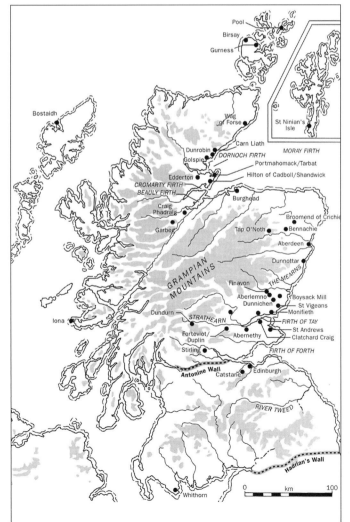

Location Map
Places mentioned
in the text.

Carving a Symbol Stone

An imaginary scene by the shores of the Dornoch Firth in the spring of AD 640. Pictish sculptors expressed ideas in symbols, some in the form of expertly drawn animals, others with distinctive and suggestive but unidentified shapes. The symbols occur all over the eastern part of Scotland and resemble each other closely, so probably relied on a small group of specialists, who travelled about, in the manner of celebrated pipers. They may have carried their patterns in their heads, But here we speculate that some images at least were carried on their bodies, by one of the very oldest forms of picture-making – tattooing with natural dyes. Dyes, or red clay or charcoal were also probably used to bring out the pattern once it had been incised onto the stone. The models for the stones are, foreground, from the Brough of Birsay, Orkney, and in the middle distance, Dunrobin 1, Sutherland.

MIKE MOORE

A Preliminary Gallop

In this book we pay a visit to the Picts, an artistically brilliant people who occupied the eastern part of north Britain around AD 300 to 900, but who then lost their identity and were largely forgotten. Who were they? What did they believe in? What became of them?

The little that was written down about the Picts is owed to authors in neighbouring lands, particularly to the Northumbrian historian Bede of Jarrow and Adomnán of Iona, the biographer of St Columba. Although the Picts left no history of their own, it can be seen from their archaeology that they were a nation of great warriors and artists, who farmed, hunted, defended their territory and set up stone monuments carved with people, animals and symbols. The meaning of the symbols, so elegant and enigmatic, is unknown but they were possibly used to mark territory and make statements about identity and belief. They survive as signposts to show us where 'Pictland' was and urge us to rediscover its people's special contribution to the history of what is now Scotland.

The people nicknamed *Picti* by the Romans patrolling Hadrian's Wall lived in extended settlements with underground stores (the 'souterrains') and buried their dead in stone-lined graves under mounds of earth or cairns of stones. Even though they were not incorporated within the Roman province of Britannia, they were in contact with it, and occasionally provoked Emperors into making punitive campaigns against them. In the 300s, as Roman control weakened, Picts raided more extensively across the Wall, sometimes in league with the *Scotti* or Scots, their neighbours to the west. By the 400s, Roman Imperial control had officially ceased, and Britain, largely a Romanised Christian island, was trying to resist takeover by pagan Germanic peoples from north Germany. It

was at this time that the southern Picts were probably visited by a British missionary, St Ninian of Whithorn, although there is little evidence for a lasting conversion. In the 500s, the northern Picts were evangelised by St Columba, founder of the Scottish monastery on Iona, whose mission may have resulted in some localised Christian communities, but probably not in the conversion of the leaders, or of the people as a whole. During his visit of AD 565, St Columba met one of the first great figures of Pictish history, Bridei son of Mailchon, who, from a base near Inverness, claimed control of a large territory spreading from Skye to Orkney. By this time, the Pictish people had begun to fortify coastal promontories (as at Burghead) or rocky outcrops (as at Dundurn), and to mark their burials or their territory with symbols carved on unshaped stones standing in the landscape.

In the early 600s, the Germanic incomers (Angles), who had been building up a kingdom in Northumbria, began to expand to west and north, and their pagan king Aethelfrith (593–617) undertook ruthless campaigns against the Scots and Britons. His successor, Edwin, also a warlike ruler, accepted Christianity in 627 and aligned with the southern English and with the Church of Rome. During Edwin's reign the disinherited sons of Aethelfrith – Eanfrith, Oswiu and Oswald – were given asylum by the Scots and the Picts, Oswald becoming a Scottish Christian and Eanfrith marrying into the Pictish aristocracy. These events had a significant effect on the subsequent history of all the peoples of the north. Under Oswald (634–641) Northumbria sided ideologically with Iona but, after the Synod of Whitby in 664, it realigned towards Rome and southern England, and began forcibly spreading the message of the Roman–English union.

Potted Picts – a timeline

PEOPLE	PLACES	OBJECTS
300–600		
297 'Picti' mentioned by Eumenius	By 500: Roundhouses with underground stores (**Newmill**)	400s–700s: **Class I symbol stones** (**Dunrobin, Easterton of Roseisle, Bransdbutt, Dunnichen, Birsay, Crichie**)
367 **Picts** and Scots overrun Hadrian's Wall	By 600: forts constructed (**Burghead, Dundurn, Clatchard Craig**); **Portmahomack** occupied	Painted pebbles
Late 400s: St Ninian at Whithorn; missions to the southern **Picts**		
c. 560 **Picts** defeat Scots in Dál Riata	Cemeteries of square-ditched burial mounds (**Garbeg, Whitebridge, Boysack Mill**)	Double-sided combs
563–597 St Columba in Iona; missions to northern **Picts**	c. 450–550: Early Christian cemeteries in Galloway (Whithorn), Lothian, Angus and Fife	500s–600s: disc-headed pins, chains and bracelets (**Gaulcross, Whitecleugh**)
565–585 **Bridei son of Mailchon king of Picts**		
600–700		
617–633 Edwin king in Northumbria; 627 Northumbria converted	634 Oswald erects a wooden cross before the victory at Heavenfield	600s: **Norrie's Law plaques**
	672 **Pictish** army massacred by Ecgfrith of Northumbria	'E-ware' reaches **Craig Phadraig** and **Clatchard Craig** from France
664 Synod of Whitby: Northumbria aligns with Roman Christians	673 Maelrubai founds Applecross	Birsay disc
672–693 Bridei son of Bili king of Picts	681 **Dunnottar** (?) and **Dundurn** under attack	
679–704 Adomnán abbot of Iona, writing his *Life of St Columba*	685 Battle of **Nechtansmere** (**Dunnichen Moss**). **Picts** defeat Angles and kill Ecgfrith of Northumbria	680 Book of Durrow illuminated on Iona
700–800		
c. 706–724 **Nechtan son of Derile king of Picts**	600s–800s: cellular houses in the western and northern isles (**Buckquoy, Birsay, Pool, Bostaidh**). Round-ended houses in Pictland (**Pitcarmick, Wag of Forse**)	c. 700 The Lindisfarne Gospels
710 Ceolfrith of Jarrow writes to **Nechtan**. **Picts** align with Northumbrian Christians		
717 Columban clergy expelled by **Nechtan**		700s–800s: **Class II stone monuments**
729–761 **Angus I son of Fergus king of Picts**. New ecclesiastical foundation at **St Andrews**	600s–800s: long-cist graves in Pictland (**The Hallow Hill, St Andrews**)	
731 Bede's *History of the English Church and People* completed	793–795 First Viking raids on Lindisfarne and Iona	late 700s **St Andrews Sarcophagus** made (perhaps to bury Nechtan or Angus I)
789 **Constantine son of Fergus king of Picts**		780–810 Book of Kells begun on Iona
800–850		
c. 811–820 Constantine son of Fergus king of **Picts** and Scots. New ecclesiastical foundation at **Dunkeld**	c. 800 Norse settlement in Shetland, Orkney, Caithness	c. 800 **St Ninian's Isle treasure**; penannular brooches (**Blair Atholl, Dunkeld**)
	807 Iona community removes to Kells	
820–834 **Angus II son of Fergus king of Picts** and Scots.	839 Major Viking victory over the **Picts**	c. 800 **Tarbat, Nigg, Shandwick, Hilton of Cadboll** stone monuments
840s Kenneth son of Alpin king of Scots and **Picts**	Pictish leaders based at **Forteviot**	
849 Relics of St Columba installed in southern **Pictland**	**Dundurn, Clatchard Craig, Burghead** abandoned	Burghead blast-horn
875 Halfdan attacks **Picts** and Strathclyde Britons	Danes attack Norse in the Isles. Some Norse migrate to Iceland	c. 820 **Dupplin Cross** dedicated to Constantine son of Fergus
895 Turf Einarr, Earl of Orkney		c. 900 Sueno's stone

Pictish people, places and objects in bold

From 670 Ecgfrith, the new king of Northumbria, began to campaign against Pictland, which was perhaps still largely pagan at that date. But Anglian expansion northwards was brought to a halt when he was killed and his army massacred by Bridei son of Bili at the Battle of Nechtansmere in 685.

In the early 700s, king Nechtan son of Derile decided to explore a Christian alliance with Northumbria and sent to Jarrow for information about its church. In the power centres of Tayside and the Moray Firth, a new model of monument appeared, carrying the cross as well as Pictish symbols carved in relief on rectangular upright slabs. But from the mid 700s, Nechtan's successor, the great Angus son of Fergus, again turned the Picts towards the west and the Scottish families of Dál Riata, the Scottish kingdom in the Argyll area. From then on the Pictish–Scottish alliance grew until little distinction could be drawn between the two peoples. In the early 800s, Constantine and Angus II, kings of both Picts and Scots, were supporting major ecclesiastical centres at Dunkeld and St Andrews, and cherishing the relics of St Columba. The new political players on the scene were now the Norse from Norway, raiding and settling in the Northern and Western Isles and coastlands. But in the old Pictish mainland, south of the Moray Firth, the Norse either never succeeded in settling or were soon absorbed.

Judging from their material culture, the Picts were a nation of individual leaders, male and female, who had access to tracts of land and the resources to put up stone memorials. Collectively they had escaped incorporation into the Roman empire, resisted English encroachment and seemed to have been unenthusiastic about the medieval political formula of a single dynastic king supported by the Christian network. When it came, the formula was delivered by their neighbours, and the people of eastern Scotland lost their separate identity. In so far as the Picts had a united view of the world, it survives in their symbols.

Britons, Angles, Scots, Norse – Christians from the west and the south, pagans from the south and the north – during their days on the international stage, the Pictish nation had plenty to cope with and to confront through diplomacy, debate, war, art or marriage. The subsequent centuries have not been kind to the Picts, and have buried them in the shifting sands of undated archaeology or under the tangled vegetation of myth and legend. But, of all the peoples who made Scotland, none had such deep roots in the prehistory of the land or left so individual a legacy. It is a legacy into which modern scholars are now energetically inquiring.

Merger at Dunfallandy, Perthsire, about AD 800

Two seated figures, apparently clerics with thrown back hoods, face each other over a cross. Above them hover the ancestral symbols of the Picts: the Pictish beast, the crescent and V-rod, the double disc. The double disc is also used to 'label' clerics at Logierait and St Vigeans.
HISTORIC SCOTLAND

Out of Prehistory
Backs to the mountains, faces to the sea

Scotland, land of lochs, mountains, moorland, forests and fields, offers many different kinds of terrain for settlers. To the south are rolling hills of rich pasture, drained by clear shallow rivers such as the Tweed. To the west, the high land drops steeply to the Irish Sea, providing a landscape of old smooth rocks and turf, with many thousands of islands. To the east, the weather is drier and there are great areas of fertile arable land, located in coastal enclaves that are almost countries of their own: Fife, the Mearns, Strathearn, the Aberdeenshire plain, the Moray Laigh, Tarbat Ness, the Golspie strip. In contrast to the west, there are few islands, but the coast is cut by three great groups of estuaries, now called by their Scandinavian name, 'firth' (equivalent to the Norse *fjord*). In the north-east, the good land clusters round the Moray Firth, with its neighbours the Dornoch, Cromarty and Beauly Firths. Together these make up a fertile coastline hundreds of miles long, with farms and estates in view of each other and in reach by boat. In the south, the Firth of Tay is flanked by more productive land still, in Angus (and Fife), and further inland by the arable and pasture lands of Strathearn. The Firth of Forth provides a southern border.

Blocking the centre of Scotland lies the mountain range of the Grampians, and the *Druim Alban* ('the spine of Britain') which defines and separates the lands of east and west. In the days before roads and railways, these hills presented a formidable barrier, crossed or avoided by three principal routes: by boat around the north coast; along the ancient routeway of the Great Glen, which by horse and boat connected the Inverness area with Argyll; or across the lowlands between Edinburgh, Glasgow and the Stirling gap – a crossroads where the peoples of the highlands and the lowlands and the North Sea and the Irish Sea have encountered each other over the centuries. In general terms, the natural regions of the Scottish peninsula also made homes for separate peoples: the Scots to the west, the Britons to the south, and the Picts to the east.

Deep roots

The eastern part of Scotland, called here 'Pictland', has had a distinctive material culture over thousands of years, the Pictish culture being only the latest we see. One of the earliest markers of this territory was the *carved stone ball*, an enigmatic artefact, Neolithic or early Bronze Age in date (*Farmers, Temples and Tombs*, p. 40). In the early Iron Age, a particular type of hill-fort was built. Dated to about 600–300 BC, these hill-forts had rubble ramparts laced with timbers which were later burnt – producing such a high temperature that the

The Stone at Broomend of Crichie, Aberdeenshire

This stone is now placed within a much earlier religious site.
RCAHMS

The Provinces of the northern Picts . . . are separated from those of the southern Picts by a range of steep and desolate mountains.

Bede of Jarrow

The Venerable Bede, England's first historian, lived most of his life at a monastery at Jarrow on Tyneside, and died there in AD 735. His writing, especially his great work *A History of the English Church and People*, contains some legends about Pictish origins, but also offers us first-hand testimony of the Picts as he saw them. Bede, being Northumbrian, had his own partisan views about his neighbours to the north.

> The population of Pictland and the Irish who lived in Britain, [were] races separated by the mountains of Druim Alban.
>
> Adomnán of Iona

Adomnán of Iona wrote an adulatory account of the work and miracles of his famous predecessor St Columba. The Life of St Columba contains a number of important contemporary observations on the northern Picts. Adomnán died in 704; Bede called him 'a good and wise man with excellent knowledge of the scriptures'.

The Vitrified Fort at Finavon, Angus
Constructed during the first millennium BC, these important Iron Age centres occupied good defensive positions, as here, and overlooked extensive areas of land. Other famous Iron Age forts include Abernethy (Perth), Monifieth (Angus), and Craig Phadraig, all of which were to have a later association with the Picts.
RCAHMS

rubble fused into a glassy mass, from which they are called *vitrified forts*. Also within our region is a group of settlements consisting of circular buildings in turf or timber, with a very distinctive type of underground store: the *souterrain* (*Settlement and Sacrifice*, pp. 38–9). Souterrains were certainly used throughout the eastern territory and, although most excavated examples date from before AD 200, they may have remained in use for longer.

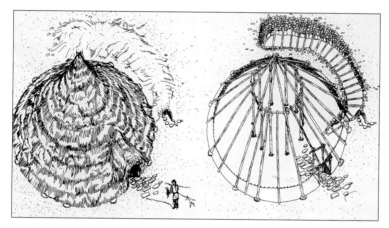

(left)
Roundhouses and Souterrains
At Newmills, near Bankfoot, Perthshire, a large roundhouse about 17.6m in diameter seems to have had a souterrain to itself. The people who lived on these sites were contemporaries of the Romans manning Hadrian's Wall, and had access to Roman objects, such as glass and brooches, although they were not part of a Roman province. The large house at Newmill, the latest in a sequence there, hints at an increase in social status.
HISTORIC SCOTLAND

(left)
The Broch at Gurness, Orkney
Brochs were constructed in the north and west during the Roman Iron Age (first century BC to first century AD), but at some sites occupation continued well into the Pictish period (200s to 800s). Here at Gurness, a Pictish group of cellular buildings was found outside the broch.
M.O.H. CARVER

On the Atlantic coasts of the north and west, there appeared in later prehistoric times a series of circular stone structures: the impenetrable tall *brochs* with their 'cooling tower' shape, and the partially underground *wheel-houses* with their radial walls inside. Such 'Atlantic' buildings continued to develop in the Dark Ages, into figure-of-eight and cellular plans; and although all the examples so far come from the Northern or Western Isles, beyond the Pictish heartland, some of them were probably adopted or adapted by the makers of the symbol stones. So, if these stones are now the main surviving markers of Pictish territory, it was a territory with roots deep in prehistory.

Prehistory of Pictland
Distribution of vitrified forts (Iron Age centres dating to the mid first millennium BC), souterrains (underground stores dating to the period 200 BC–AD 200) and brochs (fortified dwellings of the period first century BC to first century AD). The area which was to become Pictland had a number of prehistoric peoples in the same area; it is also the best arable land in Scotland.

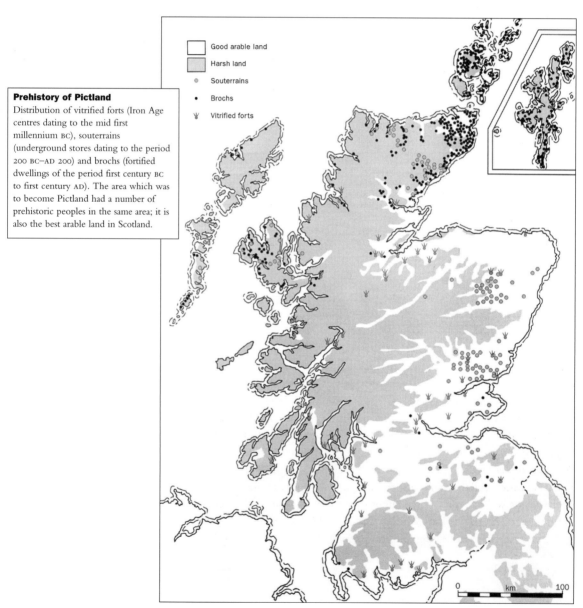

	Good arable land
	Harsh land
◦	Souterrains
•	Brochs
⚭	Vitrified forts

According to the Neighbours . . .

Calling people names

In the first century AD the Romans called Scotland 'Caledonia' – and advanced into the eastern part of it on a mission of conquest under Agricola, the Provincial Governor. In AD 82, somewhere north of the Forth, the Ninth Legion was surprised and nearly lost in a night attack. A year later at *Mons Graupius* (perhaps Bennachie in Aberdeenshire) the Romans confronted a massed gathering of Caledonians under their leader, the heroic Calgacus, and defeated them. A Roman fleet sailed round the north of Britain in a victory tour, but later emperors decided to leave the region out of the Province of Britannia, establishing the boundary first at Hadrian's Wall, then at the Antonine Wall between the Forth and Clyde, and finally at Hadrian's Wall again. The people beyond the walls were known at first by typical British tribal names – Venicones, Decantae, Cornavii – but by the 300s they had acquired a nickname: the Picts or 'the Painted People'. Giving nicknames was a widespread Dark Age habit: the 'Saxons' seem to have been named after the knives they carried and the 'Vikings' after their habit of dodging in and out of creeks.

During the first millennium AD, at least five peoples competed for territory in the land that was to become Scotland: the Britons (in Strathclyde and the southern lowlands), the Scots (in the west, the territory they called Dál Riata), the Angles (in Lothian and Tweeddale), the Picts (in the east) and, from the 800s onwards, if not before, the Scandinavians (in the far north and the west, along the 'sea road'). These peoples spoke different languages, and generally believed in different ways of living, of governing people and controlling land. Over several centuries there was a long-running debate between shifting factions, occasionally breaking into war. Ruined and defunct, but ever lingering in people's minds, was another silent contestant, the mighty ghost of the Roman Empire, a model to which every great British and European leader then, and later, was drawn. In the fourth to the ninth century, that Empire was being reborn as Christianity. These centuries, the time of the Picts, were once known as the Dark Ages because so little was known about them; now they are called the Early Medieval period or (in Scotland) the Early Historic period, a period illuminated both by documents and by archaeology.

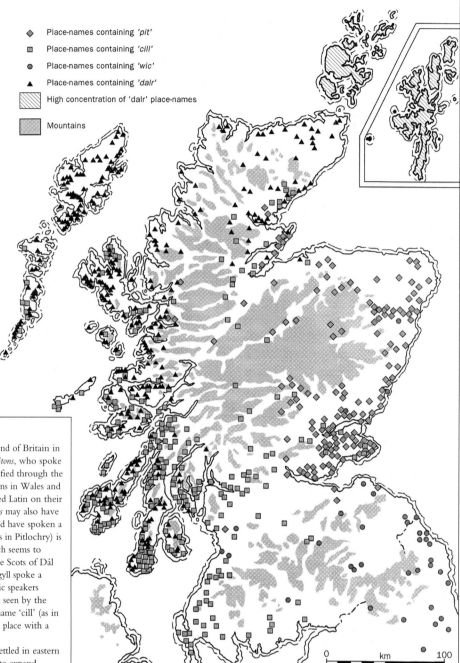

Key:

◆ Place-names containing *'pit'*

▪ Place-names containing *'cill'*

● Place-names containing *'wic'*

▲ Place-names containing *'dalr'*

▨ High concentration of 'dalr' place-names

▨ Mountains

0   km   100

Naming the Land

The inhabitants of the island of Britain in the Iron Age were the *Britons*, who spoke a p-Celtic language, modified through the Roman occupation. Britons in Wales and southern Scotland also used Latin on their memorial stones. The *Picts* may also have been of British descent and have spoken a p-Celtic language. 'Pit' (as in Pitlochry) is a Pictish place-name which seems to mean a farm or estate. The Scots of Dál Riata in the region of Argyll spoke a q-Celtic language; q-Celtic speakers spread eastwards as can be seen by the distribution of the place-name 'cill' (as in Kilmartin) which means a place with a church. The Angles were Germanic-speakers who settled in eastern England, but soon began to expand northwards. Some of their settlements are called 'wic' (as in Berwick), a market or place of exchange. The *Norse*, also Germanic-speakers, were later on the scene. 'Dalr' (valley) (as in Helmsdale) was a name given to their district centres. On this distribution, the Norse do not seem to have settled in the Pictish

What language did the Picts speak?

Contemporaries say that the Picts spoke a different language from their neighbours (the Scots, the Angles and the Britons), and St Columba (a Scot) needed an interpreter when he spoke with them. But we do not know what that language was, and posterity has left us very few examples of it. There are three main sources for the language of the Picts: inscriptions in ogham and Latin letters; a group of names of places; and the names of individuals recorded by writers outside Pictland.

Ogham was a form of writing which originated in Ireland during the first centuries AD; each letter is shown by a group of up to five strokes on a line or the edge of the stone. The scheme may have been based on a five-finger sign language, such as is still used today, where the fingers of one hand in various combinations are laid against the palm of the other. Most of the 36 ogham inscriptions found in Pictland are hard to understand, whichever way up they are read. The Glasgow scholar Katherine Forsyth has shown that many of the ogham inscriptions are in a Celtic language; while the linguist Richard Cox has argued that a number of the inscriptions are in Old Norse. If we go by other inscriptions of the times, in Wales and in Ireland, they ought to represent personal names – even more likely if the stones on which the inscriptions are found can be seen as memorial stones. The few Latin inscriptions, such as those on the Drosten stone or the St Ninian's chape, contain some familiar words but the names can be equally hard to recognise.

> At the present time there are in Britain . . . five languages and four nations – English, British, Scots and Picts. Each of these have their own language; but all are united in their study of God's truth by the fifth – Latin – which has become a common medium through the study of the scriptures
>
> Bede

The Brandsbutt Stone, Inverurie, Aberdeenshire
Two stylish symbols – the crescent and V-rod and the snake and Z-rod – are incised on the face of a stone; along the far edge is a line of ogham script, which reads (from bottom to top): IRATADDOARENS. The linguist Richard Cox believes this inscription to be in Old Norse and reads it (from top to bottom) as CQERA OLLAVAR I, which translates as 'Made by Olafr I …'.

(left)
The Drosten Stone (St Vigeans 1), Angus
This stone carries a worn inscription on its right side which begins: DROSTEN IPE UORET ETT FORCUS.
HISTORIC SCOTLAND

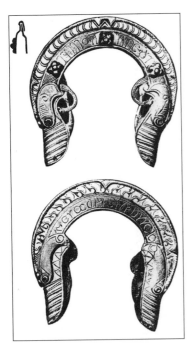

Inscribed 'Sword-chape' from St Ninian's Isle, Shetland

This object carries one of Pictland's rare inscriptions, which has been read 'IN NOMINE D[ei] S[ummi]' on one side, and on the other 'RESAD FILII SPUSSCIO'. Resad and Spusscio could be Pictish names transliterated by an Irish scribe; or Spusscio could be 'spiritus sancti'.

AFTER O'DELL

Some names of Pictish leaders are given in contemporary sources. Bede knew a Bridei son of Mailchon who was the northern Pictish king met by Columba in the 500s, and the southern king Nechtan son of Derile, who adopted the Northumbrian form of Christianity in the early 700s. For other names we have to go to some later medieval documents which are difficult to corroborate. One document says that 29 successive kings of Pictland were called Brude, a word equivalent to Bridei, which seems as though it should relate to Prydein, the Welsh name for Britain. Nine kings are called Drust, which might be the same name as the Drosten which is inscribed on a stone from St Vigeans. The Drosten stone also seems to feature the names Uoret ('Voret') and Fergus, the latter a Scottish name. Other popular names of Pictish kings were Gartnait (at least six of them), and Talorc (at least three). One southern king of the 700s was named after the Roman Emperor 'Constantine'; he was the son of another Fergus, who may have been a Scot.

Adomnán recorded St Columba's meeting with two named Picts:

During the time when St Columba spent a number of days in the province of the Picts, he was preaching the word of life through an interpreter . . . he asked a wizard called Broichan to release an Irish slave-girl, having pity on her as a fellow human-being. But Broichan's heart was hard and unbending, so the saint addressed him thus, saying: 'Know this, Broichan. Know that if you will not free this captive exile before I leave Pictland, you will have very little time to live'. He said this in King Bridei's house in the presence of the king.

An argument about the Pictish language

Expert A: We cannot understand Pictish inscriptions because the Picts spoke a much older language than Celtic or German; it was probably not Indo-European at all, but a survival from the Bronze Age or even earlier, like the language of the Finns or the Basques.

Expert B: The Picts spoke a p-Celtic language, related to British, as the place-names make clear. There was no 'non-Indo-European survival'. The reason that Bede thought Pictish was different from British may have been because the British language had evolved differently either side of Hadrian's Wall.

Expert C: The Picts spoke a p-Celtic language but made increasing use of q-Celtic words as contact with the Scots increased in the 700s, especially since ogham was an Irish method of writing. The personal names belong to a high rank of society where mixing of Britons, Scots and even English people was normal in marriage treaties.

Expert D: The Pictish ogham inscriptions are in Old Norse and commemorate people with Old Norse names. They seem to be quite late, however, perhaps eleventh century (in which case the inscriptions are considerably later than the stones they are marked on).

Where did the Picts come from?

Having no texts written by themselves, the Picts are at the mercy of many theories as to who they were and where they came from. Some believe they were mainly indigenous folk, the descendants of the people who had used the carved stone balls over 2000 years before, and not part of the later Celtic-speaking group which dominated Britain, Ireland and central Europe. This is held to provide the explanation for their apparently unusual customs: their provinces were supposedly inherited through the female line, the new queen taking a male consort for marriage and defence, generally from outside the community.

But, for most modern scholars, the Picts were Britons, just like the Britons of Wales. In this view, there is nothing particularly strange about their customs: they were not matrilinear, they just fell back on female heirs when necessary like the rest of early medieval Europe. Their weapons, forts, social organisation, marriage customs and clothing were not radically different from those of the other communities who occupied Britain and Ireland then. In practice, Irish, British, Anglian and other Scandinavian peoples all no doubt contributed to their ethnic make-up, especially given the likelihood of refugees fleeing from both the south (Britons and Angles) and the west (Irish and Scots). The Picts were not a race, although they may have been briefly a nation.

It is unlikely that new contemporary documents about the Picts will come to light, and our main hope lies in archaeology – the science of understanding people through their settlements, livelihood, burial practice and monuments. This 'material culture', which the Picts imprinted on their land, is slowly coming into focus. Archaeology certainly shows a people who in many ways resembled contemporary warrior-chiefs elsewhere in Celtic and Anglo-Saxon Britain; but in other ways they were distinctive and, whatever the neighbours may have said about them, they had minds of their own.

> *When the Britons had spread northwards and possessed the greater part of the island, it is said that some Picts from Scythia put to sea in a few longships, and were driven by storms around the coasts of Britain, arriving at length on the north coast of Ireland. The Scots refused them permission to settle so the Picts crossed into Britain and began to settle in the north of the island, since the Britons were in possession of the south. Having no women with them, these Picts asked wives of the Scots, who consented on condition that, when any dispute arose, they should choose a king from the female royal line rather than the male. This custom continues among the Picts to this day.*
>
> Bede, around 731

Imprinted on the Land
Memorials and markers: the symbol stones

The symbol stones are what makes the lands of eastern Scotland Pictish. The images are unique, graceful and expertly done – but no one knows for sure what they are intended to represent, or why the Picts etched them on metalwork, rocks, cave walls and upright stones.

The symbols fall into two main groups: the ones that consist of animals we can recognise, and which were once native to Scotland; and the ones that are abstract designs. The animals are the snake, the eagle, the fish (a salmon or cod), the wolf, the horse, the red deer, the bull, the cow and the wild boar. The abstract symbols, which have all been given nicknames, are the first group in the picture: at the top is the 'crescent and V-rod', which is also one of the most commonly occurring. A similar kind of broken rod appears again in the form of a Z in combination with a 'double disc', or with a snake, or with a 'notched rectangle', which has been seen as a chariot and horses viewed from above. The floriate rectangle looks like a metal plaque, and the 'tuning fork' reminds one of a sword. The other symbols are the 'flower' the 'dog's head', looking like a glove-puppet, and most famously the 'Pictish beast' dubbed a 'swimming elephant', which has a dolphin-like face and trails a lappet, or long curly piece from its head, like the foam of a wave; but the little tail and wheel-like feet show that it is a composite beast. The mirror and comb are amongst the most easily recognised of the symbols, since the mirror looks just like bronze mirrors found in late Iron Age Britain, for example at Balmaclellan, while the double-sided comb looks just like ones found on Pictish sites.

(above)
A Dictionary of Symbols
From top to bottom: *Left*: snake, eagle, salmon, wolf, horse, stag, bull, boar. *Right*: mirror and comb, double disc and Z-rod ('Z-rod and spectacles'), crescent and V-rod, snake and Z-rod, notched rectangle and Z-rod, rectangle, sword ('tuning fork'), flower, dog's head. *Bottom centre*: Pictish beast ('swimming elephant').
RCAHMS

(right)
The Crescent and V-rod
An ornate example of the 'crescent and V-rod' from the Hilton of Cadboll stone.
NATIONAL MUSEUMS OF SCOTLAND

The ways the symbols are displayed fall into two kinds or classes. In the first kind ('Class I'), which are the earliest, the symbols are incised onto the face of large boulders or slabs. These stones are found all over the eastern lands, generally positioned on the edge of good arable land where it meets the upland. The second kind ('Class II') are done in relief on upright slabs which are cut to a rectangle, sometimes tapering towards the top. The Class II stones carry crosses, scenes from Christian scripture, everyday life and weird composite beasts. They cluster around the Moray Firth and Tayside, two areas which appear to have been strongly targeted by the Christian missions.

Bronze plaque, Monifieth, Angus
A drawing of a bronze plaque from Monifieth, Angus, suggesting that the crescent symbol could have referred to an ornament of dress or hair (like a tiara). This one (and its owner?) was subsequently appropriated by a Viking whose name, Grimkitil, can be seen scratched on it in runes.
NATIONAL MUSEUMS OF SCOTLAND

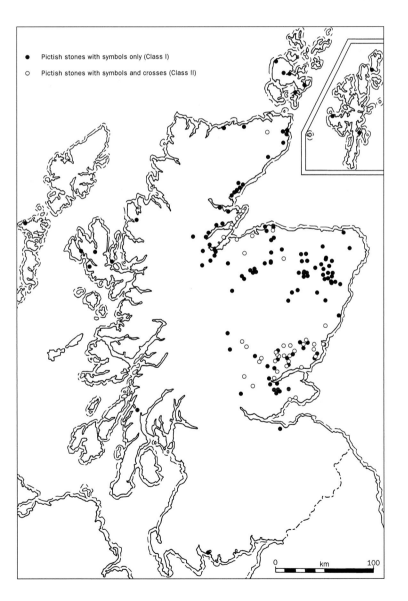

- ● Pictish stones with symbols only (Class I)
- ○ Pictish stones with symbols and crosses (Class II)

0   km   100

Distribution of Class I and Class II Stones
The Class I symbol stones are situated in the areas of good arable land. The Class II stones, which also carry Christian motifs, seem to concentrate in the two main Pictish power centres in the Moray Firth and Tayside.

What do the symbols mean?

Archaeologist Charles Thomas saw the symbols as memories of late Iron Age weapons and equipment; perhaps the symbol stones were used instead of placing these things in a grave: a broken spear, a sword, a chariot. By the time the images came to be used by the Picts, in the fifth to seventh centuries, they were symbols of rank, and indicated who was remembered and who set up the memorial. So the Dunrobin stone could mean 'Erected to a Warrior of the salmon-people by his wife'.

The anthropologist Anthony Jackson has suggested that the symbols are records of marriage treaties, typically made on boundaries of united lands, and especially necessary where descent is through the mother. The symbols refer to families or kinship groups which, occurring in pairs and triplets, record the interest that each family retains. The Dunrobin stone (below) might be interpreted as recording a marriage between the salmon and sword families. The mirror and comb indicates that bridewealth was paid by the senior family.

By contrast, the Glasgow scholar Ross Samson looked on the symbols as representing the elements of names; each symbol gives the sound of a Pictish word or syllable, which joined together make up a name. An equivalent in Anglo-Saxon would be Aethel-wulf – loosely 'Noble Wolf' – or Sigebert 'victory bright'. So in this interpretation the Dunrobin stone might mean 'In memory of a woman called Salmon-sword' or more prosaically 'Here lies Mrs Swordfish'.

Other scholars have shown how the stones are likely to mark out territory or land and most agree that the probable function of the symbols is to celebrate a named individual, in line with practice in neighbouring Celtic and German lands.

Possible Symbol Sources
(*above*) A late Iron Age mirror from Balmaclellan.
(*below*) A comb from Buckquoy.
NATIONAL MUSEUMS OF SCOTLAND

Decoding the Pictish symbols
The stone depicted is known as Dunrobin 1 and it shows a fish, a 'tuning fork' (perhaps a sword?) and a mirror and comb. Most Pictish symbol-fish are thought to be salmon.
RCAHMS

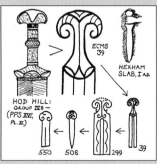

Possible Symbol Meanings
Thomas' derivation of the 'sword' symbol.

What is the date of the symbol stones?

Carving images or patterns on stones is at least as old as the neolithic period, and the Pictish symbols seem to echo Iron Age forms; but the idea of erecting stone monuments was probably learnt from the Romans. The symbols look much the same over a wide area, suggesting a common symbolic language. The symbol stones do not occur in Argyll, traditionally thought to have been settled by Scots from around AD 500, implying that the stones were a later development. However, if the Scottish settlement took place earlier, then the symbol stones could have begun earlier too. The form of the animals on the Pictish stones is close to the animals depicted in the first Insular Gospel books produced in the late 600s, and this has led some to suggest that the Picts' stone carvings started around then, when they had already been exposed to Christianity. But the Pictish symbols are not Christian, and may have been anti-Christian, in meaning.

There are no firm dates, and the story of the Pictish use of symbols is likely to have been long and complex. A beginning between the 400s and 600s is perfectly possible, the symbols being drawn on wood and textiles, or even tatooed on skin, before being transferred to stone. As time went on, the symbols acquired a style which had much in common with art in Ireland and elsewhere in Britain. Monuments bearing symbols on unshaped stones, the so-called 'Class I', were generally superseded by monuments (the so-called 'Class II') which, as well as carrying the symbols of the Picts, also featured those of Christianity. This is thought to have happened following Nechtan's overtures to the Northumbrian Church in 710 and his subsequent expulsion of the Columban clergy (see page 44). The Class II monuments were popular around the power-centres in the Moray Firth and Tayside where the meaning of the crescent and the double-disc remained current alongside the new symbol of the cross. But the erection of Class I monuments could well have continued in areas of less centralised power, like Aberdeenshire. The depiction of solitary animals may also have continued (or even started) later and could have had a different meaning from that of the abstract symbols. One could say that the Pictish symbols were in use from the 400s to the 800s, appearing on unshaped stones during the 600s, and with Christian symbols from the 700s. After about 850, they were apparently never used again, and their meaning was lost.

Burying the dead

During the Iron Age, people in Scotland, as elsewhere in Britain,
were buried in a crouched position in pits, examples being found at
Broxmouth, in East Lothian. But some time in (or after) the Roman
period, the burial rite changed: people were laid on their backs,
sometimes in graves lined with stone slabs, the so-called long-cist
burials. At the Catstane, Edinburgh Airport, excavations of about fifty
of these graves included five cist burials dated by radiocarbon to the
400s or 500s. Excavations at The Hallow Hill near St Andrews
revealed 150 cist burials, 19 of which were dated (also by radiocarbon)

to the 600s or 700s. The majority of the cist burials discovered so far cluster in the south-east of the country, and are less common in the regions which featured the Pictish Class I monuments. But this diagnosis may change: long-cists have also been encountered in Orkney, Shetland, Caithness, Sutherland and Easter Ross. There is a theory that the long-cist burial-rite denotes Christianity, and that it arrived in southern Pictland with St Ninian; on this analysis the long-cists further north may prove to be signals of spasmodic and possibly later conversions. But it may be that the long-cist has deeper roots in prehistoric practice, which favoured the use of stone slab linings, and that there is no direct equation with Christianity.

The Garbeg Cemetery

(above)
On the ground at Garbeg, with Loch Ness in the distance. An observer on this spot in the 500s might have seen the boats carrying the missionary St Columba and his party travelling slowly up the Loch to his meeting with the Pictish leader Bridei son of Mailchon.
M.O.H. CARVER

(above right)
The symbol stone found by the landowner Mr John Younie in association with Cairn no 1.
T.E.GREY FOR INVERNESS MUSEUM

(below)
Plan of the cemetery, with round and square grave-settings.
RCAHMS

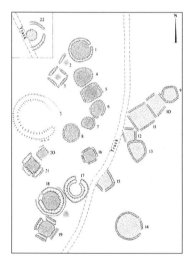

Another signature of Pictish burial recognised in recent years is the use of interrupted ditches around small burial mounds (barrows) formed of earth or stones. The barrows may be round or square in shape and can have a kerb of stones. These cluster around Inverness (for example the cemeteries known at Garbeg and Whitebridge) and Tayside and The Mearns, which puts them in the Pictish zone, but they are still largely undated. Round barrows are found everywhere in Bronze Age Britain, while square ditched barrows are found in Iron Age Yorkshire and France, some famously containing chariots. Square ditched burials have been found in early medieval British areas, such as Wales, but are also known from contemporary Scandinavia.

None of these cemeteries and very few of the mounds have been properly excavated as yet, but we can guess that the square (and round) ditched grave was used during the Roman and Pictish periods. The square ditch at Boysack Mills enclosed a deep grave containing a coffin, in which there was a corroded ring-headed pin which places the burial in the first or second century AD. At Lundin Links, Fife, long-cist burials under cairns have given radiocarbon dates of the 400s to 600s. At Dunrobin an excavated cist grave containing the skeleton of an adult female was dated by radiocarbon to the 500s to 700s. The grave was covered by a rectangular cairn of stones 9.5m by 7m, upon which had originally stood the symbol stone Dunrobin 2. Symbols stones have also been discovered to have been in association with burial mounds at Tillytarmont (Aberdeenshire), Garbeg (Invernessshire), Waternan (Caithness) and Ackergill (Caithness). So, there are now enough cases to lead us to the conclusion that symbol stones were often erected over burials.

Boysack Mills, Angus
Ploughed-down square barrow under excavation at Boysack Mills, Angus
GORDON BARCLAY

Strongholds

In the thousand years before the Romans came to Britain, the large hill-fort was a key feature of society: fortified central places where tribute in the form of food could be collected and stored, and power and ritual exercised. After the Roman Empire had collapsed, forts became important again in early historic Scotland, and took several forms. In general they were smaller and there were many more of them, implying that society was fragmented into numerous small lordships. In the west, small rocky outcrops were fortified – the *duns;* in the east, some of the old Iron Age hill-forts were re-occupied. In the north, the sites of fortified houses – the *brochs* – were re-used. To some extent, these choices were probably determined by the prehistoric sites and the different terrain and materials available. If there were hills, these were fortified and, if there were no hills, stone fortresses were built or re-used, or enclosures dug.

In the Pictish region, only a few strongholds have been investigated or dated as yet, but we can already identify several different kinds. In the southern area, Clatchard Craig in Fife enclosed nearly a hectare with a complex system of ramparts; while Dundurn is a *dun* or small fortified hillock. There are similar duns all along Strathearn, which probably indicates a time when this fertile area was divided between a number of families. Some of these land-holdings appear to have survived or developed into the historic period where they are recorded as thanages, or princely estates. On the east coast, Dunottar is an attractive seaside site, with its beach and rocky promontory, now occupied by a dramatic later castle. It is also expected, but not proved, that some of the great Iron Age forts of Aberdeenshire, such as Bennachie or Tap O' Noth, will have been re-occupied. Burghead, on the southern shore of the Moray Firth, is a promontory fort occupied from the 200s to perhaps the 800s. Craig Phadraig by Inverness was an Iron Age fort recommissioned in the Pictish period. Still further north, some of the sites of Iron Age brochs were exploited: houses of Pictish date have been found outside Carn Liath in Sutherland and Gurness in Orkney. It is not unlikely that there were also enclosures on lowland sites, fortified with palisades and earth banks, prehistoric types that were re-used or imitated in the Early Historic period.

The Fort of Dundurn
Dundurn at the head of Strathearn.
HISTORIC SCOTLAND

The Promontory of Dunnottar
Dunnottar, south of Aberdeen, has an ideal combination of an easily fortified promontory, a beach for landing cargos brought by sea, and a fertile hinterland. This is believed to be the *Dun Fother* recorded in the *Annals of Ulster* as being under attack in 681. Another candidate for *Dun Fother* could be Dinnacaer, an eroded stack north of Stonehaven where five symbol stones have been found. The castle is a much later addition.
M.O.H.CARVER

Four Forts

Craig Phadraig, now on the northern outskirts of Inverness, was an Iron Age vitrified fort, re-occupied in the Early Historic period. In the sixth century, St Columba is thought to have passed up the Great Glen towards the Moray Firth on his mission to the northern Picts. At a certain steep site he met a king, Bridei son of Mailchon, at his fortress and attempted to convert him to Christianity. Craig Phadraig is a favourite candidate for the site of this meeting, and, interestingly, fragments of pottery have been found there, of a type imported from France mainly into Christian countries bordering on the Irish Sea.

Once, the first time St Columba climbed the steep path to King Bridei's fortress, the king puffed up with royal pride, acted aloofly and would not have the gates of his fortress opened at the first arrival of the blessed man.

Adomnán

(*above*)
Examples of E-ware pottery
These potsherds, from seventh-century France, are of a type which reached Clatchard Craig and Craig Phadraig.
EWAN CAMPBELL

(*facing, right*)
Craig Phadraig Summit
The summit seen from the air in 1994.
RCAHMS

(*right*)
The path to Craig Phadraig
The path winds uphill through the woods and the old ramparts of the vitrified fort to the summit which was re-occupied in Pictish times.
M.O.H.CARVER

(*right*)

Finds from Pictish Dundurn

(a) A glass boss; (b) metal-working mould;
(c) a silvered bronze 'dangle' with an
animal-shaped terminal; (d) a decorated
leather shoe.

FROM ALCOCK ET AL.

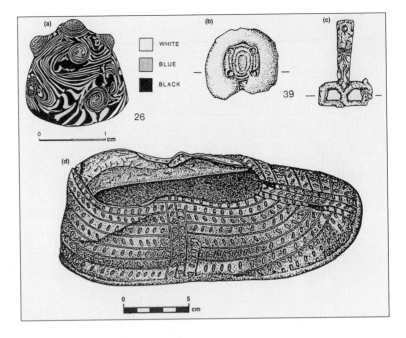

Map of Dundurn

FROM ALCOCK ET AL.

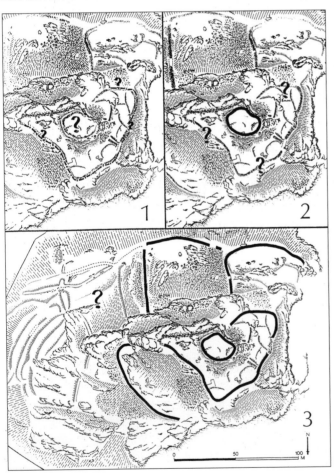

Dundurn is mentioned as being under
siege in ad 683 and its imposing mound
at the end of Strathearn makes it a natural
candidate for investigation. Excavations
by Leslie Alcock have shown that it was
fortified at least three times during a
period dated by radiocarbon to between
the 500s and 800s. The earliest
fortification had a palisade pegged into a
sill-beam anchored in a rock-cut trench.
The stockade was then demolished. Later
(around the 700s) the citadel was fortified
with ramparts built on a framework of
large timber beams (200mm square),
probably fastened together with iron
spikes. In a third phase (around the 800s),
following destruction by fire, the
ramparts were remade with dumps of
rubble. Inside the enclosed summit,
wattle and daub and a midden of animal
bone show that people were definitely in
residence. Finds of a decorated leather
shoe, fine metalwork and glass,
metalworkers' moulds and a crucible give
an exciting preview of a major Pictish
power centre.

Burghead. The great promontory fort of Burghead, on the south side of the Moray Firth, is remarkable for its complex defences. The triple rampart cutting off the headland seems to have been built of rubble and may have originally been a promontory fort of the Iron Age, while the curiously shaped double-enclosure on the headland itself is a development of the Pictish period. This inner fort had walls 8m thick, was faced with stone and built on a framework of timbers fastened with iron spikes about 200mm long. In the north-eastern half of the double-fort there is a magnificent well, originally hewn out of the living rock and approached by irregular stone steps. Excavations in the 1800s found buildings inside this enclosure, with an open space by the well.

Burghead is also famous for its very particular symbol stones: at least 30 are mentioned in old records and six have survived, every one carrying the distinctive portrait of a stocky bull, in a style belonging to the 600s. The bulls are incised on slabs of stone which must have been set up as markers inside or outside the fort. In the bend of the bay to the west is an extensive beach which probably acted as Burghead's landing place. Now the site is much altered. Between 1805 and 1809, a new

Burghead from the Air
Burghead in an air photograph taken from the north-west in 1977, showing the nineteenth-century harbour and the planned town.
RCAHMS

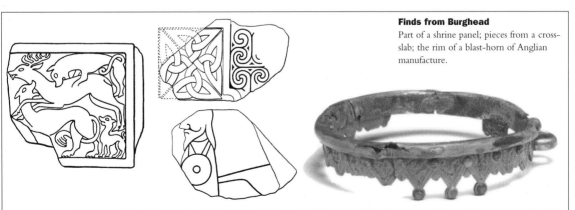

Finds from Burghead
Part of a shrine panel; pieces from a cross-slab; the rim of a blast-horn of Anglian manufacture.

The Burghead Well

The well's gloomy interior calls to mind pagan rituals and retains something of a chilling atmosphere. Adomnán of Iona reported: 'Once when St Columba spent some time in the land of the Picts, he heard reports of a well that was famous among the heathen population. Indeed the foolish people worshipped it as a god because the devil clouded their sense.' St Columba sanctified this well for Christian use, but early Christians too were highly respectful of the power of water, and continued to regard many wells in Scotland as holy places. The Burghead well has also reminded visitors of the practice of execution by drowning; a recorded victim was Talorgen son of Drustan, a king of Atholl, drowned by Angus son of Fergus in 739. However, the Burghead well was refashioned in the 1800s. Tunnelled into the rock, it no doubt followed the line of a spring, and the construction of a cistern and steps to approach the water level would have been a practical measure required to serve the large community of people and animals implied by the size of the enclosed area.
HISTORIC SCOTLAND

(*left*)

Plan and Section of Burghead

This plan was produced by General Roy in 1793. The part of the double-enclosure that lies to the south-west probably functioned as the citadel. This part was quarried away for the construction of a deep water harbour in the early 1800s. The positions of Burghead and its neighbours across the firths – Dunrobin, Tarbat Ness, Craig Phadraig (Inverness) – imply that the Picts were skilled sailors in contact with each other by sea.
SOCIETY OF ANTIQUARIES OF SCOTLAND

Inside the Fort at Burghead

At an entrance to the inner fortress at Burghead in about 800. The rampart is composed of a frame of squared oak beams joined with iron spikes. The wall is 8m thick. The famous bull symbol, virtually unique to Burghead, was incised on panels of stone. They may have been arranged as a frieze around the fort interior, or outside. At the time depicted, the bull emblems were up to two centuries old but were still in place. A war party returns: the spears and square shields of the foot soldiers and the round shields of the mounted warrior are based on images from the Class II stones. The fine sword is composed of the 'tuning fork' symbol, and its chape from the St Ninian's Isle hoard. Around the rider's neck is an Anglo-Saxon blast horn captured in some encounter with the Angles.
MIKE MOORE

harbour was built, by cutting a slice off the promontory and building a waterfront, re-using much Pictish masonry.

The churchyard at Burghead was created in the centre of the triple rampart (at 'Church Street'). Eight pieces of decorated stone from the churchyard and around the village, including fragments from a cross-slab, a cross-shaft and a stone shrine, show that there was already an important ecclesiastical establishment here in the 800s. The inner defensive wall seems also to have received attention at that time because a timber from it has been dated to the 800s. Also found at the site and dating to the 800s is a fragment of an Anglo-Saxon decorated blast-horn with a loop for a carrying strap.

Burghead, site of a significant power centre in the heyday of the pagan kingdom of the northern Picts, was thus still a major player in the complex politics of the 800s, in which Scots, English and Norse as well as Picts had an active interest in the fertile lands of the Moray Firth.

The Burghead Bulls
These are two out of six survivors, all found during repairs to the quay or the houses built in the redevelopment of Burghead in the early nineteenth century.
FROM EARLY CHRISTIAN MONUMENTS OF SCOTLAND / HISTORIC SCOTLAND

The Ramparts of Clatchard Craig

The ramparts as pictured in an air photograph taken in 1932. Excavations and radiocarbon dating show that the fort went through three main phases. In the 400s to 600s, Ramparts 1 and 3 were built on frames of oak timbers; these ramparts were then destroyed by fire. About the 600s, Ramparts 1 and 3 were rebuilt and Ramparts 4–6 added. The fort at this time received pottery imported from France. In the 700s to 800s, Rampart 2 was built, respecting Rampart 1. Inside this smaller fort was a paved hearth, probably marking the site of a rectangular building, and the occupants made penannular brooches.

RCAHMS

Clatchard Craig. Standing on a rocky promontory above the River Tay, the Pictish site of Clatchard Craig has now alas been entirely quarried away. It had probably been in use during the Iron Age and before, but excavations showed that its extant complex of six ramparts belonged to the Pictish period. Finds included imported pottery and glass and clay moulds for making brooches.

Excavations at Clatchard Craig

Excavations across Rampart 2 in progress in 1959.

HISTORIC SCOTLAND

How did the Picts make a living?
What did they eat?

Agriculture was the most important economic activity before the industrial revolution – a full-time job for most and vital for the rest. It can probably be assumed that the Picts farmed Scotland much as people did before and have done since. The native cereals were bere barley and oats. Wheat was probably rare but its cultivation was always possible in many areas of the eastern coastlands, both south and north. Grain was ground with rotary querns, which have been found on sites dated from the Iron Age to the 1800s. Cattle were of paramount importance all over Britain, but especially in the north and west; sheep, of the thin hairy kind, grazed the uplands and produced wool, milk and cheese, and pigs foraged in the woods, occasionally interbreeding with the wild boar. Salmon ran in the rivers and there were shellfish by the shore; sea-fishing was perfectly possible and on the rocky ledges there were gannets' and puffins' eggs. All these we can guess, from what there is now, what was drawn on the symbol stones, and sometimes from the collections of bones and seeds that have so far been found in archaeological work.

The principal goal of human beings is to liberate themselves sufficiently from the daily grind to enjoy the good things of life. And when agriculture produced a surplus, there was an aristocratic class ready to collect it and expend it. Some of the surplus no doubt went to feed the carvers who produced the symbol stones, who could have travelled from lord to local lord. Other surplus went to feed the metal-smiths, another group of important craftsmen. From the metal-smiths came ornamental bridles for horses, weapons and brooches which, with furs and fleeces and flowing cloaks, contrived to make wealthy men and women magnificent in their progress through the straths. Weapons were not only used for warring on the neighbours, but for hunting game, then probably, as for many since, the greatest passion of all. Judging by the pictures on the stones, stag-hunting with hounds was the top-ranking thrill. Other pastimes can be guessed at: board-games, like drafts, were a favourite with most Dark Age peoples. The Picts also painted

Drinking on Horseback
An endearing figure from Invergowrie, Dundee. Drinking from horns, pitchers and bowls no doubt extended beyond the quenching of thirst and found a role, then as now, in providing comfort to the old and supporting the young in social confrontation, ritual and recreation.
NATIONAL MUSEUMS OF SCOTLAND

pebbles, which may have had some role in a game, or were imbued with the magical properties hinted at by Adomnán. Men and women combed their hair, so that they looked good and to remove fleas and nits (the small double-sided comb is still used for this purpose today). Hunting, love-making, parties with cakes and ale: we need not doubt that, then as now, when times were good, life was good, and fun was had.

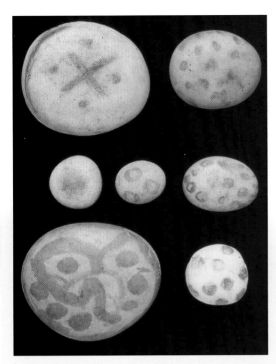

Painted Pebbles from Jarlshof, Shetland, and Keiss, Caithness

According to Adomnán of Iona: 'leaving king Bridei's house, St Columba came to the River Ness, where he picked up a white pebble from the river and said to his companions: "Mark this white stone through which the Lord will bring about the healing of many sick people among this heathen race". ...The stone was dipped in some water, where, in defiance of nature, it floated miraculously on the surface of the water like an apple or a nut....The stone was kept in the royal treasury. Whenever it was put into water, it floated and by the Lord's mercy it brought about the healing of many ailments among the people.'

NATIONAL MUSEUMS OF SCOTLAND

Hunting: The Noblest Sport

A party of Pictish aristocrats prepare to go hunting in Strathearn about AD 800. The hounds show that most will be pursuing the red deer, but one lord has been given a hawk by a lady, riding side-saddle. The drinking bowl, as a stirrup cup, is being passed round to steady excited nerves. All the images on the carved stones point to the Picts having had magnificent horses, expertly bred and schooled, and up to 15 hands in height. The wealthy youngster in the foreground shows off her bridle with its silver and niello strap-distributors.

MIKE MOORE

Pictish settlement

Within the forts, and in numerous farmsteads around them, there must have been many houses, but very few have been found and successfully excavated as yet. The type of house favoured in the later Iron Age, round and accompanied by underground storage chambers (souterrains), may have continued in use in early historic times. A new type of turf house, long and thin and round-ended like later Norse houses, has been identified in Perthshire and Angus . In the far north, houses of a similar shape are built of stone slabs, as at the Wag of Forse. In the northern and western islands, the Picts or their contemporaries built 'cellular' houses – a figure of eight as at Buckquoy (Orkney) or Bostaidh (Lewis), or round rooms surrounding a central space, like the 'shamrock' house built originally into the ruins of the Broch of Gurness.

Ploughed-down Settlement of Pitcarmick Type at Lathrisk, Fife
RCAHMS

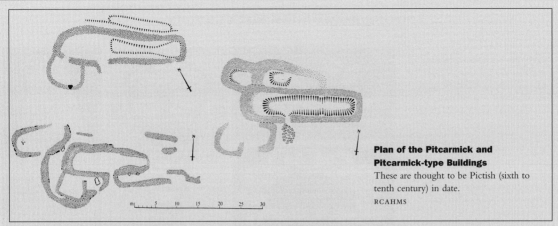

Plan of the Pitcarmick and Pitcarmick-type Buildings
These are thought to be Pictish (sixth to tenth century) in date.
RCAHMS

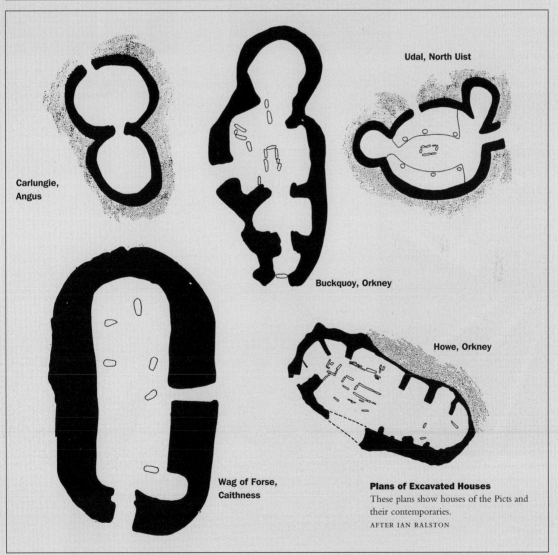

Udal, North Uist

Carlungie, Angus

Buckquoy, Orkney

Howe, Orkney

Wag of Forse, Caithness

Plans of Excavated Houses
These plans show houses of the Picts and their contemporaries.
AFTER IAN RALSTON

Looking good in the sixth century . . .

Early Pictish Accoutrements

(a) Silver bracelet with a diameter of 64 mm from the Gaulcross hoard.
(b) Silver chain 279mm long from the Gaulcross hoard. (c) Silver and red enamel pin 143mm long from the Gaulcross hoard. (d) Silver chain 480mm long with Pictish symbols from Whitecleugh. (e) Silver pin from Golspie, 60mm long, with a human head terminal. (f) Silver plaque from Norrie's Law. It is 91mm long and has no obvious means of attachment, so the idea that it could have been an ornamental pendant is purely speculative.

NATIONAL MUSEUMS OF SCOTLAND

Double-sided Comb and Pins

Comb and pins from excavations at Buckquoy, Orkney. The people seen on the Pictish symbol stones (men and women) had long hair but seem to have kept it neat, using combs and no doubt fastenings of various kinds.

NATIONAL MUSEUMS OF SCOTLAND

An Early Pictish Woman

This woman is wearing the Gaulcross pin and bracelets, and ear pendants like the Norrie's Law plaques. The Norrie's Law hoard was found about 1819 at the foot of Norrie's Law, a prehistoric mound in Fife. On discovery it consisted of 25lb (about 13kg) of silver, but most of this was dispersed and melted down. The Gaulcross hoard was found shortly before 1840 in a stone circle called Gaulcross at Ley in Banffshire. Only three pieces of the hoard now survive. These objects date from the 500s to the 600s.

MIKE MOORE

. . . and in the eighth century

(a)

(b)

(c)

Eighth-century Accoutrements
(a) A silver-gilt penannular brooch from Rogart, Sutherland: 77mm across with trilobe terminals. (b) Silver-gilt brooch-pin (pin 113mm long) found at Dunipace, Stirlingshire, but perhaps made in Ireland. (c) A silver-gilt penannular brooch from St Ninian's Isle, Shetland: 71mm across with snarling beast terminals.
NATIONAL MUSEUMS OF SCOTLAND

A Later Pictish Man
The early Picts seemed to have used handpins to fasten their clothes and worn bracelets; but in the eighth century the penannular brooch was *de rigeur*. This man's cloak is fastened with a penannular brooch similar to those found at St Ninian's Isle and Rogart. The St Ninian's Isle hoard, which included 28 silver objects, was found in 1958 under a stone slab in a ruined medieval church. The Rogart brooches were part of a large hoard largely destroyed found by workmen during the construction of a railway in 1868. The objects date from the later 700s.
MIKE MOORE

Thinking Christian

When, and how – and why – were the Picts converted to Christianity? Christianity brought clear advantages to early medieval leaders, such as a trade network with the other Christian nations and international support for the ruling dynasty; and there were advantages for the people too, such as the protection offered to women and children from the horrors of war enacted in Adomnán's Law of the Innocents. But there were also disadvantages: the church establishment had to be supported either by an extension of taxation or the endowment of land, and Christian rule ran the risk of becoming inflexible and imperious. The expectation is that the Picts would been converted when they encountered missionaries; but this does not necessarily follow. They may have deliberately reserved judgment on what was a crucial political issue.

The people of Pictland were introduced to Christianity on at least three occasions. First, in the 400s, the southern Picts are said to have been converted by Ninian, a Briton who had his headquarters at Whithorn in Galloway. The traces of this conversion may have been left in the form of the long-cist burials and the sculptured stones carrying incised inscriptions or simple crosses in low relief which are found at Whithorn and as far north as Fife. Another clue should be provided by place-names including the element 'eccles' from the Latin *ecclesia*, meaning a church. On the other hand, the stone monuments may be due to late Roman Christians,

The Skeith Stone

This stone is from Kilrenny, north-east Fife.
T.E.GREY

Long-cist Cemetery

This cemetery was excavated at The Hallow Hill, near St Andrews. The long-cists are oriented approximately east by north-east and examples were radiocarbon dated to the seventh to eighth century.
EDWINA PROUDFOOT

rather than those converted by St Ninian; and cist burial may have been a more widespread as well as a more enduring rite.

> *The southern Picts, who live on this [the Northumbrian] side of the mountains, are said to have abandoned the errors of idolatry long before [Columba] and accepted the true Faith through the preaching of Bishop Ninian, a most reverend and holy man of British race, who had been regularly instructed in the mysteries of the Christian Faith in Rome.*
>
> Bede

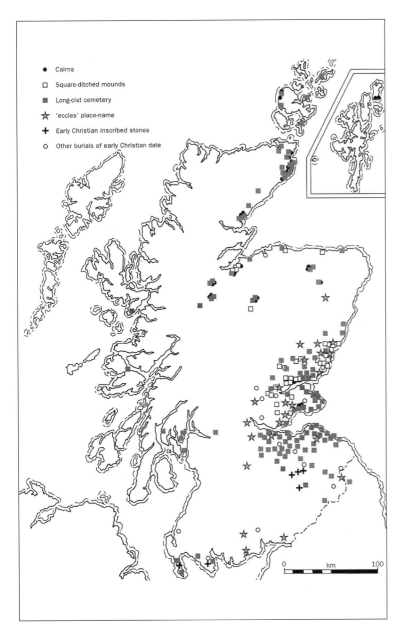

The Catstane in Midlothian
The inscription has been read: IN OC TV MVLO IACIT VETTA F[ilia] VICTI: 'In this mound lies Vetta daughter of Victus'.
HISTORIC SCOTLAND

Christian Progress
Map showing the distribution of early Christian stones, 'eccles' place-names and long-cist burials. Also shown are the locations of early historic barrows and cairns.
AFTER EDWINA PROUDFOOT

The northern Picts were visited by St Columba around AD 565. Columba travelled up Loch Ness by boat, and had the first recorded encounter with the Loch Ness monster. He then met king Bridei at his fortress and engaged in a number of competitions with his wizards. Although Columba won the magic-competition, there is little clear evidence for Christianity in the north at this time. King Bridei's

Into Pagan Lands

Columba and his companions approach the end of Loch Ness in about AD 565. Over the prow of Columba's skin boat, built in the Irish Sea tradition, a small promontory can be seen. It now carries Castle Urquhart. Then it probably had a small fort, one of those belonging to the great Pictish king Bridei whom Columba was soon to meet and attempt to recruit to the Christian cause. 'St Columba, with a great crowd of people following, came to the long loch at the head of the River Ness' (Adomnán).
MIKE MOORE

The Monymusk Reliquary

This is an eighth-century house-shaped shrine for carrying sacred relics. It is thought to be the *Brecbennoch* of St Columba, a sacred battle-box used as a rallying focus by the Scottish army. It was associated with military service owed from the lands of Forglen in Banff in the twelfth century and probably earlier.
NATIONAL MUSEUMS OF SCOTLAND

fortress has not been identified: popular candidates are Craig Phadraig, the promontory which now carries Castle Urquhart, and Torvean.

Bede felt that the mission of St Columba had been effective:

In the year of our Lord 565, when Justin the Younger succeeded Justinian and ruled as Emperor of Rome, a priest and abbot named Columba, distinguished by his monastic habit and life, came from Ireland to Britain to preach the word of God in the provinces of the northern Picts . . . Columba arrived in Britain in the ninth year of the reign of the powerful Pictish king Bridei son of Mailchon; he converted that people to the Faith of Christ by his preaching and example, and received from them the island of Iona on which to found a monastery.

Adomnán, who had closer knowledge of Columba, claims only some conversions: 'A Pictish layman heard him [St Columba] and with his entire household believed and was baptized, husband, wife, children and servants'. But he felt that Columba's reach was extensive by the late seventh century when he was writing. Recording two great plagues (probably those of 664 and 680–6), from which both the Scots and the Picts had been spared, he attributed this miraculous escape to St Columba, who 'founded among both peoples the monasteries where today he is still honoured on both sides'.

A third Christian initiative was due to the Northumbrian Angles, who tried to conquer Pictland and impose religious authority on it throughout the later 600s. The conquest failed after the Northumbrian king Ecgfrith was trapped and killed with his army at Nechtansmere (Dunnichen Moss) in 685. But a later Pictish king, Nechtan son of Derile, decided in 710 to align with the Angles after all, and sent for details of the English kind of Christianity, which, among other things, calculated the date of Easter by a different method to the church of Iona. Their monks also used a different tonsure: a circular patch on top of the head instead of a shaven forehead with long hair at the back. Advice arrived in the form of a letter from Ceolfrith, abbot of Wearmouth and Jarrow, which was swiftly promulgated in Pictland. Nechtan subsequently expelled clergy of the Columban persuasion from southern Pictland, but it is unlikely that the Picts turned their backs on Irish Christianity for long, given the named kings reigning jointly over Picts and Scots from the mid 700s. The success of this period of conversion is thought to be

Stones from the Battle of Nechtansmere

(*right and facing page*)

Dunnichen, Angus. A block of sandstone nearly 5 feet high with a flower symbol, a floriate Z-rod with double disc and the mirror and comb. The stone was said to have been found in 1811 near the marshy ground which has been identified as the site of the Battle of Nechtansmere (Dunnichen Moss) which took place in AD 685 (see frontispiece).

RCAHMS

demonstrated by the great series of
stone monuments, the Class II stones,
which, while still carrying Pictish
symbols, also carry the cross in a
prominent position.

The reverse side of Aberlemno I stone,
which is supposed to have recorded the
defeat of the Northumbrian king Ecgfrith
by the Pictish army led by king Bridei son
of Bili. Archaeologist Anna Ritchie has
interpreted the scene: (from top to bottom)
Ecgfrith flees from Bridei son of Bili,
dropping his sword and shield; Ecgfrith
confronts footsoldiers; after facing Bridei,
Ecgfrith is killed and becomes carrion for a
raven. Bede's description of this event,
disastrous for his people, speaks of 'narrow
mountain passes'.
RCAHMS

> At this time [about 710] Nechtan, king
> of the Picts, living in the northern parts
> of Britain, convinced after an assiduous
> study of church writings, renounced the
> error [the practice of the Celtic Church]
> hitherto maintained by his nation about
> the observance of Easter, and adopted
> the Catholic time of keeping our Lord's
> resurrection with all his people. In order
> to do this more smoothly and with
> greater authority, the king asked for
> help from the English people, whom he
> knew to have based their practice long
> previously on the pattern of the holy,
> Roman, apostolic Church. So he sent
> messengers to the venerable Ceolfrith,
> Abbot of the monastery of the blessed
> Apostles Peter and Paul, which . . .
> stands at the mouth of the River Wear
> . . . The king requested Ceolfrith to
> write him a letter of guidance that
> would help him refute those who
> presumed to keep Easter at the wrong
> time . . . In addition, he asked that
> architects be sent him in order to build
> a stone church for his people in the
> Roman style, promising he would dedicate it in honour of the blessed
> prince of the Apostles . . .

Bede

Ceolfrith duly replied, explaining the Roman rules, in a letter thought
to have been composed by Bede himself, who describes its reception:

> When this letter had been read in the presence of King Nechtan and
> many of his more learned men, and carefully translated into their own
> tongue by those who could understand it, he is said to have been so
> grateful for its guidance that he rose among his assembled chieftains and
> fell on his knees, thanking God that he had been accounted worthy to
> receive such a gift from England.
> The new Easter cycles were immediately sent out under a public
> order to all the provinces of the Picts to be copied, learned and adopted.

Converting the Stones

The back and front of Meigle 1 stone, Perthshire. Side 1 is a busy composition featuring a large number of symbols: a salmon, Pictish beast, snake and Z-rod, dog's head, the mirror and comb and a triquetra (a triangular knot). A group of five horsemen and a hound seem to form a hunting party, but an angel hovers in front of one of the riders. A camel-like creature and a coiled snarling beast lurk on the right of the picture. Side 2 is dominated by a cross infilled with interlace pattern; between its arms are a number of beasts which may represent the tamed forces of darkness.
HISTORIC SCOTLAND

Whether the English prescription was really welcomed with such raptures we may question. Bede was a Northumbrian Angle, and his account reflected an English viewpoint. Regrettably we have no voice which represents Pictish opinion at such a crucial moment in their history. But the significance of this incident as a change in political direction is clear. There was an issue to resolve and Pictland had resolved it in favour of the perceived allies of St Peter, among whom were the English kingdoms of the east coast. Bede felt that the measure had stuck; at the end of his book he wrote:

> At the present time [AD 731], the Picts have a treaty of peace with the English, and are glad to be united in Catholic peace and truth to the universal church.

How far the Picts had practised organised Christianity before or after this event is hard to say. As yet no certain Pictish books, churches or monasteries are known in Pictland before the 800s, by which time it had become a Scottish territory served by a Scottish church. It may be that the Picts themselves never took to the idea of an established church. Many examples of the Class II monuments, initiated at about the time of Ceolfrith's letter in the early eighth century, now stand in churchyards, but it is not usually known whether the stone was placed beside a church or a church built beside a pre-existing stone. Prominent stones were used to mark boundaries, and Class II stones could also have functioned in this manner marking the location of independent estates. Some certainly have complex Christian themes, suggesting a more than superficial knowledge of the scriptures; but examples also featured secular activities like hunting and hawking. Christian images do not necessarily have to be made by monks: the ability of the aristocracy to understand and communicate Christian ideas (as pre-Christian ones) should not be overlooked. Covered with images, personal or ceremonial, these monuments provide a marvellous archive of Pictish activities and ideas.

An argument about the Pictish conversion

Expert A: The peoples of Pictland were converted by Ninian in the fifth century. The conversion began in the south with missions from Whithorn in Lothian and Fife, as shown by the 'eccles' place-names and sculpture of Whithorn type. It later spread to the whole of eastern Scotland and up into the northern isles, as the dedications to St Ninian show. The Pictish church is a British church and traces of this British Christianity will eventually turn up all over the land . . .

Expert B: St Columba's recorded expedition in the sixth century is only the first of many penetrations of the east by the Irish church and people. As Adomnán said, and as the dedications of churches show, Columba founded monasteries in Pictland, and the conversion proceeded steadily from them during the sixth, seventh and eighth centuries. The Pictish church, when found, will resemble the monastic, Scottish church of Iona.

Expert C: The early missions from the British and Irish west were ineffective and there was little organised Christianity in the east and north of Scotland until the early

eighth century. It was then introduced from Northumbria, using Anglian religious art and following the Roman episcopal idiom. The Northumbrian conversion is signalled by the Class II stones, the only evidence for Christian Picts we have.

Expert D: All the churches, whether so-called Celtic or English or British were equally dedicated to Rome and made equal use of Bishops and monks. People did not distinguish between the western and southern churches except in matters of detail, such as the date of Easter and the tonsure. Christianity was gradually acquired by the Picts as they saw the sense in it. There are bound to have been Pictish churches, monasteries and Bishops' seats, both with and without Class II stones; they just haven't been found as yet.

Expert E: It mattered a lot to the Picts whether Christianity was adopted from Ireland and Dál Riata or from Northumbria, since this carried different political implications. The Picts probably treated every Christian overture with equal suspicion, since it threatened their independence. The Class II stones are the monuments of a secular church, retaining authority for the local lords. A centralised and established Christian church came only with Scottish political control in the later eighth century.

Christian Roadside Markers

The cross-slab Aberlemno 3 stands nearly 3m high beside the road leading from Forfar to Brechin. The cross is accompanied by angels bearing books, while on the other face (*facing page*) a hunting scene is topped by an ornate crescent and V-rod and double disc and Z-rod. Among the hunters there are images of the Biblical King David, with harp, rending the jaws of the lion (bottom right) and possibly standing with a square shield on the centre left.
HISTORIC SCOTLAND

St Ninian's Isle: an early Christian centre?

A Selection of Objects from St Ninian's Isle
NATIONAL MUSEUMS OF SCOTLAND

This St Ninian's Isle is not situated in St Ninian's homeland near Whithorn, but off Shetland. And the treasure found there dates not from St Ninian's time, or even St Columba's, but to the later 700s. By

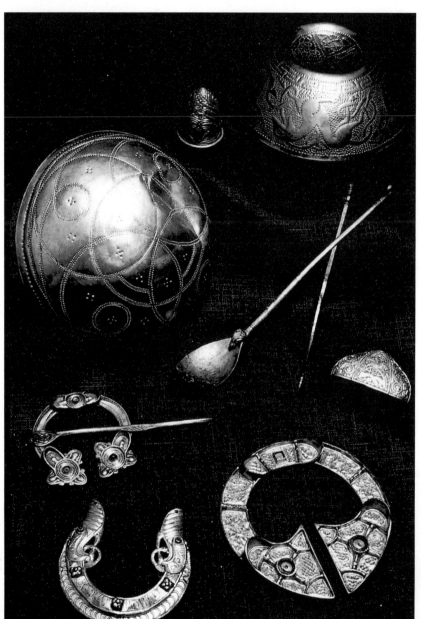

this time the people of Shetland, as in the rest of Pictland, had had plentiful exposure to Christianity from both west and south, so that we can expect to find motifs from Ireland, Northumbria and further afield embedded in Pictish Christian practice.

The famous treasure was found in 1958 during the excavation of a ruined medieval chapel. It consisted of 28 silver gilt objects and half the jawbone of a porpoise, which had been placed in a larchwood box and buried beneath a piece of a cross-slab at the east end of the nave. The objects comprise one hanging bowl, seven other bowls, two sword chapes, a sword pommel, a spoon, a hooked implement, three cone-shaped mounts and twelve pennanular brooches. The objects show strong affiliation with eighth-century Northumbrian art and were probably concealed in the church at a time of unrest due to the Vikings in about AD 800. The pommel and chapes must have already been removed from their parent objects before being put in the box, so the hoard could have been that of a metal worker, or even, given that it was covered by a broken cross-slab, of a Viking.

A Christian Burial at Portmahomack, Easter Ross, around AD 785

A man is laid to rest in a cist burial, among the memorials of his colleagues and kin. Memorials with simple crosses probably reflect the influence of Scottish Christianity from Iona and the west coast. The great monumental slab, standing some 3 metres high, is a speciality of ninth-century Easter Ross. The cemetery at Portmahomack stood on a little hill looking out across the Dornoch Firth. It had a sheltered beach which attracted settlers and traders over many thousands of years. The first chapel was probably built in the 800s.
MIKE MOORE

The 'Dragon Stone'

The stone monument found at
Portmahomack in 1995. The stone is
incomplete and once continued both
downwards and to the side. One side
features a fabulous beast, a dragon, with its
snake's-head tail and part of the
cross, infilled with peltaic
ornament. The other side
shows two lion-like animals
confronted over the
half-carcass of a deer, with
a bear slouching in the top
right-hand corner. Below
is a row of clerics, some
carrying books. These
may be intended as
monks or evangelists or,
given the space
available for the
figures, as Christ and
the apostles.

UNIVERSITY OF YORK

Tarbat – a Pictish monastery?

At Portmahomack on the Tarbat peninsula on the shore of the
Dornoch Firth is a beach ideal for landing boats. Beside it stands
Tarbat Old Church, the
site of a Pictish centre
which has produced 36
carved stones
belonging to the
700s–800s and
featuring a wide
range of styles. The
earliest burials
encountered in the church
were long-cist burials, and in
the fields beside the church a
settlement is being excavated (see page 61).
One stone carries a Latin inscription providing a
strong hint that this could be the site of a monastery.

The Carved Stones, Tarbat Old Church, Portmahomack

These stones offer an anthology of
memorial styles which look both north
and south. (a) There was a cross-slab with
a simple cross formed by four circles,
which is now lost, but is reminiscent of
the western British type which occurs at
Whithorn. (b) A grave-marker of a type
known from Iona. (c) The base of a
decorated slab (Tarbat 1) which carries
vine scroll of a type favoured in
Northumbria; Pictish symbols are carved
in relief on one edge.

IAN SCOTT

(a)

(b)

(c)

The Hilton of Cadboll: Site and Stone

This famous stone formerly stood at the site of a medieval chapel at Hilton of Cadboll. The earthwork of the ruined chapel is the rectangular shape in the centre at the foot of the photograph.

The Hilton of Cadboll sculpture is now in the National Museum of Scotland. A masterpiece of carving, it features an ornate double-disc and Z-rod, and crescent and V-rod. Below these is a hunting scene, apparently led by a woman riding side-saddle. A plant-scroll with pecking birds forms the border.

BARRI JONES; HISTORIC SCOTLAND

The Tarbat Inscription

This is one of the longest Latin inscriptions known in Pictland. It occurs on part of a memorial stone found in the garden wall of the manse of Tarbat parish church at Portmahomack, Easter Ross. The inscription is done, unusually, in relief and the form of the letters recalls those of insular manuscripts made in the eighth century such as the Lindisfarne Gospels or the Book of Kells. The ornament matches that on a large piece of a stone monument discovered at Portmahomack in 1995, the so-called 'Dragon Stone' seen on page 50.

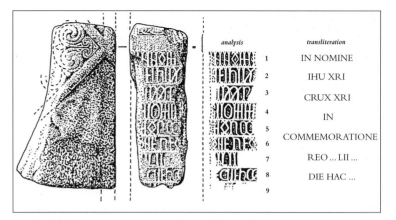

	analysis	transliteration
1		IN NOMINE
2		IHU XRI
3		CRUX XRI
4		IN
5		COMMEMORATIONE
6		REO ... LII ...
7		DIE HAC ...
8		
9		

Making a Pictish Stone

(above right)
Barry Grove carving a replica of Tarbat 1 (see page 50) in low relief in 1998. The pattern was sketched out in pencil on the slab, but the sculptor is producing the pattern by eye. As he does the interlace, he is muttering 'over', 'under' to himself. The piece of stone represents perhaps a fifth of the original monument. But it still took eight people to carry the block from the quarry on the shore to a vehicle (right).
E.R. CARVER; STEVE MILES

Open Air Archive – Windows on Pictish Life and Thought

The Class II stones provide enticing glimpses of Pictish life and thought – but must be used with care. We cannot just read off the activities, because the pictures may have originated somewhere else. This is especially true with pictures of Christian subjects, which must have been copied from books or ornamental carvings depicting people and events a long way from Scotland. So every scene on a Pictish stone has to be systematically checked to see if its images have been 'borrowed' from another culture. All the images on these pages come from carvings made in Pictland in the eighth to ninth century, but some of them may have first occurred in Roman or Byzantine art, or in England, Ireland, France or Scandinavia. The Picts were Europeans and up to date.

Some things, like the hunting scenes, can be accepted as home-grown, and used to evoke the life and ways of the real Picts; and even when exotic or Christian subjects are chosen – that choice is the choice of the Picts and not without interest in itself.

Fighting

There were mounted warriors with spears and round shields, and foot soldiers with spears and shields which might be round or square. The

Fighting
(a) Mounted warrior at Edderton, Easter Ross. (b) Three mounted warriors at Fordoun, Kinc. (c) Mounted warrior and three foot soldiers with round shields at Dull, Perth. (d) Two foot soldiers with square shields fight it out at Shandwick, Easter Ross. (e) Three foot soldiers with square shields at Brough of Birsay. (f) Benvie, Angus, showing shield, spear, bridle and sword.

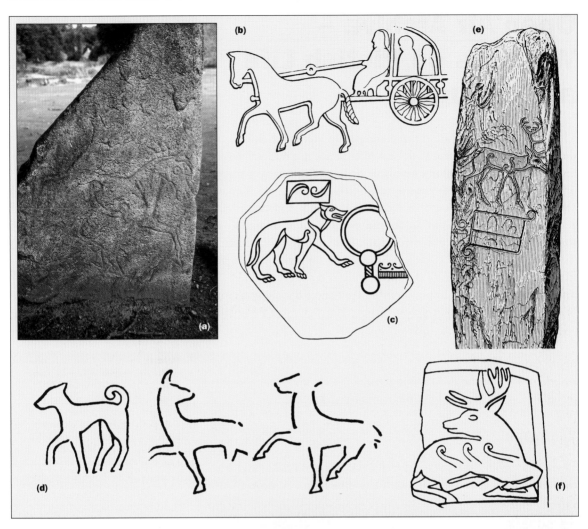

Animals

The picts loved animals: the way they
looked and the way they moved. This is
clear from the animal drawings on the
stones which for their purity of line are
arguably unmatched anywhere in the
world of art. (a) Horse running free at
Inverurie. (b) Meigle 10 (now lost) showed
a horse drawing a two-wheel cart.
(c) Dog from the stone at Newbigging
Leslie, Aberdeen. (d) Dogs from Largo,
Fife. (e) Stag at Grantown. (f) Red deer,
resting but alert, at St Vigeans.

PHOTO: GORDON BARCLAY

Tarbat Calf Stone

Bucolic scene on Tarbat 28: a family of
cattle; it seems to be the father that is
licking the new calf.

UNIVERSITY OF YORK/M.O.H.CARVER

square shields may refer to Romans or soldiers pictured in sources from overseas; the round shield is the one featured on the majority of examples, and ought to be a Pictish type. On the other hand, both might have been in use: the round on horseback and the square or rectangular on foot. The small notched shield which appears on the St Andrews sarcophagus and at Ardchattan has a prototype in the Iron Age: miniature examples were found in the Salisbury hoard, and a full-sized one at Deal in Kent. Could the Picts have 'remembered' the form of something last used in the first millennium BC? Certainly – just as techniques for building hillforts or burying the dead were revived in Pictland after an apparent interval of 500 years or more. One day we shall find a real Pictish shield . . . and also perhaps examples of the spears, bows and arrows, which occur in hunting and fighting scenes.

The St Andrews Sarcophagus, Fife
A stunning work of the late eighth century employs the ancient skill of the Pictish carver to celebrate the might of Rome in the style of the new overlords from Irish Scotland. The large figure is identified as the Biblical King David who was a favourite role model for the early medieval potentate: an active leader, fighter and decision-maker, given to regaling the company with his own compositions and beloved of the Almighty.
HISTORIC SCOTLAND

(right)
Hunting Images
(a) A horseman sounds the horn at Dunkeld. (b) Bow and arrow used against a brave stag at Shandwick, Easter Ross.

(below)
Invented Animals
Creatures with hooves, claws and a long-haired human head appear on a stone at Gask, Perth.

Scriptures

Scenes inspired by the Christian scriptures occur from time to time on the stones: King David was the one of the most popular (see p. 55), and other subjects included Samson smiting the Philistines with the jawbone of an ass, Jonah and the Whale and Daniel in the Lions' den. In addition to the meaning conveyed by the scriptures, the selected topics reflected the ethics of heroic society: the gods bless those that survive an ordeal and kings successful in battle.

Curious beasts

On the Christian memorial stones and often beside the cross itself, invented animals may be depicted. With their bits of animal, fish and bird in combination, these curious beasts may have been borrowed from classical stories which came to Pictish ears through Christianity. But the Picts, long experienced in signalling their ideas through animal forms, might simply have made them up. The point of these weird images seems to be to display a message: the beast was like a compound adjective, suggesting bravery, cowardice, triumph or death, an icon of unusual talent or terror, harbingers of good or ill luck. Perhaps heaven was thought to be populated by entertaining or scary images, the equivalent of our 'aliens'.

People and Politics

Were the Picts a tribe, a nation or a kingdom? The question is not yet answered although there is a growing number of clues. The Picts' self-awareness as a people seems to have been first stimulated by the conquest of Roman Britain to the south of them. The feeling of

On the Beach

The Picts were mainly people of the Firths and coasts, and their principal means of communication should have been by boat. According to an Irish annal, in ad 729, 150 Pictish ships were swept to their doom on the south coast of the Moray Firth. No Pictish ship has yet been found and we do not know what they looked like. A clue is provided by the image of a ship on the cross-slab at Cossins (p. 58). It looks like a standard Scandinavian clinker-built rowing boat, which is logical: the Picts should have followed a North Sea tradition of boat-building, just as the Scots with their skin boats should have followed an Irish Sea tradition. The Picts may have sailed, since the technology was well known to North Sea people. In the pre-Viking era, Scandinavian archaeologists have defined 'beachmarkets' as the principal locations for maritime exchanges. There was probably one of these at Portmahomack, Culbin, Dunnottar, and at every beach along the east coast where a boat could be drawn up.
MIKE MOORE

The Cossins Stone, Angus
This stone, the only one to feature a boat, was probably carved late enough (late eighth to early ninth century), for the boat in question to be Viking. But its six occupants do not look aggressive, and it is reasonable to assume, until we find one, that Pictish ships resembled those of other North Sea peoples.

'otherness' in the people of north-east Scotland, who were not included in the Roman province of Britannia, evolved to a feeling of being a confederacy, as the Roman province began to show its stress in the fourth century. Success in raiding may have led to a clearer sense of identity, not so much a country or a kingdom, as a 'nation' in the sense of the 'Apache Nation'. A uniformity of culture was shown by the stone markers which display common icons from Orkney to Angus. But during the early Pictish period, say the 400s to 500s, we have few obvious hints, in the settlements or the cemeteries, that the Picts had kings.

Through external or internal pressure, societies all over the island of Britain seem to have become markedly more hierarchical in the 600s. In Pictland, many rocky knolls or promontories, some of them sites originally built a thousand years earlier, are fortified, suggesting a number of small lordships. The same kind of social change is evident among the immediate neighbours, the Britons in the south-west, the Angles in the south-east, and the Scots in the west. These three peoples all adopted Christianity during the 600s or earlier, thus openly declaring common cause with the European continent. Even so, their versions of Christianity were not all of the same mould, some preferring the centralisation and regulation of the episcopal system, others aspiring to the virtues of grass-roots monasticism pioneered by the desert fathers, and others again frankly promoting a secular Christianity in the service of local lordship.

These different approaches, none of them either pure or simple, led to confrontation and enmity in which the Picts inevitably participated. We know that the Picts were exposed to Christian missions from their neighbours from the 500s onwards, and the cross appears by the early 700s on the new generation of symbol stones that we call 'Class II'. But the churches and books that are diagnostic of organised Christianity are still lacking. It may be that Pictish Christianity was a more secular affair; enough commitment to understand the message and celebrate it in art, but not so much as to lose control or revenue. The Norse seem to have embraced a Christianity of this kind from the tenth century onwards in both

England and Scotland; thus when Picts and Norse interacted in the north-east and the Northern Isles their encounters may not have been always unfriendly.

From the 700s onwards, southern Pictland became increasingly associated with the Scots, their neighbours to the west, and from an occasionally rough wooing a new political strategy was born. It was one more suited to face the main challenge of a Christian Europe – how to reap the advantages of the continental union without jeopardising independence and sovereignty. The forts did duty into the ninth century, and then became redundant. The new power centres were lowland palace complexes, of which the settlement buried at Forteviot may prove to be an example. The northerners may have cherished a hope of not committing themselves to either the Norse or Scottish camp; but, by the mid ninth century, to stay Pictish seemed to be no longer an option.

What happened to the Picts? In the clash between the Scots and the Norse, the people of the east coast, by now often intermixed and associated by arms and marriage to both, no doubt sided alternately with one and then the other. The Picts did not vanish; they simply became Scots or Norse. Upwardly mobile men and women had to express themselves in Gaelic or Norse, and soon the Pictish language became redundant. Split into many small lordships, without an ecclesiastical establishment, the Picts had no vernacular chronicles with which historians could resurrect their memory through the centuries. Soon only the stones bore witness to the genius of the Pictish era; and then their meaning too was forgotten. It is largely the late twentieth century which has discovered a mission to help the Picts to live again, through the new agenda and methods of art and archaeology.

A Dug-out of the Pictish Period
This dug-out was discovered by salmon-fishers on a sandbank at Errol in the tidal reaches of the River Tay. This kind of craft would be most effective in inland waters.
DUNDEE CITY COUNCIL –
ARTS AND HERITAGE DEPARTMENT

How Will We Find Out More?

Portmahomack and St Colman's Church

The old church of St Colman is the white building standing in its graveyard by the road (top left). A more ancient enclosure surrounding the church was discovered from the air in 1984 by Barri Jones and Ian Keiller during their survey of the Moray Firth area. The site now being investigated lies within this enclosure; occupied throughout the Pictish era, it consisted of a group of buildings on the raised ground above the beach, and seems to have functioned at different stages of its development as a stronghold, a monastery and a beachmarket. The modern village in the foreground is Portmahomack, the 'port of St Colman'.

BARRI JONES

There is so much more to discover about the Picts and eastern Scotland in early Historic times: how did the people live? How and why did they change their style of living? What became of them? The answers to many of these questions lie buried in the ground, in settlements and monuments and objects which are occasionally spotted from the air or tumbled to the surface by the plough.

Rediscovering the Picts is only a matter of time, because the archaeology of Scotland is sympathetcially managed and served by Historic Scotland, by the Royal Commission, by the Council for Scottish Archaeology and by the residents of Scotland themselves. Most casual discoveries get into *Discovery and Excavation in Scotland*, the annual report of what has been found each year. As the discoveries are made, the picture builds up and gets easier to understand.

In harmony with this careful management, research projects are launched each year, targeted on special problems. New art-historical

Excavations at Portmahomack, 1997
Excavations in progress in 1997, with St
Colman's Church in the background. The
Colman remembered here may have been
the seventh-century Irish monk and
champion of the western church who lost
the argument at the Synod of Whitby.
UNIVERSITY OF YORK/M.O.H.CARVER

work on the meaning of the symbol stones, their date and the
activities depicted on them is more or less continuous. New
archaeological field-work has to take its opportunities, but one or two
major projects are usually under way, and can sometimes be visited. At
the time of writing, there is one at *Pitcarmick* in Perthshire where a
new kind of building was identified as probably of the Pictish period
by survey work in 1990, and excavation has confirmed that the houses
and the settlement belong to the late first millennium.

The political story of the northerners, how they measured up to
the challenges of their day and dealt with the attentions of their
neighbours to the west, east and south, are being studied in the *Tarbat
Discovery Programme*, a large-scale archaeological project centred on a
site at Portmahomack on Tarbat Ness, Easter Ross (see opposite page).
The new sites like Tarbat are located by searching the land from the
surface or from the air, and in selected cases excavation may follow.
Then traces of buildings, burials, artefacts, animal bones and plant
remains are brought to light, all of which helps to answer the
questions: 'what sort of people were these? How did they live? What
did they believe in?'

Other important archaeological projects are under way all over
mainland Scotland and in the Western and Northern Isles, as well as
in Ireland and in neighbouring countries on the shores of the North
Sea. All are in pursuit of new knowledge and understanding about this
pivotal time in Europe's history: that moment when the Picts and
their contemporaries first encountered the ideas of Christianity and
began to express themselves as independent 'nations'. These were
ideas that were destined to last a thousand years.

Sites around Scotland

The main legacy of the Picts consists of hundreds of carved stones, most carrying symbols, many still standing in the open air. There are a number of excellent 'trails' but nothing quite beats the excitement of trying to find the stone you want to see, armed only with Allen and Anderson's *Early Christian Monuments of Scotland* and a map. Listed here are some of the principal collections of stones and visitable sites. At the sites of forts, cemeteries and settlements there is often nothing clearly Pictish to see, but there is plenty of atmosphere.

South

Aberlemno has three famous stones in the open air – two by the road and one in the churchyard.
Dundurn and Strathearn. A ramble along this valley will be repaid by beautiful scenery and a number of intriguing hill-forts, culminating in Dundurn itself.

Sueno's Stone

The stone in its protective box pictured at night.
HISTORIC SCOTLAND

At *Meigle* and *St Vigeans* (by Arbroath) are two of the most important exhibitions of Christian-period stones.
The *National Museum of Scotland* has many of the finest pieces of Pictish metalwork and carving in its care. Much Pictish material is now distributed within the prehistoric 'themed' display in the basement.

Centre

Archaeolink at Oyne in Aberdeenshire is a display centre designed to show off and explain aspects of the past, including the Pictish period. A short walk or drive brings you to a stunning view of Bennachie, with the Rhynie stone below it.
The *Maiden Stone* also lies a short distance from Bennachie.
Sueno's stone stands at Forres, now protected by a large transparent box.
Burghead is a modern township, but traces of the rampart still show. The well can be visited and two of the famous Bull stones can be seen in the Public Library there. Another can be seen in the fine Museum at *Elgin*.

North

Craig Phadraig is owned by the Forestry Commission and a 20 minute walk up the foot path from a car park on the north side of Inverness brings you to its summit. The Iron Age rampart is still visible and lumps of vitrified rampart lie about in the trees.

Groam House is a museum specially dedicated to the Picts at Rosemarkie on the Black Isle. The exhibition includes Rosemarkie's own intriguing collection of Christian Pictish sculpture. The Groam House Lectures form a highly successful series featuring the latest findings and interpretations. Copies of the lectures given so far may be bought from the museum.
A Pictish Trail around *Easter Ross* concentrates mainly on the great monuments on Tarbat Ness: Nigg, Shandwick, Portmahomack. At Hilton of Cadboll, a replica of the famous stone (exhibited in the National Museum in Edinburgh) is being erected.
Portmahomack is a port of call on the trail and also site of the Tarbat Discovery Centre. As well as exhibiting the 36 pieces of sculpture so far found at the site, the display describes a major archaeological research project in search of the northern Picts.
The summerhouse at *Dunrobin Castle* contains one of the most important collections of Pictish sculpture in the country, relating to both the pagan and Christian periods.
Orkney is an archaeological paradise. A famous Pictish stone stands on the *Brough of Birsay*, and artefacts of the Pictish period can be seen in the Museum at *Kirkwall*.

Further Reading

- Adomnan of Iona *Life of St Columba*, edited and translated by R. Sharpe (Penguin 1995)
- *The Early Christian Monuments of Scotland*, by J. R. Allen and J. Anderson (1903, reprinted by Pinkfoot Press 1993)
- Bede *A History of the English Church and People*, edited and translated by L. Sherley-Price (Penguin 1968)
- *The Language of the Ogam Inscriptions of Scotland*, by Richard Cox (University of Aberdeen 1999)
- *Scotland in Dark Age Europe*, edited by Barbara Crawford (St Andrews 1994)
- *Scotland in Dark Age Britain*, edited by Barbara Crawford (St Andrews 1996)
- *Conversion and Christianity in the North Sea World*, by Barbara Crawford (St Andrews 1998)
- *Scotland. Environment and Archaeology 8000 BC–AD 1000*, edited by Kevin Edwards and Ian Ralston (Wiley 1997)
- *Language in Pictland*, by Katherine Forsyth (Studia Hameliana 2, 1997)
- *Picts, Gaels and Scots*, by Sally Foster (Historic Scotland/Batsford 1996)
- *The St Andrews Sarcophagus. A Pictish Masterpiece and its International Connections*, edited by Sally Foster (Four Courts Press 1998)
- *Pictish Studies*, edited by J. G. P. Friell and W.G. Watson (BAR 125, 1984)
- *The Picts*, by Isabel Henderson (Thames and Hudson 1967)
- *The Worm, the Germ and the Thorn. Pictish and Related Studies Presented to Isabel Henderson*, edited by David Henry (Pinkfoot Press 1997)
- *A Pictish Panorama*, edited by Eric Nicoll (Pinkfoot Press 1995)
- *Picts*, by Anna Ritchie (HMSO 1989)
- *Pictish Symbol Stones: An Illustrated Gazetteer* (RCAHMS 1999)
- *Scotland. Archaeology and Early History*, by Anna Ritchie and Graham Ritchie (Edinburgh University Press 1991)
- *Warlords and Holy Men*, by Alfred Smyth (Edinburgh University Press 1984)

Acknowledgements

My thanks to Gordon Barclay for inviting me to contribute to the series, and to Mairi Sutherland for editing. I am very grateful to Sally Foster, Alex Woolf and Katherine Forsyth for their often successful attempts to save me from error and moderate my vision. Thanks also to my Tarbat co-directors Justin Garner-Lahire and Annette Roe, and most especially to Emma Carver who did the picture research and provided help and advice at every stage.

Thanks are due to the following individuals and organisations for their permission to reproduce copyright illustrations: Historic Scotland; The Royal Commission on the Ancient and Historical Monuments of Scotland (RCAHMS); National Museums of Scotland; Professor Barri Jones, University of Manchester; Gordon Barclay; T. E. Grey; The University of York; E. R. Carver; Steve Miles; Edwina Proudfoot (St Andrews Heritage Services); McManus Gallery, Dundee; Ewan Campbell; Society of Antiquaries of Scotland.

HISTORIC SCOTLAND safeguards Scotland's built heritage, including its archaeology, and promotes its understanding and enjoyment on behalf of the Secretary of State for Scotland. It undertakes a programme of 'rescue archaeology', from which many of the results are published in this book series.

Scotland has a wealth of ancient monuments and historic buildings, ranging from prehistoric tombs and settlements to remains from the Second World War, and HISTORIC SCOTLAND gives legal protection to the most important, guarding them against damaging changes or destruction. HISTORIC SCOTLAND gives grants and advice to the owners and occupiers of these sites and buildings.

HISTORIC SCOTLAND has a membership scheme which allows access to properties in its care, as well as other benefits.
For information, contact:
0131 668 8999.

The Pictish Arts Society was founded in 1988 to affirm the importance of Pictish culture. It has regular meetings, and a journal, and is based at 27 George Square, Edinburgh EH8 9LD.

Endpiece

The Pictish picture-stones have attracted some wonderfully ingenious explanations. This interpretation of the Glamis stone comes from Thomas Pennant's *A Tour in Scotland* (1776):

In the churchyard of Glamis is a stone similar to those at Aberlemno. This is supposed to have been erected in memory of the assassination of King Malcolm, and is called his grave stone. On one front is a cross; on the upper part is some wild beast, and opposite to it a centaur; beneath, in one compartment, is the head of a wolf; these animals denoting the barbarity of the conspirators; in another compartment are two persons shaking hands; in their other hands is a battle-axe: perhaps these are represented in the act of confederacy. On the opposite front of the stone are represented an eel and another fish. This alludes to the fate of the murderers, who, as soon as they had committed the horrid act, fled. The roads were at that time covered in snow; they lost the path, and went on to the lake of Forfar, which happened to be frozen over, but not sufficiently strong to bear their weight: the ice broke, and they all perished miserably.

Glamis Stone
HISTORIC SCOTLAND

how2become

HISTORY IS EASY:

STONE AGE TO IRON AGE

(KS1 AND KS2)

www.How2Become.com

As part of this product you have also received FREE access to online tests that will help you to pass History (Stone Age to Iron Age) for KS1 and KS2.

To gain access, simply go to:

www.MyEducationalTests.co.uk

Get more products for passing any test at:

www.How2Become.com

Orders: Please contact How2Become Ltd, Suite 14, 50 Churchill Square Business Centre, Kings Hill, Kent ME19 4YU.

You can order through Amazon.co.uk under ISBN: 9781911259107, via the website www.How2Become.com or through Gardners.com.

ISBN: 9781911259107

First published in 2017 by How2Become Ltd.

Typeset by Gemma Butler for How2Become Ltd.

Disclaimer

Every effort has been made to ensure that the information contained within this guide is accurate at the time of publication. How2Become Ltd is not responsible for anyone failing any part of any selection process as a result of the information contained within this guide. How2Become Ltd and their authors cannot accept any responsibility for any errors or omissions within this guide, however caused. No responsibility for loss or damage occasioned by any person acting, or refraining from action, as a result of the material in this publication can be accepted by How2Become Ltd.

The information within this guide does not represent the views of any third-party service or organisation.

CONTENTS

The New National Curriculum – Guidance for Parents 7

Palaeolithic Era (Early Stone Age) 13

   • What does 'prehistoric' mean? 15

   • What was Britain like? 19

   • The first people 22

Mesolithic Era (Mid Stone Age) 35

   • Palaeolithic traditions 37

   • New tools 39

   • People's progress 41

Neolithic Era (Late Stone Age) 49

   • The first British farmers 51

   • Advancing society 53

   • Stonehenge 56

Bronze Age 65

   • Inventing bronze 67

   • Rich and poor 69

   • Growing tribes 71

Iron Age 79

   • Working with iron 81

   • Celtic revolution 82

   • Here come the Romans 85

Mock Paper 95

2.5 million years ago

10,000 years ago

7,000 years ago

4,500 years ago

2,800 years ago

THE NEW NATIONAL CURRICULUM

(GUIDANCE FOR PARENTS)

WHY CHILDREN ARE TAUGHT HISTORY IN SCHOOLS

History is a part of the primary syllabus. Studying history gives children an introduction to the major events which have shaped Britain, and provides them with a better understanding of historical global relations. The aim of the subject is to inspire a deeper curiosity for how society has changed over the course of time.

WHAT ARE THE AIMS OF THE HISTORY SYLLABUS?

The syllabus provides children with:

- An understanding of British history as a chronological narrative, from ancient times to the present day. It focuses on how British people have been influenced by the rest of the world, and how they have made their own influence felt.

- An understanding of the history of the world as a whole, focusing on the earliest civilisations, most powerful empires, and the ways in which humanity has succeeded and failed.

- A wide historical vocabulary and an understanding of key terms and concepts such as 'civilisation' and 'society'.

- An introduction to wider historical concepts such as: continuity and change, cause and consequence, similarity, difference, and significance; and how to use them to make connections, draw contrasts, analyse trends, frame historically valid questions, and create their own structured accounts, including written narratives and analysis.

- An understanding of the importance of evidence when putting forward historical opinions. This also includes thinking about why some people interpret events or facts differently.

- An introduction to historical perspective, by considering contexts such as location, economics, politics, religion, and key points in time.

<u>Key Stage 1</u>

Below we have outlined specific criteria that should be considered when studying the History subject at Key Stage 1.

Pupils should:

- Develop an awareness of the past, using common words and phrases to describe the passage of time.

- Know where people and events fit within a chronological framework, and identify similarities and differences between ways of life in different periods.

- Use a wide vocabulary of everyday historical terms.

- Ask and answer questions, choosing and using parts of stories and other sources, to show that they know and understand key features of events.

- Understand some of the ways in which we find out about the past, and identify different ways in which the past is represented.

Key focuses

- Changes in national life within living memory.

- Historical events beyond living memory, with national and/or international significance.

- The lives of individuals who have contributed significant achievements.

Key Stage 2

Below we have outlined specific criteria that should be considered when studying the History subject at Key Stage 2.

<table>
<tr><td>

Pupils should:

• Continue to develop a chronologically secure knowledge and understanding of local, British, and world history.

• Establish clear narratives within and across the studied historical periods.

• Note connections, contrasts, and trends over time and develop the appropriate use of historical terms.

• Address questions about change, cause, similarity, difference, and significance.

• Construct informed responses that involve thoughtful selection and organisation of relevant historical information.

• Understand how our knowledge of the past is constructed from a range of sources.

Key focuses

• Changes in Britain from the Stone Age to the Iron Age.

• The Roman Empire and its impact on Britain.

• Britain's settlement by Anglo-Saxons and Scots.

• The Viking and Anglo-Saxon struggle for the Kingdom of England, up to the time of Edward the Confessor.

• A local history study (this will of course vary from school to school.)

• A study of an aspect or theme in British history that extends pupils' chronological knowledge beyond 1066. (E.g. the changing power of monarchs – using case studies such as John, Anne, and Victoria.)

• The achievements of the earliest civilisations, such as Ancient Egypt or Ancient China.

• Ancient Greece, its achievements, and its influence on the western world.

</td></tr>
</table>

- A non-European society that provides contrasts with British history, such as early Islamic civilisation, or the Mayan civilisation.

PALAEOLITHIC ERA
(THE EARLY STONE AGE)

THE EARLY STONE AGE

The Palaeolithic era is unique, as it lasted for well over 2,000,000 (2 million!) years. During this era, in Britain and indeed the whole world, the very first humans appeared, and began to develop more advanced methods of survival, adapting their lifestyles to the lands they found themselves in. But, before we look too closely at details like this, we need to have a think about what words like 'prehistoric' mean, and discuss how we know anything about this time period at all!

What does 'prehistoric' mean?

The first people

What was Britain like?

Unintelligible grunting

Our Neanderthal, Jeff, is here to offer his guidance! Good luck...

WHAT DOES 'PREHISTORIC' MEAN?

When we talk about things that are 'prehistoric', we know that means they are very old. While this is not wrong, this historical term actually means 'the time before anyone was writing things down'. In other words, 'prehistory' refers to a time before anyone was recording history. In Britain, people mostly point to the start of the Roman period as the end of prehistory, which happened around the year 43 (just under 2,000 years ago). This is because the Romans were the first people in Britain to write things down!

With no people writing down events and observations, you might be wondering 'How do we know what happened in prehistoric Britain?' The answer to this question lies in the field of archaeology!

What is archaeology?

Archaeology is the study of both recent and ancient human history. It is conducted by looking at the physical remains which people have left behind. These can either be remains of objects used by humans, or of their bodies themselves. Such remains are then studied for clues, which can tell us a great deal about the lives of the people who have left them behind. Archaeologists can then analyse the remains, and find out how old they are, placing them at a specific point in history. This means that archaeologists can work out when objects such as tools and weapons were used or even invented. They can then compare objects from different time periods to each other, to investigate how things have developed over time.

So, finding more and more archaeological evidence can paint us a picture of how people's lives changed across years, decades, and centuries. It is for this reason that archaeological finds are often very exciting. What's more, scientists suspect that there is still a lot of ancient archaeological evidence we haven't found yet, containing secrets of history that we are yet to explore.

Dorothy Garrod

Dorothy Garrod was a British archaeologist who was at the forefront of some of the world's first investigations of the Palaeolithic and Mesolithic Periods. She was born in 1892, and died aged 76 in 1968, after a long and illustrious career in science.

Her best work took place during the 1920s, during which time she carried out excavations (digs) across the Middle East, focusing on a collection of caves located in an area called Mount Carmel in Israel. Here, she found a wealth of evidence proving that ancient people had once lived there.

The best find of these investigations was a near-complete skeleton of a human woman, who was a 'modern human' – she had an identical body to humans of today. She was around 40,000 years old. Garrod and her team also found much more. For example, as well as several more human remains, a variety of ancient tools were found. Some of the tools resembled modern sickles, a farming tool which is used to harvest grains such as wheat and barley.

These were incredible discoveries, and led Garrod to name this group of people 'the Natufians', after a cave in the area called Wadi Natuf. Garrod believed that the Natufians may have been the first humans who farmed, and there was even evidence that the Natufians enjoyed making things like jewellery – they certainly enjoyed creating through carving.

Garrod's discoveries and explanations of what they might mean are still an important part of how we understand the lives and activities of ancient humans. Due to her expertise and pioneering work in her field, Garrod was appointed as professor of archaeology at Cambridge University in 1939.

This appointment was a historic one, because it meant that Dorothy Garrod became the first woman to be any kind of professor at the university. Her contributions to archaeology, as well as this breakthrough for women, has caused her to be remembered as a vital figure in British science.

WHAT WAS BRITAIN LIKE?

Of course, Dorothy Garrod is known for her findings in the Middle East, which shed huge amounts of light on ancient people's lives in this area. However, it does not tell us about what people's lives were like during the Stone Age in Europe or other parts of the world. Let's change our focus onto what the Palaeolithic Era was like in the land we now call Britain.

Doggerland

Until around 6,000 years ago, Britain was actually connected to Continental Europe by a huge bridge of land that has since been named 'Doggerland'. When it was above sea level, Doggerland stretched eastwards, meeting the lands we now call France and Germany. It also extended northwards, nearly reaching what we now call Norway. Archaeologists and researchers believe that Doggerland was once home to a wide variety of life, including humans. This is because ancient remains of mammoths and lions (yes, they used to live in Europe as well!) have been found, as well as early human tools and weapons.

Today, Doggerland sits far below sea level, forced there following huge amounts of ice melting during the various ancient Ice Ages. This rising sea level affected many places of the world, submerging huge amounts of land. Of course, this changed the face of the world forever.

Ice Ages

As just mentioned, Britain was caught up in several Ice Ages during the Palaeolithic Era, the longest of which lasted for around 400,000 years! Ice Ages can also be called 'glacial periods', after the glaciers (bodies of ice) that formed and hung around during these long and extreme winters.

Scientists today know that the world went through three different Ice Ages during the Palaeolithic Era. The longest (and oldest) one lasted for around 400,000 years, and the shortest (and most recent) one lasted for around 60,000 years. Of course, because we know that there were three separate glacial periods, we know that Britain experienced pockets of warmer weather in between them. These warmer ages can be called 'interglacial periods'.

The first Ice Age began around 750,000 years ago and ended around 350,000 years ago.

The second Ice Age began around 200,000 years ago and ended around 120,000 years ago.

The third and final Ice Age began around 70,000 years ago, and ended around 10,000 years ago.

Of course, Britain itself went through huge change from Ice Age to Ice Age. For example, during the glacial periods, sea levels would be very low, and it would be much harder for humans and animals to survive. The warmer weather of the interglacial periods would give rise to different species of plants and animals, whose remains we have found and dated.

THE FIRST PEOPLE

As we have covered, Dorothy Gerrod was responsible for the discovery of the body of one of the oldest 'modern humans'. In other words, Gerrod's work has proved that humans who were the same as us lived around 40,000 years ago.

However, other archaeologists have also found evidence of several different groups of people whose bodies are not quite the same as ours today. Many of them even lived thousands of years before Gerrod's Natufians. These groups of people, who were many years older than the Natufians, were less developed than modern humans – they did not have many of the favourable characteristics that we have today. For example, their brains were not as well developed, and they were not as good at communicating.

Such groups represent earlier stages of human evolution; they are our ancestors. Before we look at the specific changes our ancestors went through to become us, it is important to know what the theory of evolution actually is, and what 'evolving' means in a scientific sense.

What is evolution?

Evolution is the widely-accepted theory to explain why life on earth looks and behaves the way it does, and both how and why all species of animals and plants on Earth have very slowly, over millions of years, changed; thereby increasing their chances of survival in their particular environments.

How do the species change?

Species change through random genetic variation – this means that animals' offspring (children) are sometimes born with different physical features to their parents. This happens by chance.

Why do they change?

Sometimes, these random changes give the offspring an advantage in the animal's habitat. This means that the offspring with the features that give them this advantage are more likely to survive, and have offspring of their own.

So, the favourable feature is passed on again and again. Eventually, the only animals that survive in the habitat are those who possess this favourable feature, because those who do not have it are unable to compete. This is called natural selection. One of the pioneering humans in observing this phenomenon was Charles Darwin *(the man on the £10 note)*. He looked at birds on the Galapagos Islands, and noticed that each species of bird had evolved to have different shaped and sized beaks, which helped them eat the different kinds of food that appeared in the islands. This enabled the species to excel in their habitat. It is by the same process that our ancestors began to change into us – only not involving beaks!

Finch 1 is good at cracking hard nuts, Finch 2 is good at feeding on seeds, and Finch 3 is good at catching small insects. (Sketches by Charles Darwin!)

How do we know that evolution happens?

Once again, archaeology is involved! Remains of plants and animals that were not as well-adapted as their modern relatives have been discovered, which help scientists put together timelines of how certain species have changed over millions of years. Archaeologists have found huge numbers of fossils that prove the theory of evolution – and they expect to find many more as time goes on.

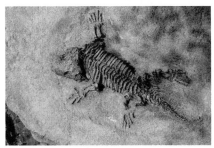

Human Evolution

The first thing to know about human evolution is that it took an extremely long time – several million years. The second thing is that humans did **not** evolve from chimps or gorillas. While these animals and humans are closely related in terms of the makeup of their brains and bodies, this is because they share a common ancestor. So, it is incorrect to think of chimps and gorillas as 'less evolved humans'.

Also, you might have heard of a group called the Neanderthals, which are often portrayed in films and TV programmes as being our cavemen ancestors. However, this is not really the case. While Neanderthals did exist, again it is more accurate to say that they share a common ancestor with us. So, Neanderthals did not evolve into us, but we're related to them. Modern humans (us!) were probably the reason that Neanderthals became extinct – we were a lot cleverer and more organised, so we took all their land and food.

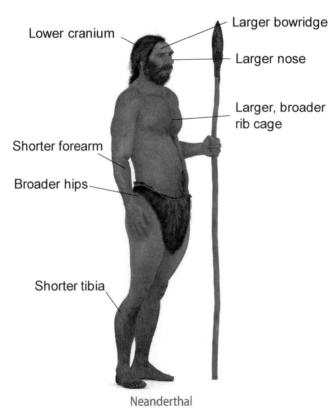

Lower cranium

Larger bowridge

Larger nose

Larger, broader rib cage

Shorter forearm

Broader hips

Shorter tibia

Neanderthal

Neanderthals' bodies compared to ours!

Here is a timeline to represent how and when our earliest ancestors began to change into us:

The disappearance of the dinosaurs.

— 65 million years ago

The appearance of modern mammals, mainly rodents and other small land dwellers.

— 65 million– 1.5 million years ago

The appearance of modern apes (chimps and gorillas). Soon after, the lines of heritage between humans and apes split, when the oldest human ancestor who walked on two legs (unlike apes) appeared.

— 10 million – 4 million years ago

Homo habilis appears, resembling modern humans much more than its ancestors. *Homo habilis* is also much smarter, and knew how to use basic stone tools.

— 2 million years ago

Homo erectus appears. It has a much larger brain even than *Homo habilis*. As its name suggests, *Homo erectus* stood up much straighter than its ancestors, and were much better hunters as well.
They were probably the first people to discover fire. Neanderthals also began to appear.

— 1.9 million years ago

Homo sapiens appears. This is what you are! Finally, modern humans appear, and soon becomes the dominant species on Earth, even causing its relatives like *Homo erectus* and the Neanderthals to become extinct. Scientists believe this is because *Homo sapiens* were much better communicators, and therefore, could develop more efficient societies.

— 200,000 – 100,000 years ago

The first people in Britain

As we have already discussed, during the Early Stone Age, Britain looked very different to how it looks today. It was even still attached to continental Europe! Of course, it was also exposed to many Ice Ages, during which times every form of life struggled to survive.

However, before the Ice Ages, as well as during the warmer periods between them, life was able to exist, and even thrive. Included in this were early humans!

Who were they?

Only a few years ago, researchers found evidence of a group of very early people who lived in Happisburgh, Norfolk. The most exciting piece of evidence that was discovered was a set of humanlike footprints, which had slowly been revealed after many years of coastal erosion. In other words, the footprints were so old that they had sunk far below the surface of the Earth, and only rose to the top (where they could be discovered) after years of the sea washing away the soil and sand above it.

The Happisburgh coast as it's seen today – you can see how the land has been eroded back.

The footprints told scientists huge amounts of information about the ancient people who lived in Happisburgh. For example, the footprints were either 850,000 or 950,000 years old – nearly a million! In fact, these are the oldest footprints (left by ancient people) that have been found outside of Africa.

Also, there were several prints of different sizes, which has led researchers to suggest that the prints belonged to one large family. Also interesting was that the largest prints were very similar in size to those that adults have today.

The footprints are not the only major archaeological discovery to have been made in Happisburgh. Stone tools have been uncovered, as well as animal and plant remains which can give us lots of information about their lifestyles. For example, the findings proved that people had begun living in this area from a much earlier point than first thought – scientists had believed that the conditions in Britain around 850,000 years ago had been too cold for humans to survive. This is why the footprints and other discoveries were so exciting and important.

Archaeologists believe that humans around the time of the Happisburgh people, knew how to use fire for warmth and to cook food; which included large animals they often hunted for. Also, it is believed that humans at this time could build simple shelters, using both wood and rock.

You might be wondering how similar the Happisburgh people were to us. Luckily, scientists have thought a lot about this as well. Their age indicates that the Happisburgh people were at a stage of evolution somewhere between *homo habilis* and *homo sapiens*. This means that they were very similar to us, but not quite as clever. As a result, the Happisburgh people, as well as people of the same subspecies, probably went extinct (died out) around 800,000 years ago.

Question Time!

QUESTION 1

Choose the best answer for the following multiple choice question, by writing **A**, **B**, or **C** in the box underneath.

"What is archaeology?"

A	Archaeology is the study of buildings, both old and new.
B	Archaeology is the art of building huge wooden ships, designed to provide shelter to humans and animals during floods.
C	Archaeology is the study of ancient remains which can give us huge amounts of information about living things that were around thousands of years ago.

Your answer:

QUESTION 2

Why is it said that British 'prehistory' ended with the start of the Roman Era?

_____

_____

_____

_____

QUESTION 3

Below are three of the Galapagos finches researched by Charles Darwin. Look at the information, then write **1**, **2**, and **3** in the table below to decide which bird eats which food!

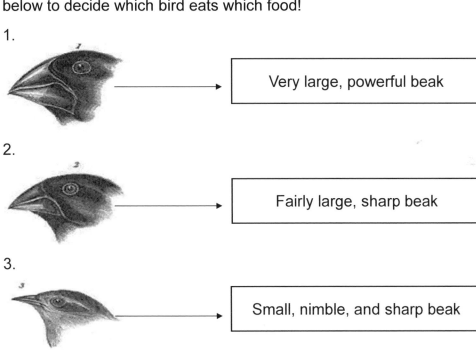

1.

Very large, powerful beak

2.

Fairly large, sharp beak

3.

Small, nimble, and sharp beak

Eats insects	Eats nuts	Eats seeds

QUESTION 4

Why is it **not** correct to say that humans evolved from chimps or gorillas, although the three species are closely related?

_____

_____

_____

_____

QUESTION 5

Look at the following statements, and decide whether you think they are correct. Circle '**TRUE**' or '**FALSE**' for each one.

The dinosaurs became extinct around 65 million years ago.	TRUE	FALSE

Homo habilis was cleverer than _Homo erectus_.	TRUE	FALSE

Modern humans are also called 'Neanderthals'.	TRUE	FALSE

Homo sapiens were much better communicators than Neanderthals.	TRUE	FALSE

QUESTION 6

Write down a few reasons why you think the Happisburgh footprints were such an exciting and important discovery.

_____

_____

_____

_____

_____

ANSWERS

QUESTION 1

In the box, you should have written:

QUESTION 2

It is said that British 'prehistory' ended with the start of the Roman Era, because the Romans were the first people to write things down in Britain. Before this, no one was recording events, which meant that no history was being recorded!

QUESTION 3

To show what the birds eat, this is what your table should look like:

1.   2.   3.

Eats insects	Eats nuts	Eats seeds
3	1	2

QUESTION 4

It is not correct to say that humans evolved from chimps or gorillas, because it is much more accurate to say that we share a common ancestor with these animals. In other words, humans, chimps, and gorillas evolved from the same ancient species; chimps and gorillas did not change into humans.

QUESTION 5

You should have answered the true or false statements like this:

| The dinosaurs became extinct around 65 million years ago. | (TRUE) | FALSE |

| *Homo habilis* was cleverer than *Homo erectus*. | TRUE | (FALSE) |

| Modern humans are also called 'Neanderthals'. | TRUE | (FALSE) |

| *Homo sapiens* were much better communicators than Neanderthals. | (TRUE) | FALSE |

QUESTION 6

These are some of the reasons that you could have written down for why the Happisburgh footprints were such an exciting and important discovery:

- The footprints were around 900,000 years old, which proved that people were living in Britain at this time. Before this, it was thought that Britain was too cold for people to survive 900,000 years ago!

- The largest Happisburgh footprints were very similar in size to modern humans, telling us a lot about the bodies of people who lived such a long time ago.

- The footprints are the oldest footprints (left by people) that have ever been found outside of Africa.

HOW ARE YOU GETTING ON?

MESOLITHIC ERA
(THE MID STONE AGE)

THE MID STONE AGE

As you might expect, the early stages of the Mesolithic Era (the mid Stone Age) have lots of similarities to the latter stages of the Palaeolithic Era, often making it difficult to compare one to the other. Today, we tend to say that the Mesolithic Era began after the last Ice Age ended. Also, while it's true that modern humans (*homo sapiens*) appeared towards the end of the Palaeolithic Era, it is not until the Mesolithic Period where people started to get really clever! That is to say, people were getting much better at communicating and adapting to their environments. This chapter will cover these changes in detail, so read on!

Palaeolithic traditions

People's progress

New tools

More grunting

Our cave-dwelling friend, Jeff, is still here. We still don't know what he's saying though.

PALAEOLITHIC TRADITIONS

Post Ice-Age Britain

After the final Ice Age, which ended around 10,000 years ago, Britain itself went through major changes. Of course, this was caused by the huge amount of water that descended on Britain after all the ice melted! Not only did this water eventually cause Britain to become an island (see page 19), but it also gave rise to dense forest and grasslands across Britain, which steadily grew over many years. Of course, this changed Britain forever, transforming it from a marshy area with few plants to a vibrant land thick with trees and wildlife.

Soon, humans would start to depend on the forest for survival, as it would provide home to the plants and animals that made up their food supply. It is for this reason that humans living in the Mesolithic (and Palaeolithic) came to be called 'hunter-gatherers', because they hunted animals for their meat, and gathered plants, berries, and nuts to eat as well. In the forest, humans would also find many of the useful materials that they used to build and create things, meaning that their new landscapes provided them with new opportunities to thrive.

So, as Britain itself gradually changed, human behaviour had to as well. This is why researchers say that human behaviour at the start of the Mesolithic Era was very similar to that during the later stages of the Palaeolithic Era – humans had to learn how to survive in their new surroundings, it didn't just happen!

Development Begins

However, although this change of behaviour was slow, it was incredibly significant. Have a look at the details that define the lives of humans in the Mesolithic Era.

▶ Where did people live?

People lived in small families, occupying simple wooden shelters or even caves. At first, families had to move around a lot as the seasons changed, in order to follow where food was. For example, when snow melted and the weather became warmer, animals like fish and birds would change habitat to be as warm as possible for as long as possible. However, as time went on, people learned to settle more permanently in strategic locations – close to food and water but out of danger.

▶ How did they hunt?

People could craft spearheads and other weapons out of sharp stone. However, tools and weapons were also made out of bone, wood, and even the antlers of slain deer. (For more on tools, see the next section of this chapter.) Humans in the Mid Stone Age also began to tame wolves and use them for hunting – they would be trained to chase and corner deer. This was the start of humanity's friendship with dogs!

▶ Did they have free time?

Due to the harsh nature of their lives, Stone Age people were not able to enjoy much free time as we know it today – all their decisions were made with survival in mind. However, there is evidence that people enjoyed creating art – ancient paintings have been found (often on the walls of caves), showing drawings of animals. It is not clear whether they did this out of sheer joy, or if it was also a form of worship to the creatures that provided them with food.

NEW TOOLS

As mentioned previously, humans during the Mesolithic Era were developing more and more advanced tools and weapons. These new tools reflected the new environments people found themselves in. For example, animal bones and antlers were fashioned into tools: deer antlers were hard and could be sharpened with rocks.

This development in craftsmanship shows how people were getting better and better at dealing with their surroundings, and how humans (although already dominant) were increasing the distance between themselves and other species from the top of the food chain. In other words, humans were getting better at surviving because they could more easily kill and eat other animals! This was also due to the fact that humans could outsmart animals – they would trick them into running into traps and even off cliffs!

Types of weapons and tools

The most important material for making tools and weapons from was a stone called flint. Flint was an incredibly good choice to make things like axeheads and spearheads from because it is both durable and easy to shape. So, it is possible to carve it into a sharp point that is strong enough to cause damage and not easily break. It was also common and easy to find! People would then attach the stone to wooden handles and poles to the flint to create weapons and tools. In the Mesolithic

Era, people were crafting tools with much more expertise than they were in the past, meaning the tools were much higher quality.

These are the tools that people were starting to design and craft during the Mesolithic Era:

- Axes (the tool on the left is an axe head)

- Spears (the tool on the right is a spearhead)

- Knives

- Carving tool

- Bow and arrow

- Fish traps

Using these tools, Mesolithic people would hunt for deer, cattle, boar, rabbits, and rodents. Fish (including shellfish) and foraged plants also appeared in their diets.

PEOPLE'S PROGRESS

As mentioned earlier, people just lived in families during the Mesolithic Era – there were no permanent communities like modern villages, towns, or cities.

Families tended to have nomadic lifestyles – this meant that they travelled around a lot. This movement had a lot to do with the changing of the seasons. People learned that staying in different locations during different seasons was beneficial, so they often returned to the same place year on year.

This is more information that points to the fact that human society was developing. Another aspect of this is to do with what some historians have referred to as an early form of religion. In other words, ancient humans during the Mesolithic Era started to behave in ways that can be compared to more recent religious ceremonies, many of which still take place today.

For example, people were burying those close to them when they died, often alongside items that belonged to them during their lives. For instance, archaeologists have found Mesolithic graves containing jewellery and other prized possessions.

Why would they do this? Many historians believe that this showed that people were starting to think about some form of afterlife, or heaven. The idea was that a person would be buried with their favourite belongings, so they would still have them in the next life. Although it is not clear what people specifically believed about what happened after death (or if they even had specific beliefs), the buried belongings showed that they were at least beginning to consider it.

Question Time!

QUESTION 1

Other than the fact that it became an island, how did the ending of the Ice Age change Britain?

_____

_____

_____

_____

QUESTION 2

Look at the following possible responses to the question: 'How did Britain's new landscape following the Ice Age, allow its people to thrive like never before?'

Put a tick (✓) in the box next to the response you think is best.

The new forest environment provided habitats to many animals which people could hunt, wood people could use for building, and plants and berries people could eat.	
The new forest environment meant that people could start building luxurious log cabins to stay in during the cold winter months.	

QUESTION 3

How did taming wolves allow people to become better at hunting?

_____

_____

_____

_____

QUESTION 4

Create your own drawing of a Stone Age cave painting. Remember that they often drew animals and their favourite food!

QUESTION 5

In the box below, you will see several potential adjectives (describing words) for flint, the stone used by Mesolithic people to make tools. However, some of them are not suitable! Circle all the ones that you think are correct.

Bendy

Sharp

Easy to shape

Soft   Rare

Hard

Easy to find   Blunt

QUESTION 6

Why did people start to bury those close to them with their belongings?

_____

_____

_____

_____

_____

_____

_____

ANSWERS

QUESTION 1

The ending of the Ice Age caused Britain's landscape to change dramatically. The huge amounts of water left by so much ice melting, caused grasslands, forests, and plant life to appear. This provided people and animals with a habitat and lots of resources.

QUESTION 2

You should have ticked the first statement, like this:

The new forest environment provided habitats to many animals which people could hunt, wood people could use for building, and plants and berries people could eat.	
The new forest environment meant that people could start building luxurious log cabins to stay in during the cold winter months.	

QUESTION 3

Taming wolves allowed people to become better at hunting, because in doing so, they gained another advantage over their prey. Of course, being able to control wolves meant that people could use the wolves' natural hunting abilities (like their speed, sense of smell, strong jaws) to catch prey for themselves more easily and quickly.

QUESTION 4

Show someone your drawing! Did they like it?

QUESTION 5

You should have circled the following adjectives:

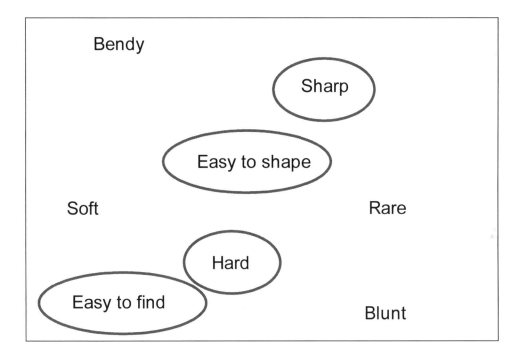

Bendy

Sharp

Easy to shape

Soft   Rare

Hard

Easy to find

Blunt

QUESTION 6

People began to bury people with their belongings because they
started to consider what happens to people when they die, such as the
possibility of the afterlife. Perhaps people thought that the dead would
be able to take their belongings with them to the next life (if that's what
they believed in), if they were placed in the graves alongside them.

HOW ARE YOU GETTING ON?

NEOLITHIC ERA
(LATE STONE AGE)

THE LAST STONE AGE

As we have travelled throughout the Stone Age, you will have noticed how fast humans were developing, and becoming more and more dominant over their surroundings as the Mesolithic Era came to an end. However, humanity was yet to make its biggest breakthrough, that was to spell the end for the hunter-gatherer lifestyle. What was this breakthrough? The answer is all to do with farming! That's right, humans working out how to farm would change history forever.

The first British farmers

Advancing society

Stonehenge

Even more grunting

Yes, Jeff is here again. No, we haven't worked out what he's saying yet...

THE FIRST BRITISH FARMERS

Although it is unclear exactly when or where the first farmers in the world lived, historians believe that farming spread to Britain around 6,000 years ago, and became commonplace by a couple of thousand years after. This revolutionary moment marks the start of the Neolithic Era – the late Stone Age! It was such a major change because it meant that people began to grow plants themselves to eat, rather than simply forage for plants where they grew by chance. So, what were these early farmers doing, and what did this mean for their everyday lives?

Early farming techniques

A big part of this farming revolution was the invention of the sickle. A sickle is a curved farming tool with a blade attached to it, ideal for cutting fruits from the top of plants.

The image on the right shows a Neolithic sickle. It is made from wood, and its blades are made from flint. It even has a rope string attached to the handle to make it easier to grip.

The sickle would have been used to harvest grain from wheat plants, which has many different uses in Stone Age foods, like bread.

In addition to harvesting grain, Neolithic farmers would grow vegetables and other crops like barley. They would bake bread, and even start to make things like butter and cheese. Also, they would start to look after animals like sheep, cows, and pigs, which farmers still do today. While they used the farm animals for food and their products, they continued to keep dogs as helpers and pets.

Changing lifestyles

Of course, this change from a hunter-gatherer lifestyle to a farmer lifestyle greatly affected how people spend their days. For example, people no longer had to travel around following the food – so they could control where it grew! Soon, people started to settle down permanently, and stay in one place all year round. This meant that slowly, people began to cluster together, forming small communities and villages.

Eventually, people got so good at farming that they started to produce more than they needed to survive, so they were able to store food and focus on other things. This period in history represents one of the first in which people didn't have to spend 100% of their time worrying about pure survival!

ADVANCING SOCIETY

As a result, other human activities like building and crafting began to flourish. It also gave rise to a new form of trading. See the next chapter for more detail on how society was changing during the Neolithic Era.

So, with people no longer having to spend all their time hunting and foraging, what did they do?

Crafting

With more time to practise and experiment with different crafting techniques, people began to make more and more advanced tools and weapons. This led to people being able to build and craft more intricate and useful things.

For example, around 5 years ago, researchers revealed just how skilled Neolithic people were at working with wood, with the discovery of four water wells in Germany.

The wells were constructed out of many pieces of wood interlocked together, which had been designed and shaped to fit together perfectly. The wells were around 7,000 years old.

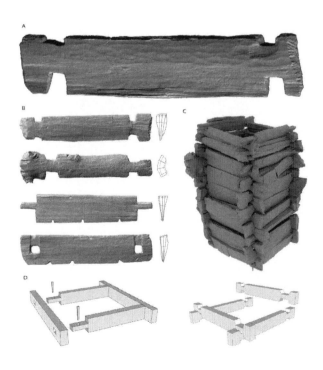

This was such a huge discovery, because it was previously thought that carpentry of this complexity was not yet possible. Researchers had previously believed that such intricate design and building was possible for early humans without metal nails, which would not be invented as we know it for thousands of years!

Trading

As people became better at farming, they could grow food more and more efficiently. Eventually, the best farmers found themselves with more food than their families needed to survive. So, they were able to store it as spare. Soon, people realised that they could offer this spare food to others who needed it more them. They did not do this for free of course – they looked to see what they could get in return for their food. Perhaps the people who wanted the spare food had extra resources, like flint and other materials, which they were willing to swap for it. This basic idea gave rise to early forms of trading!

As years passed, people began to travel longer and longer distances with the goods they wanted to trade. This meant that people were becoming able to get hold of things that did not come from their area. For example, materials like gold, silver, and obsidian started to spread across Asia and Europe as traders travelled in search of customers!

We know this because archaeologists have found ancient goods native to Asia (such as jewellery and precious metals) in Britain, suggesting that they were gained by trading with a travelling salesman!

Housing

All the while, people's living conditions began to improve. Due to the fact that people did not travel around as much as they did during the Mesolithic Era, they started to make their permanent homes nicer and nicer – they no longer had to live in caves or simple wooden huts!

One of the best examples of how permanent homes developed during the British Neolithic Era can be found at Skara Brae, in Orkney, Scotland. In 1850, a severe storm eroded away enough of its landscape to reveal an astonishingly well-preserved Neolithic settlement.

An inside view of one of the houses

In total, the storm revealed 8 houses, made from stone bricks, with rooves made from wood. They even contained furniture, like dressers and beds, all made from stone and wood. In the centre of the houses, there would have been fires to cook food on, as well as to heat the house.

Perhaps most amazing of all is that the houses were equipped with an early system of sewers and toilets! The fact that the houses shared this technology shows that they lived as a community of families, representing an early village-like settlement. Clearly, the houses at Skara Brae, which were eventually dated as being around 5,000 years old, can tell us a lot about how people in Britain were living their lives during the Neolithic Period.

A view of the houses from the outside

STONEHENGE

However, surely the most famous construction to come out of the Stone Age is none other than the stone circle of Stonehenge, in Western England. The famous Stone Circle is around 5,000 years old. Even today, it doesn't fail to amaze or prompt questions like: 'How did they move these huge slabs of stone?', 'How did they make the stone stand upright?', and 'Why on Earth did they bother?' Fortunately, historians believe they've been able to answer most of these questions.

Firstly, researchers believe that the only way it would be possible for ancient people to build the stone circle is very slowly, and in huge teams. Certainly, construction of the stone circle began with a round trench dug in preparation. As for how they made the slabs stand upright, we only have speculative theories – guesses! Some historians believe that people would have had to use a series of wooden scaffolds and rope, and dozens of people pulling as hard as they could. The horizontal slabs are able to stay lying across two vertical ones due to a system of round knobs and holes – like how Lego bricks fit together!

As for the reason the stone circle was built, historians are more confident they know what it is: it marked when the winter solstice occurred, and when the summer solstice occurred. In other words, the shortest day of the year, and the longest day of the year. When the sun set directly in-between a certain archway of rock, Neolithic people knew when these dates were. But, why was this important to them?

In their new lives as farmers, knowing when these days occurred was vital for Neolithic people. This is because the solstices mark the seasons, and where they begin and end. For example, the winter solstice marks the turning point where winter starts to become spring. Knowing this meant that Neolithic people could begin preparing for planting and growing season, something that was impossible during winter.

Conversely, the summer solstice marks the end of growing season and the start of harvesting season. This is because the shortening days mean that time is running out before winter returns. So, it is possible to look at ancient stone circles as being like early calendars!

Spirit Stones

Stone circles like the one at Stonehenge also give us an insight into Neolithic spiritual practices, which you could say were like early religious ceremonies. For example, people cremated their dead at the site of the stone circle for hundreds of years, showing they believed it to be a place of significance.

Also, archaeologists have found evidence that Neolithic people held festivals and ceremonies at the time of these solstices. At Stonehenge, archaeologists have found an abundance of pig and cow bones all clustered in one area. This suggests that huge feasts were held in the area. Some researchers have suggested that people in Britain travelled from many miles away, even as far as Scotland, to attend these gatherings. This could show how important the solstice events were for Neolithic people, and could even suggest how British people were starting to unite under one culture, something that had not been seen before.

Question Time!

QUESTION 1

What do historians say marks the start of the Neolithic Era?

_____

_____

_____

_____

QUESTION 2

Label the following Neolithic sickle in terms of the material each of its components are made from.

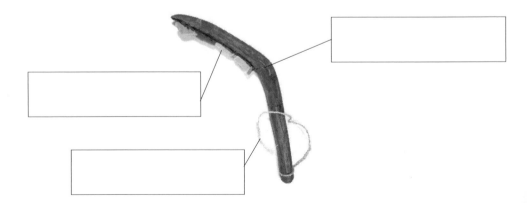

QUESTION 3

Look at the following statements, and decide whether you think they are correct. Circle '**TRUE**' or '**FALSE**' for each one.

When farming spread to Britain, people could start settling in one area all year round.	TRUE	FALSE
After farming spread to Britain, most people became vegetarians.	TRUE	FALSE
People had lots of farming to do, meaning they had less time to build, craft, and trade.	TRUE	FALSE
Farming gave rise to larger communities being established.	TRUE	FALSE

QUESTION 4

Why was the discovery of the four Neolithic wells in Germany such a huge one?

_____

_____

_____

_____

QUESTION 5

How do we know that people in Britain began buying things that came from abroad?

_____

_____

_____

_____

QUESTION 6

Look at the photograph below. It was taken on the longest day of the year at Stonehenge.

What is this day called, and why is it important?

_____

_____

_____

_____

ANSWERS

QUESTION 1

Historians say that the time when farming spread to Britain (around 6,000 years ago) marks the start of the Neolithic Era.

QUESTION 2

The materials that make up a Neolithic sickle are as follows:

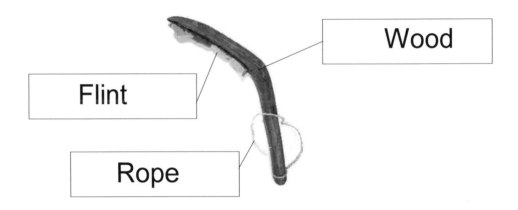

Wood

Flint

Rope

QUESTION 3

You should have answered the true or false statements like this:

When farming spread to Britain, people could start settling in one area all year round.	(TRUE)	FALSE
After farming spread to Britain, most people became vegetarians.	TRUE	(FALSE)
People had lots of farming to do, meaning they had less time to build, craft, and trade.	TRUE	(FALSE)
Farming gave rise to larger communities being established.	(TRUE)	FALSE

QUESTION 4

The discovery of the four wells in Germany was such a huge one, because historians previously thought that Neolithic people were not capable of such intricate and complex work with wood. Until the find, it was assumed that people could not build such items without the use of metal nails.

QUESTION 5

We know that people in Britain began buying things that came from abroad, because archaeologists have found items such as jewellery in Britain that could only have come from other parts of Europe and Asia.

QUESTION 6

The longest day of the year is called the summer solstice. It is important, because it marks the end of the planting and growing season for farmers, because it shows the days are getting shorter and shorter. At the same time, it marks the beginning of harvesting season, which was and is often celebrated with festivals.

HOW ARE YOU GETTING ON?

THE BRONZE AGE

THE BRONZE AGE

The end of the Stone Age was a huge moment in human history – it had lasted for well over 2 million years. As you might be thinking, the event to bring such an age to an end must have been massive! Well, you'd be right. Although the invention of metalwork was not one single event, it undeniably changed Britain, and indeed the world, forever. It would go hand in hand with the rise of trading, which in itself would transform people's lives and living situations. It may have taken a while, but metal was here to stay in Britain.

Inventing bronze

Rich and poor

Growing tribes

Metal!

Jeff has gone! Now, our bronze age tribe leader is here!

Meet Paul. He likes metal.

INVENTING BRONZE

Towards the end of the Neolithic Era, as humans began to get even better at crafting, they eventually made a huge breakthrough. It involved working with metal, and would bring about the end of the Stone Age – which had lasted for millions of years!

What was the breakthrough? In mainland Europe, people realised that they could mine copper ore (a naturally occurring rock) in order to extract the copper metal itself from it. People would then smelt the copper (melt it down to a liquid), then pour it into moulds, which were carved into stone. The moulds would be in the shape of tools and weapons, so when the liquid cooled down and hardened, a copper tool would be the result!

Working with copper in this way spread to Britain about 4,500 years ago, and changed people's lives hugely – people no longer used stone tools and weapons. However, soon copper would be improved upon and left behind! That's right, the Copper Age was not to last for very long at all, because people worked out how to make bronze, a much harder and more useful metal than copper.

Here's a flowchart to show the process of making tools and weapons.

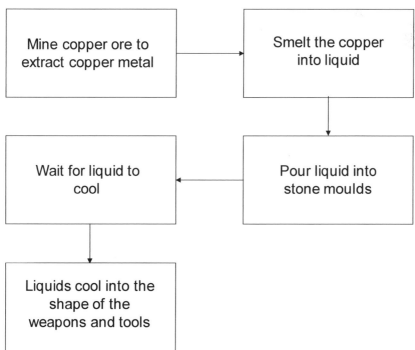

How did people make bronze?

The method people used to produce bronze was very similar to the method used to produce copper, with a key difference. It involved adding an extra ingredient, tin mined from tin ore, that gave the metal all its superior qualities over copper.

So, people would make bronze tools by adding melted copper mixed with melted tin to their moulds. When this mixture cooled and hardened, bronze would be the result. This was important because bronze turned out to be much more useful than copper, which was a fair bit softer.

Soon, people had to dig deep mines in order to find the tin and copper ore they needed. These were very dangerous places, which could collapse and crush whoever was inside digging. To make it worse, children were often sent down into the mines, as they were often the only ones who could fit down certain tunnels.

Despite this, being able to create and work with metal tools was a monumental step forward for humankind, with this new technique marking the start of the Bronze Age, which would last for over 1,000 years. During this time, people's lives would change dramatically, for a number of reasons. Read on to discover how and why this happened!

Why is metal better than stone?

There are a few reasons why Bronze Age people preferred to use tools and weapons made of metal rather than stone. For example, swords, axes, daggers, and spearheads began to be made in bronze. The advantage of this was that metal was more durable – it could not crumble or shatter in the same way many rocks did. Also, due to the fact that it was made by pouring liquid into moulds meant that people could make things of any shape out of bronze, something that is impossible with stone. This meant that people could make wearable things out of bronze, like armour and accessories. In short, there was a lot more people could do with bronze!

However, this did not mean that people stopped using stone entirely. It was still very useful for building things out of – like the furnaces people would use to melt copper and tin!

RICH AND POOR

As mentioned before, the invention of bronze and its arrival in Britain had a dramatic effect on people's daily lives. Pretty quickly, it would also begin to change the equal nature of human society – for the first time, major differences between the lives of 'rich' and 'poor' people would start to appear.

How did this happen?

As you might imagine, creating and working with metal was a task that took a lot of skill. This, along with the fact that they were of a higher quality, meant that bronze tools and weapons were more valuable than the old stone ones – people were willing to trade more to get hold of them!

As a result, people who did this work (a more modern word for them might be 'blacksmiths') were able to gather wealth much more quickly than people who did other things. Gradually, people began to become proud of their wealth. Wearing accessories made from valuable materials like bronze and gold became fashionable – as did exotic foreign items like amber and decorative beakers.

For example, an extremely intricate and precisely designed cape, made out of solid gold, was found in 1833 in Mold, Wales. Researchers found that it was from the Bronze Age, and that it was discovered in a burial mound belonging to someone who must have been very rich and powerful, like a tribe leader. However, it would have restricted the wearer's arm movements, so it was not used as armour. Most likely it was simply decorative – worn to show off one's wealth!

The Mold Gold Cape

The arrival of trading in this way was another major development in the human story – people have never stopped trading goods with each other since! Traders in control of the best trade routes (like between southern England and northern France) were also able to become very rich and powerful.

GROWING TRIBES

All the while, settlements were growing bigger and bigger. This had continued ever since farming had arrived in Britain during the Neolithic Era – people no longer had to roam around for food.

Eventually, the settlements people lived in became larger than single families – villages of tribes started to appear. Within these tribes, different people would have different roles – some would bake bread, some would farm, some would make metal, and some would work with wool to create clothes.

Soon, the richest people in these villages started competing with one another, each trying to prove that they had the most money and desirable possessions. This led to people lunging for power – competition for the position of tribe leader was intense!

As tribe leaders and the people they controlled became more established, wider conflict became more and more common. In other words, tribes would start fighting in groups against each other, for land, wealth, and resources. Tribe warfare had come to Britain.

All of these elements were at play when humans made yet another major breakthrough, and ushered in yet another brand-new age! That's right, the Iron Age was almost here.

Question Time!

QUESTION 1

Below you will find all of the steps that people in the Bronze Age would have had to take to make bronze! However, they are in the wrong order! Put them in the correct order in the space underneath, using the blank boxes on the next page.

Melt down the copper and tin using fire in a furnace, which were often made with stone.

Let the liquid cool and harden, and remove your bronze product!

Mine copper and tin from the rocks (ore).

Pour the liquid into a mould (which is carved into stone) in the shape of what you are making.

1.

2.

3.

4.

QUESTION 2

Using the bullet points below, write down two advantages bronze has over stone.

- _____

  _____

- _____

  _____

QUESTION 3

Look at the picture of the Mold Gold Cape. What does it tell us about whoever owned it?

_____

_____

_____

_____

QUESTION 4

During the Bronze Age, one major change in people's lives was that trading became more and more common and made people rich, as did working with bronze. What was another major change that affected how people lived with one another?

_____

_____

_____

_____

ANSWERS

QUESTION 1

Steps for making bronze in the right order:

1.

> Mine copper and tin from the rocks (ore).

2.

> Melt down the copper and tin using fire in a furnace, which were often made with stone.

3.

> Pour the liquid into a mould (which is carved into stone) in the shape of what you are making.

4.

> Let the liquid cool and harden, and remove your bronze product!

QUESTION 2

Two advantages bronze has over stone:

*   Bronze is more durable in that it cannot crumble or shatter like rock does.

*   You can make things of any shape out of bronze: anything you can make a mould of!

QUESTION 3

The intricate design, as well as the fact that it was made from solid gold, shows that whoever owned the Mold Gold Cape was very rich, and therefore very powerful. The fact that its only purpose was to make the wearer look fancy and show off wealth shows that whoever had it made had money to burn.

QUESTION 4

At the same time that trading between long distances was becoming more and more common, people were starting to live in larger and larger communities. In other words, people moved away from just living in their own families, and started forming tribes. This led to fighting – not only when deciding tribe leaders, but between tribes themselves.

THE IRON AGE

THE IRON AGE

Although copper and bronze changed people's lives forever, their time at the top was not to last for that long at all! Instead, a new metal would start to assert its dominance in Britain, at the hands of a new group of people we call the Celts. The Celts had become the dominant tribe in Europe, and before too long they would have Britain as well. The Celts would have a huge impact on Britain's history, due to their expertise working with iron and their rich cultural traditions – Celtic influences are still seen across Europe today. However, a certain Italian empire would not stand by and watch them prosper for too long...

Looks like Paul has already been forced out! This is Brian, a Celtic warrior. He likes fighting.

WORKING WITH IRON

As you might have guessed, the Iron Age began when humans learned how to work with iron, and so started to use less and less bronze. Before we talk about why iron was (probably) better than bronze, let's have a look at how people living during the early Iron Age managed to use it to their advantage!

How do you make iron tools?

Working with iron had many similarities to working with bronze and copper, with a couple of key differences that made it a lot harder. Firstly, it was a lot more difficult to extract iron from iron ore – it took a lot of precise and hard work. Also, iron is much more difficult to melt than bronze – you need to heat it to much higher temperatures for it to turn into liquid. These differences meant that people had to invent and perfect new techniques to produce iron tools, something that took many years. Of course, when people did work out how to achieve this, a whole new era of history was born.

Why is iron better than bronze?

Iron tools and weapons have a few advantages over bronze ones. Firstly, iron is a lot tougher, making it even more durable than bronze. It also only requires one type of ore to make, giving iron production an advantage over bronze production, which needs both copper ore and tin ore. This meant that once people perfected the technique of collecting and smelting this ore, it was a more efficient process, as resources only had to be collected from one place.

However, some believe that iron tools and weapons were not actually that much better than bronze tools. Although it is harder than most of the bronze being made at the time, it's not sharper or more easily shaped. Iron tools also had problems that bronze tools did not, like being at risk to rust.

So, why did working with iron become so many people in Britain's favourite? Many point to the arrival of a new group of people in Britain for the answer – the Celts. The Celts were extremely good at working with iron, and soon they would take over.

CELTIC REVOLUTION

Who were the Celts?

The Celts were a group of people who appeared in Western Europe towards the end of the Bronze Age. Quickly, due to their skill and efficiency working with iron, their power grew and they began to dominate. Naturally, this meant that they eventually became the dominant people in Britain.

However, Celts did not identify themselves as belonging to a whole nation. Rather, people in Iron Age Britain still lived in separate tribes, as people did in the Bronze Age. Celtic tribes were ruled by chieftains and warrior kings and queens, who often fought with each other for power and land.

What was life like in Iron Age Britain?

Due to how much land they occupied, a Celtic way of life eventually became well-established in Britain, as it had done across Western Europe. This represented a major change in how people spent their time and lived their lives – a new culture had arrived in Britain.

One example of this is that people's living spaces were developing. The largest tribes in Britain now lived in impressive hill forts, which were dug into the earth and looked like steep, giant staircases, to slow down any attackers. At the top of the hill forts were communities of large round houses made using timber, sticks and clay (a method called wattle-and-daub). The thick, cone-shaped rooves would be made from thatch straw.

Inside the houses, you would even find small rooms, cordoned off around the outside. The rooms were used for storage of weapons, as well as sleeping. At the centre of the house would be a large hearth and fire, which would be used to provide heating, as well as cook food. A loom, to work with cloth and wool, would also be a feature of most Celtic homes. Finally, families would keep farm animals in small areas akin to a modern back garden!

You can see how people's living areas were developing over time, all becoming more like our ones today! Look back at page 55, where a Stone Age house is described, and compare it to the Celtic house!

Celts also had a proud tradition of artistic culture. For example, Celts loved storytelling and poetry. Bards would tell tales about great victories in battle, and heroes of years gone by. These stories would always be told using the spoken word, as reading and writing as we know it had not become commonplace in Britain yet.

As touched upon, the Celts were master craftsman. However, this went beyond making tools and weapons. Celtic Britons loved making beautiful jewellery out of gold, which they were able to twist into complicated shapes and patterns. Celts also loved to decorate anything and everything with bright colours, using dye from a plant called woad. They would colour their clothes, creating patterns with the blue paint. Famously, Celtic warriors would also dye their skin with woad to intimidate their enemies – applying war paint would become a vital stage in any tribe's preparations for war.

Could the Celts fight?

Celtic warriors learned to fight from a very early age. Children trained with swords, spears, and even slingshots! Some tribal warriors covered themselves in mud and dyed clay to appear intimidating. In addition to this, they would shout and blow trumpets to mark the start of a battle.

The Celts also knew how to use horses and chariots to cause chaos in battle, charging at their enemies and forcing them to scatter and break rank. However, the Celtic warriors, while led by their king or queen, had no official formations or hierarchy. Still, their fearsome fighting techniques, as well as their expert use of iron swords and chariots, meant that they were feared throughout Europe.

Celtic Religion?

Historians also believe that the Celts had more advanced religious practices than people seemed to have during the Stone Age or even the Bronze Age. Tribes had religious leaders (called Druids) who would carry out ceremonies in the name of many gods that people believed in. Each god would represent a different part of Celtic life – be it to do with nature (god of water, god of trees) or otherwise (god of war).

Celts can be said as being early followers of paganism, which means we cannot say that they would have belonged to any of the major religions that people follow today. Many other ancient pagans believed in many different gods as well – it was certainly a form of worship that would dominate Britain until the rise of Christianity – which would take centuries and centuries longer yet.

HERE COME THE ROMANS

However, while the Celts were doing well across Western Europe and Britain, another European force was building in the distance. By around the year 30 BC, the Roman Empire, beginning in what we now call Italy, had evolved into a mighty and uniquely advanced nation, living lives that humans in Europe could never have imagined only years before.

The Romans in power were writing down laws and history, becoming extremely rich trading and invading, and inventing 'sports' like gladiator fighting and chariot racing. Their lives and living situations soon became very different to those of the Celts, who still lived in separate warring tribes – not in big cities as a country. An important part of the Roman nation was their incredibly well-drilled and effective army – it was allowing them to conquer huge areas of Europe and Asia with ease.

However, for a while, the rich Romans were happy just to trade with the British barbarians (as they called them), taking their goods and resources in return for wine and pottery. However, as their Empire grew further and further westward, the powerful Romans' priorities changed. Their armies had easily conquered so much land around them, why not take the British Isles as well? At the forefront of this priority change was a certain Julius Caesar.

Celtic life in Britain was soon to change forever – the Roman Era was about to begin. This would have massive consequences, including bringing an end to the Iron Age forever!

Question Time!

QUESTION 1

What are the two key differences between producing bronze and producing iron?

1.

2.

QUESTION 2

Discuss the things about iron that make many say that it is not better than bronze.

_____

_____

_____

_____

QUESTION 3

Look at this picture of an Iron Age hill fort.

How would digging this fort have helped the tribespeople living at the top?

_____

_____

_____

_____

_____

_____

_____

_____

QUESTION 4

In the box below are things that you would have found in both Stone Age homes and Iron Age homes. Sort the things into columns in the table underneath – look at each thing and decide whether it would be in a Stone Age home, an Iron Age home, or both! Use page 55 to help you.

Fireplace

Small rooms

Wooden rooves

A loom

Thatched rooves

Beds

Stone Age home	Iron Age home	Both

QUESTION 5

Why were Celtic stories told using the spoken word, not written down?

_____

_____

_____

_____

QUESTION 6

Look at the following possible definitions for the word 'paganism'. Choose which one you think is best by putting a tick (✓) next to one of the options.

| Paganism means believing in one god, like followers of most of the major world religions of today do. | ☐ |

| Paganism refers to a form of worship that does not fit with the beliefs of any major religions that are still followed today. Pagans often worshipped many gods that represented different aspects of their lives. | ☐ |

ANSWERS

QUESTION 1

The two key differences between producing bronze and producing iron are:

1.

> Iron is much more difficult to get from the rock it comes from – iron ore.

2.

> Iron has a much higher melting point than bronze.

QUESTION 2

People can say that iron is not better than bronze, due to the fact that is it harder to extract from its ore than bronze, and has a much higher melting point. At the same time, it is not even sharper or easier to shape. Also, iron suffers from rusting, which bronze does not.

QUESTION 3

Digging the hill fort would have helped the Iron Age tribespeople who lived on it, as it would have slowed down anyone trying to run up and attack them! It would have made an attack a lot harder, their enemies and their horses would have had to put a lot more effort into reaching them.

QUESTION 4

Your table should have ended up looking like this:

Stone Age home	Iron Age home	Both
Wooden rooves	Small rooms	Fireplace
	Thatched rooves	Beds
	Loom	

QUESTION 5

Celtic stories were told using the spoken word, not written down. This is because writing as we know it had not spread to Britain yet. In other words – they could not read or write!

QUESTION 6

You should have ticked the second statement, like this:

Paganism means believing in one god, like followers of most of the major world religions of today do.	
Paganism refers to a form of worship that does not fit with the beliefs of any major religions that are still followed today. Pagans often worshipped many gods that represented different aspects of their lives.	

HOW ARE YOU GETTING ON?

Total Score

out of 32

Mock Paper:

Stone Age to Iron Age

35 minutes

First Name	
Middle Name/s	
Last Name	
School	
Date of Birth	D D / M M / Y Y Y Y

⭐ **1** Answer these questions about the end of the Iron Age:

a) How did the Roman Empire's priorities about Britain change?

_____

_____

_____

_____

b) How did the Roman Empire pose such a serious threat to Iron Age people in Britain?

_____

_____

_____

_____

⭐ **2** Answer these questions about Stonehenge:

a) How do historians believe people managed to make the stone slabs stand upright at Stonehenge?

_____

_____

b) How did the people who built Stonehenge make sure the horizontal slabs did not fall off the vertical ones?

_____

_____

3 Answer these questions about evolution:

a) Give 2 favourable characteristics that modern humans have, which early people did not have?

_____

_____

1 mark

b) During evolution, how do species change in the first place?

_____

_____

1 mark

c) What part did *homo sapiens* (modern humans) play in the extinction of the Neanderthals?

_____

_____

_____

_____

2 marks

Explain how we know that evolution occurs.

_____

_____

_____

_____

2 marks

4 Answer these questions about the Bronze Age:

a) Other than the invention of bronze, what other major development in the human story happened at this time?

_____

_____
1 r

b) How did the invention of bronze lead to some people becoming richer than others?

_____

_____

_____

_____
2 r

5 Answer these questions about early British farming:

a) When people started to move from a hunter-gatherer lifestyle to a farming lifestyle, how did this affect the amount they moved around?

_____

_____
1 r

b) What is a sickle?

_____

_____

_____

_____
2 r

6 Answer these questions about the Celts.

a) How were the Romans' views on nationhood different to those of the Celts?

_____

_____

_____

_____

2 marks

b) Discuss how the Celts liked to fight.

_____

_____

_____

_____

2 marks

c) What did Celtic druids do?

_____

_____

_____

_____

2 marks

d) What did Celtic bards do?

_____

_____

_____

_____

2 marks

Answer these questions about the Palaeolithic Era:

a) Explain the difference between a 'glacial period' and an 'interglacial period'.

_____

_____

_____

_____

2 m

b) What was Doggerland, and why does it no longer exist?

_____

_____

_____

_____

2 m

c) In relation to *homo habilus* and *homo sapiens*, where do the Happisburgh people appear on the evolutionary timeline? (i.e. before them both, after them both, or in-between them.)

_____

_____

1 m

d) What happened to global temperatures after the end of the last Ice Age?

_____

_____

1 m

ANSWERS

a) Just before the end of the Iron Age, the Roman Empire's priorities about Britain changed in that they no longer wanted to trade with the Celts. Instead, they wanted to invade them and take over their land.

b) The Roman Empire posed such a serious threat to Iron Age people due to their extremely efficient and well-drilled army, which had taken over other parts of the world with ease.

a) Historians think people managed to make the stone slabs of Stonehenge stand up, via large groups of people using a system of wooden scaffolds.

b) The people who built Stonehenge made sure the horizontal slabs did not fall off the vertical ones, by using a system of round knobs and holes that fit together.

a) Two favourable characteristics that modern humans have that earlier people did not have, include bigger brains and better communication skills.

b) During evolution, species change due to random genetic mutation.

c) *Homo sapiens* played a major role in the extinction of the Neanderthals; they were better suited to their environment due to their better communication skills and larger brains. This meant that *homo sapiens* were far better at hunting and keeping hold of resources – so much so that there was none left for the Neanderthals, who died out.

d) We know that evolution occurs, due to fossils and ancient remains that have been found by archaeologists. Using dating techniques on these remains, researchers have been able to construct a timeline of how species have changed over millions of years.

a) During the Bronze Age, along with the invention of bronze, the arrival of trading represented a major development in the human story.

b) The invention of bronze gave rise to the idea of people being rich and poor, because it was a highly skilled task that produced useful and desirable items. So, people who could not produce bronze were willing to trade valuable goods in exchange for bronze, meaning that those who made bronze could become rich.

a) The change from a hunter-gather lifestyle to a farming lifestyle meant that people moved around less than they did before.

b) A sickle is a farming tool which is designed to make harvesting grain easier. Its curved shape, as well as the fact that it is equipped with a sharp blade, means that cutting plants becomes much faster and takes less effort than just using your hands.

a) The Roman view on nationhood was different to the Celts' in one key way: the Celts lived in separate tribes, and did not see themselves as belonging to a wider nation. On the other hand, the Romans united under one nation: The Empire.

b) The Celts liked to fight with strong iron weapons, using horses and chariots. They also liked to cover themselves in war paint to intimidate opponents. However, although they were strong fighters, they were not organised, and did not have clear tactics or shape.

c) Celtic druids were the spiritual heads of the Celtic pagan religion. They would perform ceremonies and sacrifices in the name of their many gods.

d) Celtic bards would perform poems and sing songs to people in their tribe. Their stories would often be about great heroes and battles of times gone by.

a) A 'glacial period' means a time when an Ice Age is occurring. An 'interglacial period' refers to a time when an Ice Age is not happening. Most commonly, it is used to refer to the periods in-between the three major Ice Ages that took place on Earth.

b) Doggerland was the stretch of earth that used to connect Britain to mainland Europe in ancient times. Doggerland disappeared under rising seas after the last Ice Age: the water levels got too high for it to remain poking out as land. This is when Britain became an island.

c) Researchers believe that the Happisburgh people were at an evolutionary stage that comes in somewhere between *homo habilus* and *homo sapiens*.

d) Following the end of the last Ice Age, global temperatures rose – it got warmer.

WANT MORE HELP WITH KS1 AND KS2 HISTORY?

CHECK OUT OUR OTHER HISTORY GUIDES:

How2Become have created other FANTASTIC guides to help you and your child learn all they need and want to for history at primary level

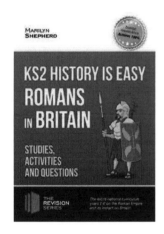
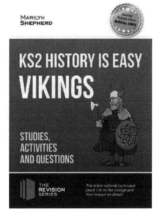
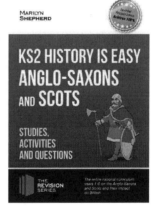

These exciting guides are filled with engaging facts and fun activities to ensure that their study is interesting, and their learning is improved! Invest in your child's future today!

FOR MORE INFORMATION ON OUR KEY STAGE 1 AND 2 (KS1 and KS2) GUIDES, PLEASE CHECK OUT THE FOLLOWING:

WWW.HOW2BECOME.COM

Get Access To

FREE

Online History Tests

www.MyEducationalTests.co.uk

Printed in Great Britain
by Amazon

BLOODY SCOTTISH HISTORY

EDINBURGH

GEOFF HOLDER

The
History
Press

DEDICATION

Dedicated to the memory of my grandparents – those I knew, and those I didn't.

⸺∞⸺

ACKNOWLEDGEMENTS

With thanks to Ségolène Dupuy, Cate Ludlow, and a bloodied battalion of librarians.

The History Press
The Mill, Brimscombe Port
Stroud, Gloucestershire, GL5 2QG
www.thehistorypress.co.uk

ISBN 978 0 7524 6293 6

Typesetting and origination by The History Press
Printed in Great Britain
Manufacturing managed by Jellyfish Print Solutions Ltd

CONTENTS

	Introduction	5
600-700	'And There Was Slaughter'	7
1296-1357	A Barricade of Dead Horses!	10
1437	Tortured to Death Over Three Days – for Killing the King!	14
1440	Murdered at the Sign of the Black Bull!	17
1520	Slaughter on the Streets!	19
1544	'Burn Edinburgh to the Ground!'	22
1560	A Tapestry of Naked Corpses!	25
1566	Stabbed to Death – in Front of the Queen!	28
1567	Death of a King – Blown up and Strangled!	31
1571-1573	Siege!	34
1581	Death and the Maiden	36
1622	A Sea Battle – Inside the Harbour!	39
1628	Buried Alive in the Loch!	41
1603-1670	Burn the Witch!	45
1645	Plague!	47
1638-1679	A Concentration Camp – in the Middle of Edinburgh	50
1650	The Dismembered Marquis!	53
1670	The Wizard of West Bow	56
1682	The Hangman was a Murderer!	59

1707	He Roasted the Servant on a Spit – and Then Ate Him!	62
1736	He Fired into the Crowd – and was Lynched by the Mob!	64
1745-1746	Jacobite Conflicts and the War of the Chamber Pots	67
1811	Riot!	70
1821	Piracy and Murder on the High Seas!	73
1822	Duel!	77
1824	Fire!	80
1828-1829	Burke and Hare – Serial Killers!	83
1850	Edinburgh's Deadliest Residents!	86
1864	Hanged by the Neck until ye be Dead	88
1916	The Night of the Zeppelins	92

| AND INCLUDING | Ranger's Impartial List of Ladies | *between pages* 64-65 |
| | *Bibliography* | 95 |

INTRODUCTION

MURDER. MASSACRE. BATTLES. Wars. Sieges. Riots. Rebellions. Assassinations. Anarchy. Plague. Bodysnatching. Fire and devastation. Beheadings and hangings. *Bloody Scottish History: Edinburgh* is a journey into the heart of darkness that lies within one of the most beautiful and visited cities in the world.

The Penguin *Buildings of Scotland* series – the definitive work on the nation's built heritage – states quite bluntly that Edinburgh has the most spectacular landscape of any city. And it's true. The castle sits upon Castle Hill, a volcanic plug that overshadows the low-lying land around. The Old Town perilously straddles a steep-sided ridge that slopes down to the east, leading into the Canongate plain on which stand the new Scottish Parliament and Holyrood Palace, the former home of kings. The direct route from castle to palace is known as the Royal Mile. Immediately south, ancient thoroughfares such as the Grassmarket and Cowgate occupy a valley spanned by tall viaducts, so what appears to be a 'ground-floor' shop on George IV Bridge can actually be an upper storey of a building that starts many floors below on Cowgate.

To the north, across what used to be a stinking loch but is now a delightful garden, lies the shopping Valhalla of Princes Street and the wide elegant avenues and crescents of the Georgian New Town, a geometrical contrast to the cramped and higgledy-piggledy Old Town. Further east, the rugged grandeur of Calton Hill and Arthur's Seat dominate the skyline, while to the north-east the land descends to Leith and its port, opening on to the breezy vastness of the Firth of Forth. Add to this some of the most magnificent buildings of any city, anywhere, and you have a truly spectacular cityscape – a fitting theatrical backdrop for a history steeped in dramatic and stirring events. Not to mention bloody ones.

The castle, towering over the streets in the valley below. (From Modern Athens *by Thomas H. Shepherd, 1829)*

Edinburgh in the 1820s, viewed from Princes Street. From the left, North Bridge, Arthur's Seat and Salisbury Crags, then the Old Town climbing the ridge of Castle Hill. (From Modern Athens *by Thomas H. Shepherd, 1829)*

A view from the Cowgate, showing the difference in height between various parts of the city. (From Modern Athens *by Thomas H. Shepherd, 1829)*

Most of our tales centre on the Old Town, the medieval core of the city that grew up in the shadow of the castle. Here, narrow closes, wynds and lanes run off the Royal Mile, some dropping precipitously to the depths below. Here, within a confined, walled world, artisan and aristocrat, professional and pauper, all once lived cheek-by-jowl in tall tenement buildings: Europe's first skyscrapers. Here, street life was an intense experience, where mob rule often prevailed, and public executions provided welcome entertainment. Here, the stink would have been so strong as to make any modern visitor's eyes water. Since the nineteenth century, Edinburgh has traded on its image as a haven of culture and respectability, but before that it was one of the most violent and volatile capital cities on the planet.

Welcome to Edinburgh. There shall be blood!

'AND THERE WAS SLAUGHTER'

THE PROUD WARRIORS marched out from the great hall of Dun Eidyn, the fortress on what would later be known as Castle Rock. Three hundred mounted chieftains, each with their personal warband of hardened foot soldiers. They had been carousing and boasting in the drinking hall as their numbers swelled with allies from not just the whole of Scotland but as far away as Yorkshire and North Wales. Now they set out in a great army to face the enemy, confident of victory.

Only a handful returned.

DARK AGE WARRIORS

It was sometime around the year AD 603, and the Edinburgh and Lothian area was ruled by the kingdom of Gododdin. At this period in the Dark Ages, the British Isles were a confused mix of different kingdoms and ethnic groups – concepts such as 'England' or 'Scotland' did not yet exist, and even the names of peoples were still evolving. The Gododdin were Britons, a Celtic people who spoke a form of Welsh. The north of what would later be known as Scotland was the homeland of the Picts, while the west, Dalriada, was occupied by the Scots, a tribe recently arrived from Ireland. And to the south lay the new power in the land

– the Angles – who, in the course of time, eventually became known as the English.

Along with their fellow Germanic invaders the Saxons, the Angles had emigrated from northern Europe in the period after the Romans had abandoned Britain. Territorially aggressive and militarily powerful, they moved against the Britons, taking over a hotchpotch of kingdoms from Yorkshire to

A Victorian view of Dark Age warriors. (From Wilson's Tales of the Borders, 1884)

7

Cumbria. Under King Ethelfrith – known to his British enemies as 'Twister' – the Angles started to move further north. Recognising a common enemy, the Britons of Gododdin allied with other British tribes and even their traditional foe, the Picts, and launched a pre-emptive assault on the Anglian forces of the kingdoms of Deira and Bernicia.

The Britons were a Celtic warrior culture, where aristocratic honour depended on prowess in battle and masculine virtues at home. In the time that it took their forces to gather, the various chieftains got riotously drunk in the pine-built hall of Dun Eidyn, enjoying the hospitality of the Gododdin king, Mynyddog the Wealthy. Boasting, conviviality, and contests of skill and muscle were the order of the day.

RED WERE THEIR SWORDS

The two armies clashed at Catraeth (Catterick) in North Yorkshire. The proceedings were poetically recorded by Aneirin, Mynyddog's court bard. His epic poem, *The Gododdin*, is one of the earliest surviving documents in Welsh. 'Three hundred men hastened forth, wearing gold torques, defending the land, and there was slaughter.' It eulogises the courage, fighting skills and bloodlust of the Britons – 'Red were their swords, May their spears never be cleansed' – and then it points out that their entire force was wiped out, almost to a man.

Aneirin witnessed the slaughter first hand, and, according to him, was one of a tiny number of survivors: 'None escaped save three, through feats of combat ... And I, with my blood streaming down, For the sake of my brilliant poetry.' The bard was captured and held prisoner until his ransom was paid.

The poem exists in different versions, each giving varying facts, so it is impossible to get an accurate figure of how large the respective armies were, but what is certain is that the British forces were utterly annihilated. A short time later the Angles also wiped out an army of Dalriadan Scots at the Battle of Degsastan. The Anglian advance northwards was relentless and it was only the internal difficulties following Ethelfrith's death that slowed their depredations. But the kingdom of Gododdin was tottering. In the year 638, after years of exacting tribute and bleeding the kingdom dry, the Angles finally besieged and took the British stronghold of Dun Eidyn (if this date seems late, it is possible that the Battle of Catraeth took place not in the year 603 but in 617, perhaps even 626; no one knows for sure). With the Britons out of the picture, the Angles entered into decades of conflict with the Picts, often allying with the Picts' neighbours and enemy, the Scots of the west coast. In the Anglo-Saxon language, Dun Eidyn became *Edwinesburh*, which became Edinburgh.

At its height in the seventh century, the triumphant kingdom of the Angles stretched for 350 miles from the Humber to the Tay. In the tenth century, the Angles of Northumbria were weakened by the incursions of the Danes, and the Gaelic-speaking Scots of Dalriada, seeing a power vacuum, took Edinburgh and Lothian. By this point the proud Welsh-speaking kingdom of Gododdin was little more than a memory.

King Mynyddog's wooden hall of Dun Eidyn, where the boisterous Celtic warriors feasted, swilled mead and bedded serving girls in the weeks before the massacre, is lost somewhere beneath the centuries of stonework that make up the various stages of Edinburgh Castle.

WHAT DID THE ROMANS DO FOR US ...?

Castle Rock had been a stronghold long before the Gododdin. There was a settlement on the crag in at least 900 BC, during the late Bronze Age. Later, the inhabitants were

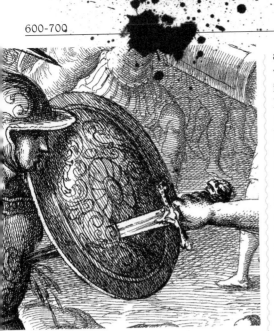

an Iron-Age Celtic tribe called the Votadini, who had a second hill fort on Traprain Law in East Lothian. The Votadini appear not to have resisted when the Romans invaded, and they were largely free to go about their business without military occupation. As a client nation of the Roman Empire the Votadini received many benefits, such as trading privileges and payment in valuable silver – many of these silver objects can be seen at the National Museum of Scotland. The Romans finally quit the area in the fourth century AD, leaving behind a culture that could be described as 'Romano-British'. The Gododdin of the Dark Ages were actually the direct descendants of the Iron-Age tribe – 'Gododdin' is a version of 'Votadin'.

'Red were their swords.' Blood spurts on the battlefield. (Courtesy of the Thomas Fisher Rare Book Library, University of Toronto)

A BARRICADE OF DEAD HORSES!

THE EXHAUSTED SURVIVORS of the running battle could find no cover. In a last desperate tactic, they slaughtered their steeds and built a barricade of horseflesh. Surrounded, and lacking food or water, they had little hope ...

By the Middle Ages the kingdoms of Scotland and England were firmly established, more or less on today's borders. And, like other close neighbours, they were frequently at each other's throats. Between 1296 and 1357 the Scots fought two long-drawn-out Wars of Independence to avoid becoming a vassal state of England. This condition of semi-permanent warfare saw crops burned, areas evacuated, and fields left fallow, as the Scots pursued a scorched earth policy in the Lowlands, denying the invaders food and supplies. In Scotland the growing season was shorter than further south, so, with agricultural output curtailed, the fourteenth century had its fair share of hungry years.

Edinburgh was not yet the capital – in truth, the capital was where the King happened to be at the time – but it did possess one of the finest castles in the kingdom. The original site, now the Old Town, was built on what is known as a crag and tail. The crag is a hill of hard volcanic rock that resisted the power of the glaciers, while the tail is a sloping ridge of softer rock protected from glacial erosion by the crag. With the crag towering 260ft above the surrounding countryside, and protected by sheer cliffs on three sides, Castle Rock was a perfect defensive position. The part of the Royal Mile formed by Lawnmarket and the High Street runs along the spine of the tail. Salisbury Crags and Arthur's Seat, a favourite hill walk on the eastern edge of Edinburgh, form another example of crag and tail.

MEDIEVAL BOMBARDMENT

The first castle was almost certainly built of wood, but it appears to have acquired a curtain wall of stone by the twelfth century, making it one of Scotland's first enclosed stone castles. We have no idea what the castle looked like at this time, as endless wars and rebuilding have erased all the original traces. Between 1174 and 1186 the castle was held by Henry II of England, at a time when the Scottish King, William the Lion, was a prisoner south of the border.

In 1296, during the First War of Independence, Edward I of England subjected the castle to bombardment by ballista and trebuchet (stone-throwing catapults). The garrison surrendered after three days. The records and the movable treasure were taken to London, and an English garrison of more than 300 men was installed. The castle was rebuilt in stone by Edward's master masons, fresh from constructing a ring of fortresses around Wales for 'The Hammer', as Edward was known.

COMMANDO RAID BY NIGHT

Edinburgh Castle remained in English hands for eighteen years. But from 1310 onwards a Scottish warrior-aristocrat, Robert the Bruce, waged a successful guerrilla war against the occupation, taking English-held castle after castle. On the night of 14 March 1314, Thomas Randolph, the 1st Earl of Moray and Bruce's nephew, led thirty men on an ascent up the 'impregnable' north cliff of Castle Rock. Guided by a turncoat member of the garrison, William Francis, the attack took the defenders by surprise, and the castle was once again in Scottish hands. The Scots did not have enough forces to man it, however, and so Bruce ordered the castle to be demolished, thus denying it to the enemy. The only structure that survived the destruction was St Margaret's Chapel, which remains as the oldest building in Edinburgh. Three months after Randolph's commando raid, Bruce defeated the forces of Edward II at the Battle of Bannockburn, thus expelling the English for another two decades.

THE ENGLISH INVADE (AGAIN)

In 1335 Edward III of England decided that a major invasion of Scotland was required. In this he was assisted by a group of Scottish aristocrats who had lost their estates to Robert the Bruce. As with most conflicts of the period, there were no 'good guys' or 'bad guys', no easily spotted heroes and villains – Bruce and the disinherited Scottish nobles had been engaged in a vicious power struggle for years, and the former got the good press simply because he was the winner. His minor misdemeanours – such as stabbing to death one of his rivals in a church, a violation of holy sanctuary – were generally edited out of the propaganda. But now Bruce was dead, his pre-teen son David II was on the throne, and the sons of the Scots who had suffered under Bruce wanted revenge (and their profitable estates back). All of which suited Edward III down to the ground.

THE MERCENARIES ARRIVE

Edward and his Scottish allies marched as far north as Perth, meeting little opposition. Meanwhile, a different group of ambitious knights disembarked at Berwick, looking for some action. Their leader was Guy, the Count of Namur, a tiny Flemish state in what is now Holland. Namur had always had to play power-politics with its more powerful neighbours, and technically was a client state of France – Edward's invasion was not Guy's war. But this was the age of knightly chivalry, and Guy was a

A medieval knight in armour. (From Chambers's Encyclopaedia, *1888-1892)*

twenty-three-year-old in search of adventure and excitement. He formally swore allegiance to the English king, and headed for the heat of the battle with around 100 knights dressed in their full armour, equipped with splendid warhorses and carrying pennants and lances. Accompanied by perhaps another 200 archers and men-at-arms, the force set forth to link up with Edward's army further to the north.

Guy's armoured column was moving through unknown territory in a foreign land. They were probably shadowed from the moment they landed. Somewhere south of Edinburgh, they were ambushed by a party of Scottish knights and archers. The Flemings established a battle formation on the open space of the Burgh Muir south of Edinburgh, and carnage ensued, with bodies falling under sword, battle-axe, mace and arrow. The Scottish force was larger, but the disciplined Flemings fought fiercely. At one point Richard Shaw, a Scottish squire, was challenged to single combat by a Fleming in a closed helmet. Each killed the other – and when their armour was removed, in a true Hollywood epic moment, the Namur knight was found to be a woman.

The Flemings were slowly beaten back and retreated north into the city, some being cut down in fierce hand-to-hand combat in the narrow lanes of Friars' Wynd and St Mary's Wynd. Finally they reached the top of Castle Hill. But the castle itself had been demolished twenty years earlier. In a scene reminiscent of a Wild West movie, the desperate knights killed their injured and exhausted warhorses and created a semi-circular rampart of horseflesh among the ruins.

For the moment, they were safe. But they were also trapped. Lacking water, food and shelter, they spent a miserable night in the open, surrounded on all sides. The following day, 31 July, they surrendered. It was a capitulation under the rules of chivalry. The Flemings were all allowed to go free on payment of a ransom and swearing a promise

A fanciful view of mounted warfare in the past. (Courtesy of the Thomas Fisher Rare Book Library, University of Toronto)

that they would never again take up arms against the Scottish King David II. The leader of the Scottish force, John Randolph, the Earl of Moray, even personally escorted the Count towards the border, although this was not so much an act of chivalry as a recognition of the power of Guy's political godfather, Philip VI, the King of France.

Guy embarked from Berwick and sailed to Perth, where he made homage to Edward III. Under the rules of chivalry, the promise given by Guy to Randolph could not be broken, and so the valorous Flemish knights were of no further use to Edward. Guy received a royal pension of 400 merks a year and a protection order was issued for the Flemings, allowing them to return home unmolested by any of

THE BATTLE OF ROSLIN ... THE TRUTH

Another local fourteenth-century battle has entered contemporary patriotic folklore as a 'David and Goliath' story. According to the legend, at the Battle of Roslin on 24 February 1303, 8,000 poorly armed Scots defeated a better-equipped army of 30,000 English. In reality, the numbers involved were in the low hundreds, there were no infantry, and the two sides were equally matched in terms of equipment, knights, men-at-arms and archers. Propaganda and exaggeration are the handmaids of warfare.

the King's subjects. In other words, Edward paid them off and quickly showed them the door.

THE AFTERMATH

Guy of Namur lived less than a year after the Battle of the Burgh Muir, dying from wounds suffered during a tournament in Flanders. Randolph, the Earl of Moray, was captured in an English ambuscade near Jedburgh, and spent the next five years in prison. The Battle of Burgh Muir was a minor incident in the Second Scottish War of Independence, which continued for another two decades.

The Burgh Muir once extended for around 5 square miles, covering much of modern south Edinburgh, from Morningside to Dalkeith Road. We shall meet this former open space again and again in this book – as a quarantine refuge, as a place of plague burials, and as a site of execution and criminals' graves. In 1867, a large number of

skeletons were dug up at what is now Glengyle Terrace. These were probably the men (and one woman?) who died in the battle. There is no record of what happened to the horses.

THE TROJAN HORSE

Constantly swaying between English and Scottish occupation, Edinburgh Castle was the ball in a deadly game of ping-pong. The Scots regained it in 1341 in a masterpiece of 'Trojan Horse'-type covert assault. William Douglas, the 1st Earl of Douglas, disguised himself as a merchant delivering supplies to the garrison. Once through the gates, a band of Scots leaped out of the cart and slaughtered around 100 English soldiers.

From 1356 onwards the castle was completely rebuilt, but very few of the medieval structures from that date survived later sieges. Most of what visitors to the castle see today dates from the eighteenth and nineteenth centuries.

TORTURED TO DEATH OVER THREE DAYS

– for Killing the King!

THE ASSASSINATION OF a king rarely goes unpunished – as Walter Stewart, the Earl of Atholl, found to his cost. Stewart was part of a conspiracy of disaffected aristocrats who murdered James I in the Dominican Friary of Perth on 20 February 1437. The King, who was Walter's nephew, had tried to take refuge in a drain, but it had been blocked up, and he was run through whilst hiding in sewage.

The plotters, however, had miscalculated the support for their attempt at regime change, and the coup faltered almost immediately. The murderers were quickly captured, brought to Edinburgh and found guilty of regicide. The Middle Ages was a period of often hideous tortures and punishments, but what Walter Stewart suffered in March 1437 was extreme even for those times.

'KING OF ALL TRAITORS'

On the first day, he was hoisted up high, his arms and legs tied to a crane. He was then violently dropped until his body was jerked to a stop just before hitting the ground. After repeated bouts of this, virtually all his joints were dislocated. He was then propped upright on a pillory at the Mercat Cross and a heated crown, inscribed with the words 'King of All Traitors', was placed upon his head. The hot iron bonded with his skin, so that when it was taken off much of his scalp was ripped away.

On the second day Walter Stewart was tied naked to a hurdle, attached to a horse, and dragged through the streets. One reference claims he was also burned with red-hot iron pincers, and even blinded, but this is unconfirmed. On the third day of his torment, the old man was again tied to the Mercat Cross. The executioner cut open his abdomen and wound out his intestines. The agony made Stewart pass out often – at which point a bucket of water was thrown in his face to wake him up again. All the organs of the abdominal cavity were then burned before the victim's eyes. Astonishingly, he was still alive. In the final act, the executioner cut out the still-beating heart from the chest and added it to the fire. The corpse was then beheaded – the head placed on a spike – and all four limbs chopped off, one each to be nailed up in Stirling, Perth, Aberdeen and Dundee as an exemplar of what happens to king-killers.

BREAKING ON THE WHEEL

Elaborate, long-drawn-out executions such as this were the exception rather than the norm – hanging, beheading, burning and drowning were much more common, and logistically easier to arrange. On two other occasions, however, we find an example of an extended execution – the breaking of the condemned on a wheel. This incredibly vile act was common on the Continent but, other than these two episodes, unknown in Scotland. The breakings took place during the reign of James VI, and it seems His Glorious Majesty was experimenting with new ways of keeping his subjects in line.

On 30 April 1591, John Dickson of Belchester in Berwickshire was found guilty of murdering his father three years previously, although we have no details of the crime itself. The Dicksons were one of the Border clans who gave so much trouble to the rulers of both England and Scotland, so perhaps there was a political motive behind the nature of Dickson's execution. John Dickson was brought to the Mercat Cross, set up on a scaffold and 'broken' – all his limbs shattered – before being strangled to death. The corpse lay exposed to public gaze for a day, and was then taken to the Burgh Muir, the burial ground for criminals. It was not interred, however, and the rack or wheel on which he had been tortured was set up again, with the body left exposed to the elements and the crows and ravens.

THE REVENGE OF AN ABUSED WOMAN

The second and last time a man was broken on the wheel in Scotland took place on 26 June 1604. Four years earlier, John Kincaid of Warriston, one of Edinburgh's wealthiest individuals, had been murdered, strangled in his own bedroom. The instigator of the crime was Kincaid's beautiful twenty-one-year-old wife, Jean Livingstone, who claimed Kincaid had frequently beaten and abused her, one time even sinking his teeth into her arm. Jean was herself of high status, being the daughter of the Laird of Dunipace. Through the agency of her nurse, Janet Munro, Jean persuaded a Livingstone

A sixteenth-century German woodcut showing torture with red-hot pincers, breaking on the wheel, beheading, and burning at the stake. (Author's collection)

family retainer, Robert Weir, to murder her husband. It seems the faithful servants were more than willing to help their mistress and right the wrongs she had suffered. On the fateful night, Jean secreted Robert in a cellar within the Warriston mansion. At midnight she guided him through the stairwells and corridors to her husband's chamber. John Kincaid put up a stout resistance but was overwhelmed by the stronger man.

It seems all the focus had been on revenge, and not on the practicalities of avoiding arrest. Robert Weir fled, but a mere four days after the murder, the Lady of Warriston was led to the Girth Cross at the foot of the Canongate and beheaded. Her execution took place at four in the morning, deliberately timed to avoid attention from the populace – her family did not want to suffer the shame of public humiliation, and their money had persuaded the authorities to change their usual pattern of afternoon executions. At the same hour, the nurse Janet Munro and another serving woman who was implicated in the conspiracy were strangled and burned a mile away at the Mercat Cross on High Street, the more usual place of execution. Thus, if any inhabitants of the town had been up and about at 4 a.m., they would have been drawn to the flames further up the hill, and not to the quietly delivered beheading down on the Canongate.

After four years on the run, Robert Weir was apprehended and sentenced to an appalling death. He was bound to a cartwheel, and the hangman proceeded to break both of his legs and both of his arms with the coulter (iron furrow) of a plough. It is not recorded whether the victim was relieved of his suffering by being strangled to death, or whether he was left to slowly expire from his injuries. Weir's body was displayed at the Mercat Cross for twenty-four hours, after which the wheel was hoisted vertically on the roadside between Warriston and Leith, and the corpse was allowed to decay over a number of months.

1440

MURDERED AT THE SIGN OF THE BLACK BULL!

TREACHERY WAS A way of life amongst the aristocrats of medieval Scotland. Allies became enemies overnight, long-standing friendships were betrayed, and ideals of honour and chivalry were cast aside in the struggle for power. The *realpolitik* of a weak monarchy and a vipers' nest of feuding nobles meant that human decency was at a premium. Which is why two youths, their safety guaranteed under the ancient rules of hospitality, were slaughtered in front of their ten-year-old host.

In the late 1430s, following the murder of James I, a political tug-of-war took place over the new king, James II, who was still a young boy. Whoever controlled the child basically ruled the country. By 1440, after various imprisonments, escapades and political manoeuvring, the battle lines were drawn. On one side in an uneasy alliance were Sir Alexander Livingston, father of the governor of Stirling Castle, and Sir William Crichton, governor of Edinburgh Castle: between them they controlled the most powerful fortresses in the country. On the other side was the King's mother, Joan Beaufort, who had gone on to marry Sir James Stewart, a supporter of the House of Douglas, probably the most powerful Lowland clan in the country.

Crichton had kidnapped James from Stirling Castle and taken him to Edinburgh, and so the two rival governors had come to a mutually beneficial arrangement. Between them they wanted to keep the ten-year-old king in protective custody, and hence rule Scotland as *de facto* regents. However, Livingston and Crichton feared that the Douglases, with the King's mother as their ally, would attempt to take the King and strike for power.

As it happened, Clan Douglas had just acquired a new chief – William, the 6th Earl, who was fifteen or sixteen years old. Under the guise of an offer of reconciliation and a new era of co-operation, Sir Alexander Livingston and Sir William Crichton invited the young earl to a dinner with the King at Edinburgh Castle. Suspecting nothing, William agreed, and arrived at the castle with his younger brother David on 24 November 1440. The grand banquet took place in the Great Hall of Edinburgh Castle. The food was excellent, the wine flowed, and the boy king enjoyed the company of the two teenagers.

THE BLACK DINNER

Then a servant appeared with a platter laden not with sweetmeats but the head of a black bull. It was a symbol of death. The young earl and his brother were seized, subjected to

A sixteenth-century German image of a beheading with a sword. (Author's collection)

the briefest of mock trials for high treason, and beheaded on Castle Hill in front of the King, whose protests could not save his new friends.

The Black Dinner, as it came to be known, struck horror into the hearts of later generations as it violated the almost sacred laws of Scottish hospitality, which made it clear that a guest in your house was safe from harm.

On the surface it seemed a straightforward piece of violent treachery. But it was more complicated than that. The power behind the plot was actually a member of Clan Douglas itself: William's great uncle James, known as 'James the Gross'. He had conspired with his enemies Crichton and Livingston for his own ends. With his nephews out of the way, James became the 7th Earl and the Chief of Clan Douglas, with all the wealth and power that implied. Crichton and Livingston went unpunished, even when James purged his nobles when he was finally able to rule in his own right in 1448.

The Douglases continued to be a thorn in the side of the Scottish monarchy. In 1452, for example, King James II in person stabbed and killed William Douglas, the 8th Earl, and proceeded to dismantle the Douglas power base through extended military campaigns. In Edinburgh, the Douglases, infamous for their raiding and destruction, lived on as bogeymen in children's lullabies:

> Hush ye, hush ye,
> Little pet ye,
> Hush ye, hush ye,
> Dinna fret ye,
> The Black Douglas
> Shanna get ye.

EAT, DRINK ... AND BE STABBED

Another murderous breach of hospitality took place in Edinburgh Castle in 1485. Alexander, the Duke of Albany, was imprisoned there for rebellion against his older brother King James III. One day Alexander received two flagons of malvoisie wine. In one was hidden a rope, while the other contained a letter informing him that the King had secretly ordered his execution the following morning. Alexander invited the captain of the guard and three functionaries to share the wine with him, and they gladly accepted, sitting convivially around the blazing fire in the chamber. When all four guards were sufficiently drunk, Alexander casually lifted the captain's dagger and stabbed them all to death, throwing their bodies onto the fire. With a servant he then scrambled down the rope and headed for the safety of a ship waiting in Leith Harbour.

1520

SLAUGHTER ON THE STREETS!

WHEN THE SMOKE cleared on 30 April 1520, at least seventy corpses were strewn around the closes and pends leading off the Royal Mile. The men had been gutted with billhooks and spears, stabbed by swords and daggers, and blown apart by shot fired from primitive guns. The gutters ran with blood.

The 'Cleansing of the Causeway', as it was known, was yet another in the long list of rumbles, skirmishes and battles between rival clans – only this one had been fought not in the heather-clad mountains or mossy glens, but in the hemmed-in streets of Edinburgh, turning it into a combination of street brawling and urban warfare. Following the Scottish defeat at the Battle of Flodden in 1513, the upper part of Edinburgh had been ringed by a defensive wall, in anticipation of an English invasion that never came. The wall was not particularly effective at keeping invaders out – but it did make the cramped city a trap for anyone trying to escape from within.

MURDEROUS ARISTOCRATS

Most Scottish nobles at this time were a little rough around the edges, preferring daggers to diplomacy, and murder to manners.

GANGS, MEDIEVAL STYLE

Fatal brawls between noblemen were a common sight on the streets of Edinburgh, a consequence of rival armed factions being shut up together in the cramped city. In 1588 the Earl of Bothwell and Sir William Stewart of Monkton had something of a spat in court at Holyrood, but only words were exchanged. Three weeks later, Sir William and friends were coming down the High Street while Bothwell and his party were heading up. Swords and daggers were produced. Stewart stabbed one of Bothwell's friends, losing his sword in the process. Stewart fled into Blackfriars Wynd – Bothwell pursued him, and ran the unarmed man through from behind. Such was the tenor of the times that the blood had scarcely been washed off the cobbles of the Royal Mile before Bothwell was back in public life, and no murder charge was ever brought.

Several generations of kings had despaired of controlling their tempestuous aristocrats, who in truth were often scheming thugs only distinguished from street criminals by their relative wealth. In this case, a long-running dispute between the House of Clan Hamilton and the House of Clan Douglas had come to the boil over the regency.

As had happened too many times before, Scotland had a child king. As a result, a regent was appointed to govern the country until James V was old enough to rule. Regents were king in all but name, and so, in the snakepit that was Scottish politics, the competition to be regent was fierce – and often fatal. In 1520 Archibald, the head of Clan Douglas, had the upper hand. The regent was the Duke of Albany, a close ally of the Douglases, and the

A man holding an arquebus, an early sixteenth-century gun. (From Chambers's Encyclopaedia, *1888-1892)*

young king and his mother, Queen Margaret, were in their custody. Archibald's rival, James, chief of Clan Hamilton, assembled a small army of supporters and descended on Edinburgh, determined to wrest the royal family from the grip of the Douglases.

Each party had perhaps 500 armed men. Tension mounted in the city as the two factions circled each other for a day, neither wanting to be accused of starting the violence. An attempt to broker a peace deal between two bishops – one from either side – came to nothing, and Archibald Douglas decided to strike first. He sent his men to block the narrow entranceways into the pends and lanes leading to the lodgings where the Hamiltons were sleeping. But before the ambush could begin, Patrick Hamilton, a hot-headed duellist and an illegitimate son of the Hamilton chief, decided to start a one-man war. He rushed up to Archibald Douglas and attempted to kill him. There were shouts, there was the clang of sword on armour, and there was such a disturbance that all the sleeping Hamiltons were roused.

THE KILLING LANES

They rushed out along the confined closes and wynds – and into a hell of edged weapons and arquebus fire. The chronicler George Buchanan described the scene vividly: 'They [the Douglases] set upon their enemies as they came out of several narrow alleys at once; first they slew, and drove the rest back headlong, tumbling one upon another in great confusion.' As the desperate Hamiltons sought sanctuary wherever they could, the Douglas men set fire to the buildings to smoke them out. The realities of urban warfare became all too evident: Hamiltons and Douglases alike killed their own men, being unable to tell friend from foe.

Even when the Hamilton men escaped the killing lanes, they were not out of trouble. James Hamilton had been the Provost of

A Victorian impression of the 'Cleansing of the Causeway'. (From A History of the Scottish People *by Thomas Thomson, 1893)*

Edinburgh since 1517; he had recently taken the side of the merchants of Leith during a trade dispute with the merchants of Edinburgh, and hence was a figure of hate for many of the residents of the city. His soldiers could find no hiding place. James Beaton, Archbishop of Glasgow and an ally of the Hamiltons, fled for his life and took refuge in a church, only to be dragged out at sword-point. His life was spared only because his opposite number in the Douglas camp, Bishop Gawain of Dunkeld, threatened to excommunicate anyone who harmed a prince of the church. James Hamilton, the clan chief, escaped by stealing a packhorse laden with coal and riding panic-stricken down the slope and across the marshes of the Nor Loch.

No one really knows how many were killed in the melee. George Buchanan estimated that the Hamiltons lost seventy-two men, although another historian thought the figure was nearer 300. Whatever the numbers, the truth was that the Hamiltons were utterly defeated. By nightfall all their remaining supporters had quit the city on pain of death, and the Douglases had ensured they were firmly in control not just of Edinburgh but also of the young king.

1544

'BURN EDINBURGH TO THE GROUND!'

OVER A FEW days in May 1544, much of Edinburgh was put to the torch. Holyrood Palace and Abbey, Craigmillar Castle, Newbattle Abbey, and many dwellings were either burned or plundered. Leith Docks were looted and then dismantled. But the castle held out, and after a fortnight the invading force sailed away, loaded with booty and leaving a smoking ruin of a city behind them.

The burning of Edinburgh was the result of yet more political chicanery. With King James V dead, the control of Scotland was once again in the balance – and the tipping point was James' daughter, the infant Mary, Queen of Scots. One party of Scottish nobles favoured a dynastic union with Protestant England, and to this end a marriage had been arranged between Mary and the five-year-old Edward, son of Henry VIII of England. Another faction within Scotland supported an alliance with Catholic France, and wanted to marry Mary off to François, the heir to the French throne, and at the time a baby even younger than Mary. In either case the future child of any union would be the joint ruler of either Scotland and England, or Scotland and France. With England and France in a semi-permanent state of war, both countries saw the east coast ports of Scotland as strategic resources. If Scotland and France were permanently allied, England would have to

fight on two fronts. And if Scotland united with England, France would find it harder to operate in the North Sea and the Atlantic. It was a prize worth fighting for.

SHOCK AND AWE

Soon civil war broke out between the various Scottish nobles. When the Scottish Government broke the marriage treaty with England, Henry VIII first attempted to get his own way through bribery. When that failed, he went for the military option. A full-scale invasion was not logistically possible, however, and so a series of short, sharp punitive raids took place. Henry's instructions were brutally explicit:

Put all to fire and sword, burn Edinburgh town, so raised and defaced when you have sacked and gotten what you can of it, that there may remain forever a perpetual memory of the vengeance of God upon them for their falsehood and disloyalty. Do what you can out of hand, and without long tarrying, to beat down and overthrow the castle, sack Holyrood house, and as many towns and villages about Edinburgh, as you may conveniently. Sack Leith and burn and subvert it and all the rest, putting

Henry VIII. (Courtesy of the Thomas Fisher Rare Book Library, University of Toronto)

man, woman and child to fire and sword without exception where any resistance shall be made against you, and this done, pass over to Fife and extend the same extremities and destructions to all towns and villages which you may reach conveniently.

The attack on Edinburgh involved an army of 6,000 men transported from Newcastle by 200 ships. They landed on the south shore of the Firth of Forth and marched against Leith, winning a small victory over the defenders in an engagement that lasted less than thirty minutes. Once the port was taken, the larger ships docked and unloaded their heavy cannon.

With Leith fully under English control, the Scots closed the city gates of Edinburgh and fortified the castle. On 6 May 1544 the English mounted an assault on the Netherbow Port, the barrier in the city wall that marked the boundary between the low-lying Canongate and the High Street that climbed up Castle Hill. Both sides exchanged artillery fire. Then a suicide squad of English infantry engaged the defenders in fierce close combat, pinning them down with pistol shot and arrows. Under the cover of this withering fire, the English gunners brought a cannon up close to the wall and blew the wooden gate apart. The English army poured through, killing perhaps 300 or 400 Scots. The English cannon were pulled through the gap and trained on the castle. The castle gunners, however, had not just a clear zone of fire down the High Street, but also the advantage of the high ground. They rained down cannonballs onto the English, who were forced to withdraw.

FIRE AND PLUNDER

The cannon-bedecked castle was deemed impregnable, and so the English turned their attention elsewhere – plundering all movable goods, and burning everything else. Most of the Canongate, including the royal palace at Holyrood, was set aflame, along with the suburbs, and many of the houses in the High Street. Pilrig, Restalrig, Duddingston and Lauriston were all devastated. The English commander, Lord Hertford, described in a report to his king how he had stood upon Calton Hill to view the vast conflagration, and could hear an endless wailing – the lament of the women and children burned out of their homes.

At this point a force of 4,000 mounted Borderers arrived by land, further swelling the English army. The burning and looting continued for three days, and raids were made on other Forth ports; Musselburgh, Dunbar, Newhaven, South Queensferry, Kinghorn, St Monans, Burntisland and Pittenweem were all hit. Then, having given the Scots a bloody nose, the English started to withdraw. The ships at Leith were loaded with booty estimated to be worth £10,000 (around £3 million in today's money) and sailed away, but not before the docks were themselves smashed up and burned. Two high-quality Scottish ships were also taken – one, the *Salamander*, being a gift from the

King of France. The English army marched back across the border, burning villages and castles as they went.

From Henry VIII's point of view, the raid was an almost complete success, at least in the short term. But it did not bring the Scots to heel, and many of the pro-English nobles re-joined the pro-France party when large bribes changed hands. It looked as if the child-queen Mary would still end up married to the son of the King of France. What was later known as the 'War of the Rough Wooing' was called at the time the 'War of Nine Years', as first the English and then the Scots gained the advantage. Finally, after seemingly endless bloody conflict, the six-year-old Mary was taken to France in 1548. The English had lost. But before too long, Mary, Queen of Scots, was back in Edinburgh, former enemies became allies, and allies enemies, and the cycle of bloodletting was to begin all over again ...

1560

A TAPESTRY OF NAKED CORPSES!

THE YEAR 1560 saw Scotland change forever. Firstly, in a religious revolution forged in blood and fire, the Reformation saw Protestantism replace Catholicism as the state religion. And secondly, the 'Auld Alliance' between Scotland and France, an informal pact based on their mutual hatred of the English, came to an end. And Scotland's new ally was – England.

The fulcrum of this epoch-making change was Edinburgh – or, more exactly, its port, Leith. Following the attack on Edinburgh in 1544, Scotland suffered more incursions from English forces. An appeal was made to France for protection – an appeal that had great force, because James V's widow was Mary de Guise, a member of the French royal family. And her daughter, the future Mary, Queen of Scots, was betrothed to the Dauphin, François, the eldest son of the King of France. So in 1548 a large contingent of French troops arrived in Scotland and started to fortify Leith, the strategic port facing the Continent. Shortly afterwards Mary was spirited across the Channel. France now had a strong interest in protecting Scotland, which, it was believed, would soon become a province of the French Empire. The numbers of Frenchmen in Leith grew, swelled by the families they brought with them. In 1554 Mary de Guise became Regent of Scotland.

Four years later her daughter married François. It seemed as if a long-plotted takeover of Scotland by France was becoming a reality.

But religious conflict now reared its ugly head. More than two decades after the Reformation in England, the Protestant religion was now in the ascendant in Scotland. The Catholic Mary de Guise found herself embattled, and only retained her power with the help of French troops. The Protestant lords called on help from their old enemy – England.

ENEMIES BECOME ALLIES

It was as if the world had turned upside down. Protestant Scots were now allied with an army from Elizabeth I's Protestant England, together fighting the Catholic French in Scotland, who were led by the Catholic widow of the former Scottish king. Religion had changed everything.

By 1560 Leith was a fully fortified town, surrounded by high earthen ramparts harbouring perhaps 3,600 French soldiers and around 600 of their wives and children, as well as the townspeople. The fortress was superbly designed, the troops battle-hardened and disciplined. Several assaults by the forces of the Protestant lords were simply

Sixteenth-century cannon. (From Chambers's Encyclopaedia, *1888-1892)*

brushed aside. During one attack the French routed the ill-equipped and poorly trained Scots back into Edinburgh, and returned triumphant, laden with plunder. On another occasion the French ambushed a Scottish supply column en route from the port at Musselburgh to Edinburgh, thus gaining several weeks' worth of food. The only route left to the Scottish Protestants was to invite an English army to undertake the difficult task of winkling out the French from Leith.

THE SIEGE OF LEITH

From the spring of 1560 English gunners and engineers were throwing up siegeworks designed to encircle the French defences – when completed, they stretched for a mile, with six substantial gun platforms and numerous trenches. At their closest the English and French positions were less than 500 yards apart. On 12 April the French made a pre-emptive strike, cannonading an English platform and killing sixteen men. Two days later the English heavy artillery was finally in place, and the bombardment of Leith began. Although much destruction was caused to the town, the ramparts resisted the heavy cannonballs. There was to be no easy solution to the Siege of Leith. To make

matters worse, on 16 April a large force of French infantry and cavalry sallied out and destroyed an unfinished gun platform, killing many English soldiers and taking a number of officers prisoner.

Generals often find themselves undertaking risky operations because the politicians back home want speedy results. On 7 May, under pressure from the government of Elizabeth I, the English commander, the Duke of Norfolk, ordered a full-scale assault. It was a disaster. The plans, poorly conceived in the first place, were betrayed. The combined English and Scottish force may have lost as many as 1,500 men. By this point Mary de Guise was ensconced in Edinburgh Castle, sending secret messages to the French in letters written in code and invisible ink. When she looked out from the castle and saw the piled-up naked corpses of the dead English soldiers, she 'hopped with mirth' and exclaimed: 'Yonder is the fairest tapestry that ever I saw; I would that the whole fields between me and them were strewn with the same stuff.' Or, at least, that's what her arch-enemy John Knox *said* she said. The French claimed they had only suffered fifteen casualties in the assault. Both sides exaggerated enemy deaths and downplayed their own losses, so it is difficult to reach an

'The fairest tapestry that ever I saw.' (Courtesy of the Thomas Fisher Rare Book Library, University of Toronto)

accurate assessment of how many actually perished.

Through May, the siege tightened. The English fleet blockaded the port. Within the ramparts, food became short. A group of some forty or fifty French soldiers and Leith citizens were massacred when they ventured onto the beach in search of cockles and periwinkles. The defenders were reduced first to eating their horses, and finally rats and weeds. A brief armistice was called in June, and, in a scene reminiscent of the Christmas Day truce between German and British troops during the First World War, French and English soldiers ate together on the beach at Leith. According to one report, the English turned up with beef, bacon, poultry, wine and beer, while French cuisine was represented by horse pie and roasted rats.

THE FRENCH KICKED OUT

On 11 June Mary de Guise died of a long-term illness. The French saw it as a symbol of the hopelessness of their cause, and sued for peace. Under the terms of the Treaty of Leith, all French soldiers and civilians in the port were evacuated to Calais – 4,195 people in total. They had arrived as invited guests and twelve years on they were expelled, unwanted baggage from yesterday's politics. The Auld Alliance was severed, and France never again had a part in supporting the Scottish state. Although the English troops also withdrew, Protestant Scotland and England were now, if not partners, then at least allies, and England came to play an increasingly important political role in Scotland. The era of the Anglo-Scottish wars was over; future conflicts were often fought along lines of religion, not nationality.

On 20 August 1560 Mary, Queen of Scots arrived from France, disembarking at a virtually annihilated Leith. With her young husband François dead, and the Auld Alliance extinguished, she was now

Mary, Queen of Scots, bids adieu to France and sails for Scotland and a lifetime of troubles. (From A History of the Scottish People *by Thomas Thomson, 1893)*

of limited value to the French and had been manoeuvred out from the royal succession in Paris. Desperate, she returned to Scotland expecting to find a welcome as the nation's rightful monarch. Instead, she encountered a country divided, and the seventeen-year-old queen quickly discovered that her Catholicism was a key source of that division. Civil war was to be Scotland's lot for the near future.

The Siege of Leith had lasted for almost six months, and had cost thousands of lives. As soon as it was over, the siege fortifications were demolished, and very little physical evidence of this historically crucial episode now remains.

1566

STABBED TO DEATH
– in Front of the Queen!

MARY, QUEEN OF Scots was at supper in Holyrood Palace when the conspirators charged in, her husband Lord Darnley among them. A loaded pistol and dagger were pressed to the breast of the pregnant queen, and she was warned not to cry out on pain of death. The target of the conspirators, Mary's secretary, David Rizzio, tried to cling to her dress, begging for mercy – 'Justice, justice, save my life, Madame!' It was to no avail: his first stab wound was received from over the Queen's shoulder. Rizzio was dragged off into an adjoining chamber, where he was hacked to death. His corpse had fifty-six separate wounds. In the frenzy, some of the plotters accidentally wounded each other.

The assassination of David Rizzio was a combination of high politics and base emotions. On the one hand it was a *coup d'état*, another in a long series of grim events from Scottish history where one powerful group removed the monarch from power – and in this case, the point was to neutralise Mary and make Darnley the ruler. On the other hand, Darnley was insanely jealous of Rizzio, whom he suspected of having an affair with the Queen. So the murder served two purposes – even though Darnley did not realise he had been played as a patsy.

At the time, Italy was not a nation-state – or even a single kingdom. As a result, many ambitious Italians found little opportunity for advancement at home and so sought success abroad. Many of them had migrated to the court of the French kings, and when the teenage Mary married her first husband, François II, in Paris, she became used to the idea of Italians as courtiers. When François died and Mary returned to Scotland as Queen of Scots, she found herself a pawn in a country violently divided by religion and competing noble families. It was natural for her to turn to someone such as David Rizzio for support. Rizzio assisted the Queen in filtering out the many approaches from would-be husbands from across Europe; both Rizzio and Mary were of the opinion that her first cousin Henry, Lord Darnley, was the best choice politically, as he was a candidate for the throne when Queen Elizabeth I died, and Mary hoped to unite the two kingdoms of England and Scotland. He was also passably good-looking, and so he got the nod. Mary married Darnley in 1565. During the 'honeymoon period' of their marriage, they seemed genuinely fond of each other.

Unfortunately, however, Darnley – a gambler and drinker with scant respect for the vows of marriage – had a weak character, and became the dupe of a number of Protestant nobles who wished to replace Mary. Mary was Catholic, as was Rizzio, and the rumour was put around that they were

Holyrood Palace in the nineteenth century. (From Modern Athens *by Thomas H. Shepherd, 1829)*

plotting with the Pope and foreign powers to return Protestant Scotland to the Catholic Church. Furthermore, Italians were widely distrusted, being regarded as poisoners or even necromancers. In addition, as 'Seigneur Davey' gained more power and influence over the Queen, even becoming her private secretary, Darnley became more and more convinced that the child Mary was carrying was Rizzio's.

A QUEEN HELD AT KNIFEPOINT

The plot came to its bloody climax on the evening of 9 March 1566. Mary's supporters were scattered – many of them escaping from the palace by means of ropes thrown out of windows. The Queen was held at knifepoint and prevented from communicating with the outside world, despite fears that she was on the edge of miscarrying the child. Darnley assumed supreme executive power

Mary's apartments in Holyrood. From the top: supper-room, bedroom, the private staircase, and Lord Darnley's room. (From Cassell's Old and New Edinburgh *by James Grant, 1880)*

Rizzio, his lute abandoned on the floor, attempts to hide behind the Queen from the assassins. (From The Great Events by Famous Historians *by Rossiter Johnson, 1905)*

and started issuing proclamations, one of them designed to restrict the movements of Catholics (including any who might have come to the Queen's aid). The coup had been successful. It seemed as if Mary would be forced to hand over power to Darnley permanently.

But then personal issues arose. Several of the rebellious Protestant nobles had always detested Darnley, seeing him as merely a cloddish mouthpiece who could be manipulated to their own ends. As Darnley started to ease into the role of king, that dislike became manifest. Darnley realised the plotters only wanted to use him as a puppet. Trapped together in Holyrood Palace, he and Mary were briefly reconciled, and they escaped together. He betrayed his former fellow conspirators. Mary gathered her forces. In a dramatic reversal of fortune, she returned to Edinburgh and reasserted her power. Two of the minor players in the conspiracy were caught and executed, and others were imprisoned or pardoned, but the major plotters fled to England, vowing vengeance on the man who had double-crossed them.

Darnley himself protested that he was innocent of any part in Rizzio's murder. A proclamation was read out at the Mercat Cross stating that to suggest otherwise was to be guilty of treason – which meant anyone making the claim would be executed. The citizens of Edinburgh wisely kept their mouths shut and laughed behind their hands. Meanwhile, the rebellious lords, being too powerful to keep as enemies in exile, were slowly allowed back to Scotland. Mary was determined to bring peace to her troubled country, and if that meant forgiving a rabble of treacherous and murderous nobles, then so be it.

THE QUEEN'S SPEECH

The relationship between Mary and Darnley had broken down, however. On 19 June 1566, three months after the assassination of Rizzio, the Queen gave birth to a son at Edinburgh Castle – the child who was to be the future King James VI of Scotland and James I of England. When Darnley called to see the infant, Mary – in a loud voice so that everyone could hear – told him that the boy was his son. She also made it clear that she would not forget his role in the murder of her friend.

Darnley refused to attend the baptism of his son at Stirling Castle in December 1566. He left for Glasgow, where he fell ill with smallpox, although there were rumours that one of his enemies had tried to poison him. Mary came to visit and nurse him, and their on-again off-again romance seems to have been rekindled. The royal couple travelled together back to Edinburgh. Little did Henry, Lord Darnley, suspect that he was riding to his doom ...

1567

DEATH OF A KING
– Blown up and Strangled!

THE MARRIAGE OF Mary, Queen of Scots and Lord Darnley reached its grim climax in the early hours of 10 February 1567. As darkness still lay over Edinburgh, a huge explosion was heard. The citizens, shaken from their beds at 2 a.m., found that a building known as Kirk o'Field, just inside the city walls, had been blown up. Further investigation revealed the body of the self-proclaimed king in the garden; he had been strangled. Immediately suspicion fell on the Queen: had she been part of the conspiracy to murder her husband?

The gunpowder plot has preoccupied historians and amateur detectives ever since. It was the JFK assassination of its day, and even after all this time it is still not clear exactly what happened.

A PLOT TO KILL THE KING

What is known is that the previous year a group of Scottish nobles had gathered at Craigmillar Castle in the south-east of Edinburgh, and gave their 'bond' to a plot to kill the increasingly unpopular Darnley. Principal among the conspirators was James Hepburn, the Earl of Bothwell, one of the nobles closest to Mary. It was suggested at the time that Bothwell and the Queen were, in fact, lovers, although this is uncertain.

The conventional version of events sees Bothwell as the main actor in the drama. Darnley was resting at Kirk o'Field following his illness in Glasgow. It may be that the building was chosen as part of the conspiracy because it made an easy target, but that is speculation. On the evening of the 9th, Mary spent some time in the mansion, then bid a farewell to her husband, with whom she seemed to have been reconciled yet again. Around 9 p.m. she walked back to Holyrood Palace, accompanied by Bothwell. Meanwhile, Bothwell's servants were assembling barrels of gunpowder beneath Darnley's bedroom, Bothwell having obtained counterfeit copies of the keys to help them get in. The servants lit the fuses and returned to their base, and the explosion took place a little while later.

Mary wrote to the Bishop of Glasgow, her ambassador in Paris, the next day:

The house wherein the king was lodged was in an instant blown into the air, he lying sleeping in his bed, with a vehemency that of the whole lodging, walls and other, there is nothing remaining – no, not a stone above another, but all carried far away, or dung in dross to the very ground-stone. It must be done by force of powder, and appears to have been a mine. By whom it has been done, or in what manner, it appears not as yet ... [but] the same being discovered, which we wot God will never suffer to lie hid, we hope to punish the same with such rigour, as shall serve for example of this cruelty for ages to come.

A MURDER MYSTERY

It is supposed that Darnley, hearing strange noises below him and suspecting a plot, climbed out of his bedroom window via a rope, accompanied by his servant. In the garden they were set upon by unknown assassins and strangled. The fact that both bodies were naked apart from a nightshirt supports the idea of a hurried exit.

In another version of events, Darnley and the servant were strangled first, and the gunpowder was set off in an unsuccessful attempt to disguise the real nature of the murders. Then we come to an entirely different theory, which claims that it was Darnley who blew up the building, as part of his own plot to murder his wife.

In truth, no one knows for certain. The consequences, however, were plain for all to see. With her husband dead, Mary realised she was once again a pawn in the powerplay of brutal aristocratic politics. The Earl of Bothwell was put on trial for the assassination, but was acquitted in an

A sketch made at the time of Darnley's murder, showing the semi-naked corpses of the King and his servant. (Author's collection)

obviously rigged trial. A mere three months after Darnley's murder, Mary married Bothwell. Historians are split as to whether Mary did this willingly, or whether Bothwell kidnapped and raped her and forced her into the marriage. Whatever happened, Bothwell was now on his way to becoming the King of Scotland.

EXILE AND ABDICATION

Bothwell's personality and ambition had made him deeply unpopular with the other

THE STOLEN SKULL!

As for Darnley, the self-proclaimed King of Scotland, his remains were buried in the chapel at Holyrood.

In 1768 the roof of the chapel collapsed, and Darnley's skull was stolen. Along with a femur, it is now in the museum of the Royal College of Surgeons in London. The bone structure shows the distinctive pitting associated with syphilis. Darnley was twenty-one when he was murdered; judging by the advanced stage of the disease, he may not have had that long to live. The guilt or innocence of his wife regarding his murder remains unresolved.

lords, and they did not want to see him as king. A revolt of nobles in June 1567 forced Bothwell into exile in Denmark, and saw Mary imprisoned in Loch Leven Castle near Kinross. She was forced to abdicate in favour of her one-year-old son, James. Whilst on her island prison she had a miscarriage, losing twins; Bothwell was almost certainly the father.

The following year she escaped and raised an army, which was defeated at the Battle of Langside in Glasgow. Lacking any support, Mary fled to England and threw herself on the mercy of her cousin, Queen Elizabeth. Mary lived out the rest of her life as a prisoner in the English castle of Fotheringhay. The Scottish nobles produced 'proof' that she had been directly involved in the plot to murder Darnley. The authenticity of this evidence has been debated ever since – there is a good chance that it was faked. But it served to keep her in jail and out of the hair of the Scottish nobles. With the Queen out of the picture and the King still a child, the Scottish earls were able to exercise power and accumulate wealth without any pesky royals getting in the way. The way Mary had been brushed aside led to a profound change in the relationship between kings and nobles in Scotland, resulting in a loss of power and prestige for the monarchy.

After nineteen years in prison, Mary was implicated in a Catholic plot to assassinate Elizabeth. She was executed on 8 February 1587. Bothwell spent a decade chained to a low post in a Danish dungeon; he died insane. Four of his servants and associates were

Mary, Queen of Scots, at her execution. (From A History of the Scottish People *by Thomas Thomson, 1893)*

found guilty of the gunpowder plot. After being horribly tortured, they were drawn backward on a cart to the Mercat Cross on 24 June 1567, and hanged and quartered, their various body parts sent to be nailed up in different cities around the kingdom.

SIEGE!

THE FORTRESS OF Edinburgh Castle has often been the key to military success in Lowland Scotland. Not surprisingly, it has changed hands many times. It also dominates the heights of Castle Rock, which means that if the castle was occupied by one side, and the city by another, then the former could rain fire and cannonshot down on the latter. Conversely, defenders could find themselves trapped in the castle while besieging forces cut off food and supplies.

In 1400 the forces of the English King Henry IV commenced another siege, but were forced to withdraw due to a lack of supplies. Further short sieges took place in 1445 (besiegers: Clan Douglas) and 1544 (besiegers: the army of Henry VIII of England). The principal siege in the castle's

history, however, took place during the bloody civil war between the friends and enemies of Mary, Queen of Scots. Because it lasted two years, from 1571 to 1573, it is known as the Lang (long) Siege.

THE LANG SIEGE

At the time, Scotland essentially had two monarchs. On the one side there was the Queen's Party, supporters of Queen Mary. On the other side were the King's Party, the forces of the regent, the aristocrat who 'owned' the infant King James VI and ruled Scotland in his name. Being regent was not a particularly enviable role, with being murdered something of an occupational hazard. When the first regent, the Earl of Moray, was assassinated in Linlithgow, the keeper of the castle, Sir William Kirkcaldy, changed his allegiance and declared for the Queen's Party.

For the King's Party, this unexpected reversal was a disaster. Kirkcaldy occupied not just the stronghold of the castle but also the walled city leading up Castle Rock, and had installed cannon on the town walls and church towers. The King's Party did not have enough cannon to effectively attack the castle or walls, and so, a few skirmishes aside, they resolved to starve the defenders out.

CASTLE VS CITY

In 1640, during the religious civil wars, the Royalists held the castle against the Covenanters. The defenders bombarded the city, but were forced to surrender after three months because of disease brought about by lack of food.

In July 1572, after more than a year of siege, a truce was negotiated and the blockade was lifted. Kirkcaldy withdrew from the city and holed up in the castle, which he continued to fortify. An uneasy peace reigned.

On 1 January 1573 the truce ran out. Terror tactics were employed by both sides. From his vantage point, Kirkcaldy bombarded the town and sent out troops to burn swathes of houses to the ground; the castle garrison then fired on anyone who tried to contain the blaze. Meanwhile, the King's Party employed biological warfare – poisoning the source that supplied much of the castle's drinking water, St Margaret's Well. We are not told how the water was rendered undrinkable – a standard practice of the time was to throw human or animal corpses or faeces into well water, but the attackers may have used something else, perhaps a chemical.

The castle from The Mound in the early nineteenth century. Almost the entire structure was rebuilt after the Lang Siege of 1573. (From Modern Athens *by Thomas H. Shepherd, 1829)*

TEN DAYS OF ARTILLERY

The King's Party valued victory over their fellow Scots more than they hated the English. They forged an alliance with Elizabeth I of England, who supplied troops and the all-important cannon. Six artillery batteries were constructed around the castle. 17 May 1573 saw the commencement of ten days of continuous bombardment. One by one the castle's fortifications fell to the onslaught. It is estimated that at least 3,000 pieces of ordnance were fired. The noise must have been insupportable. As late as the 1870s, cannonballs were still being found embedded in walls and rubble.

Inside the castle, the beleaguered garrison had run out of water, food and ammunition. Their situation was hopeless, especially when the attackers captured an outer fortification and took their last well. Realising that his soldiers would soon be overwhelmed and slaughtered to a man, on 28 May Kirkcaldy lowered a messenger with a parley over the wall by a rope, as all the entrances were blocked by cannon-smashed stones. The keeper of the castle, however, chose to surrender not to the bloodthirsty Regent Morton of the King's Party, but to the English commander, Sir William Drury, in the hope that he would be granted the professional courtesy of one officer to another. In this he was to be thwarted. Although Drury accepted the surrender, his hands were tied, and he had to pass over control of the castle to the King's Party. The majority of the garrison were, surprisingly, allowed to go free, but Kirkcaldy and his brother James were to suffer the full wrath of a triumphant Regent Morton. Along with two Edinburgh burgesses who had been minting Mary's coins inside the castle, they were trawled backwards through the streets by a cart to the Mercat Cross. There they were hanged, their limbs cut off (to be exhibited in other parts of the kingdom) and their severed heads exposed upon the castle wall.

The devastation of the Lang Siege was so great that the vast majority of the fortress had to be completely rebuilt.

DEATH AND THE MAIDEN

THE IRON BLADE was 13in long and more than 10in high, its cutting edge faced with sharpened steel. Above it lay a lead ingot 75lb in weight. With a rope and pulley the lokman or executioner pulled the lethal combination up through the vertical grooves of the upright oak shafts and secured the blade and ingot at the very top. The prisoner was placed, face down, over a wooden block, an iron chain and adjustable bar preventing any movement or attempt to escape. At the signal, the lokman released a catch. The tension on the rope was instantly released and the heavily weighted blade shot downwards, decapitating the prisoner in an instant. The Scottish Maiden had claimed another victim.

Long before the guillotine became the symbol of the French Revolution, Edinburgh had its own execution machine. The Maiden was constructed in 1564, and was used regularly until it was retired in 1710. It was a kind of IKEA guillotine, being a flat-pack device that could be stored when not in use and quickly assembled when occasion demanded. It could thus be set up wherever it was required, and the Maiden made the rounds of Castle Hill, the Grassmarket, and at the Mercat Cross on the High Street part of the Royal Mile.

Before the advent of the Maiden, any beheadings took place with a two-handed sword, and there was ample opportunity for the act to be bungled – it sometimes took three or four strokes before the head was finally severed from the body. By tradition, beheadings were reserved for the gentry, while the common people were hanged: a severed head was usually a sign that its

The Edinburgh Maiden. The dotted line marks the position of the bar used to hold the head in place. (Author's collection)

A woodcut of 1539 shows a German Maiden in use. (Author's collection)

possessor had been a person of quality. The Maiden seems to have changed this practice, and although it gave many an aristocrat a shave above the shoulders, it was also used to despatch murderers, conspirators and thieves from all classes. The Maiden democratised death.

THE EARL OF MORTON LOSES HIS HEAD

One of the Maiden's most prominent victims was James Douglas, the Earl of Morton. Morton had been the regent while King James VI was too young to rule. His regency had been merciless, and when he later fell foul of the King's displeasure (over a mutual mistress) his various pigeons came home to roost. Morton was yesterday's man. He was accused of eighteen charges, including 'comprising the murder of King Henry [i.e. Darnley]'. At 4 p.m. on 2 June 1581, Morton met the Maiden. His body remained on the platform for a further

four hours before being removed for burial in the Burgh Muir, where the corpses of the worst criminals were disposed of. His head was fixed on the highest spike of the Tolbooth on the High Street. This was a common fate for the most notorious traitors and murderers, although some trophies were treated differently. In 1649, for example, the head of James Wilson, a coalminer executed for incest, was taken away and wrapped in an 'ell of buckram' (37in of stiff linen).

Morton's ending, combined with his unpopularity, created a folk legend that not only had he commissioned the Maiden, but also that he was its first victim. This legend had widespread appeal because of the 'poetic justice' story it tells – a wicked men meeting the cutting edge of ironic retribution. However, neither part of the story is true. Morton did not suggest the construction of the Maiden – although he may have seen similar devices during his travels in Europe – and his blood did not baptise its blade. That honour may have gone to Thomas Scott of Cambusmichael, the under-sheriff of Perth, who on 3 April 1566 was executed for his part in the murder of David Rizzio, the secretary of Mary, Queen of Scots. The Maiden was definitely present on the scaffold, but another account does not mention the device, and states that Scott was hanged, drawn and quartered. Perhaps the Maiden was used at the end of the ordeal, or possibly it was not working correctly. Certainly Scott's severed head was fixed on a spike at Holyrood Palace, while that of a fellow conspirator, Henry Yair, ended up attached to the Netherbow Port at the entrance to the city. Whatever the truth, the Maiden did not remain thirsty for long: by the following January it had despatched murderer Robert Aitken, the first of more than 150 victims to experience its weighted blade plummeting down the shafts.

Where the crimes can be clearly identified, we find that about 50 per cent of all those executed had been found guilty of murder. Thirteen were convicted of treason or plotting against the state. Nine people were executed for incest, four for adultery and one for rape. Two others were thieves or burglars, one a forger and another a pirate. One man was beheaded for 'cruel oppression', another for besieging Glasgow Castle. Thomas Ross, a minister of the church and a man of good family, was beheaded in 1618 for writing rude things about King James VI. James VI was notoriously averse to criticism: between 1596 and 1615, at least four other men were hanged or strangled to death in Edinburgh for verbally criticising the King: freedom of expression was not something the Stuart kings had much time for.

THE SWEET KISS OF THE MAIDEN

One of the enduring legends associated with the Maiden took place on 30 June 1685.

Archibald Campbell, the 9th Earl of Argyll, had taken part in a rebellion against King James VII of Scotland and II of England. So, like his father, the 8th Earl before him (beheaded in 1661), Archibald had an appointment with the Maiden. The Earl was a flamboyant character, and his execution was his finest performance. When placing his head on the rest, he declared it was uneven, took out a rule to measure it, and instructed the lokman to find a carpenter to smooth out the wood to a comfortable level. He then inspected the rest of the device carefully, delighting the huge crowd with his claim that it was 'the sweetest maiden I have ever kissed'.

The execution machine can now be inspected in all its gory glory in the National Museum of Scotland. It used to be traditional for citizens to tip their hat when they passed the Maiden in the street, and some visitors to the museum do the same to this day.

1622

A SEA BATTLE

– Inside the Harbour!

SOMETIMES BLOOD WAS shed in Edinburgh that had nothing to do with Scotland or Scottish conflicts. In the dark early hours of 6 June 1622, two Dutch warships took anchor within the safety of Leith Harbour. When dawn came the sailors were appalled to discover that, lying right next to them, was a frigate belonging to their sworn enemies – the Spanish.

Within minutes of daylight breaking, the Spanish ship had run up its ensign, a symbol of readiness for action. The provisions they had taken on at Leith were cleared away. On the Dutch flagship, Mynheer de Hautain, the Admiral of Zealand, ordered his own vessels to battle stations. The fighting started almost immediately.

HAND-TO-HAND COMBAT

The single Spanish ship and the two Dutch vessels were lying virtually side-by-side, and so the below-decks cannon could not be used.

Instead, small deck-mounted brass cannon raked the enemy with lethal grapeshot, while matchlocks, culverins, pistols and other projectile weapons were fired almost muzzle to muzzle. The Spanish tried to board more than once, but were repulsed by sword and cutlass in fierce hand-to-hand fighting. It was a full-scale sea battle, only it took place between stationary ships at anchor within the docks.

Not surprisingly, the damage was not confined to the opposing vessels, and soon dockside buildings were suffering as well. The Leith authorities, unwilling to act against two nations with whom Scotland was officially on friendly terms, tried to mediate by sending out a herald on a small boat, but both sides ignored the peace mission. The next step was for a battery of heavy cannon from Edinburgh Castle to be brought down to the dockside, and used to menace the two combatants into submission. This was a huge logistical exercise – and by the time the cannon had arrived, it was too late.

A matchlock. (From Chambers's Encyclopaedia, *1888-1892)*

A culverin. (From Chambers's Encyclopaedia, *1888-1892)*

BOMBARDED AND BEATEN

After many hours of smoke and bloodshed, the Spanish captain, Don Pedro de Vanvornz, tried to manoeuvre into a more protected part of the harbour, but this only exposed his hull to further bombardment. The Dutch vessels relentlessly pounded the frigate out of the harbour, this time firing with full cannon. The shattered ship grounded on a dangerous reef, and it was all over. The majority of the Spanish crew were dead.

A party of mariners from Leith boarded the stricken vessel and claimed it for Scotland, flying a Saltire from the mast. But it was to no avail. Under cover of darkness the Dutch burned the ship all the way down to the waterline, and by dawn the victorious warships had sailed away.

THE DUTCH ARE COMING!

Five years later there was almost a repeat experience. On 16 August 1627 Spanish and Dutch warships engaged in a battle off the east coast of Scotland, while the fishing boats that the Dutch were protecting fled to the safety of the Firth of Forth. Observing the close formation of ships approaching, the citizens of Leith feared it was a Spanish armada come to bombard the port. All the men of Edinburgh and Leith were ordered to take up arms at the seashore, while the heavy cannon were once again laboriously brought down to the dockside. The town remained in a state of nervous apprehension until 10 p.m., when it was finally discovered that the supposed Spanish invasion was merely the Dutch fishing fleet.

BIG BANGS

In December 1613 another warship was destroyed at Leith – but not through enemy action. The 48-gun English man o'war, a battleship of its day, had been at anchor for six weeks. Captain Wood and most of his officers were on shore when, for no definable reason, a crew-member laid trails of gunpowder throughout the vessel, kindled a fire, and blew the great ship sky-high. The conflagration was made even larger by all the powder, shot and other ordnance catching fire and exploding, which meant no one could get near until the ship had burned out. Out of the crew of around sixty, twenty-four died. It is not known whether one of the dead was the arsonist's son, who was also on board.

Another explosion, this one in 1702, caused even more damage in Leith. Thirty-three barrels of gunpowder were accidentally set alight. Eight people died, all the adjacent buildings were reduced to matchwood, hundreds of other dwellings were damaged, and the bang could be heard many miles away. The damage was estimated at £36,936 Scots, around £2,841 in English money, or £220,000 in modern terms.

A warship aflame. (Courtesy of the Thomas Fisher Rare Book Library, University of Toronto)

1628

BURIED ALIVE IN THE LOCH!

THE WORKMEN FOUND the coffin on the second day of digging the trench through the thick mud. It was made of thick fir timbers, and was obviously old. It crumbled apart as they opened it. Inside were three skeletons – one of a tall man, the others shorter, probably women. They had been drowned.

The greenery of Princes Street Gardens is an oasis of peace between the endless busyness of Princes Street and the beetling crags of the Old Town. There are benches with splendid views of the castle, floral displays, and popular strolls. At lunchtime on a fine day it can seem that half the city is out in the gardens, soaking up the precious sunshine. Further down in the dip runs the main Haymarket-Waverley station railway line.

HUMILIATION IN FOUL WATERS

But up until 200 years ago this shallow valley was the site of a stinking, polluted and vile slice of water – the Nor Loch. The loch stretched from below the western edge of the castle, past what is now The Mound, and as far as where North Bridge now stands. It may have been created as a defensive measure in the fifteenth century, but another school of thought suggests that the water flowing through the small Craig Burn was simply accidentally dammed by the vast landslide of human faeces and discarded rubbish that slid at glacial speed off the sloping sides of the medieval city on the Rock. Whatever the original cause, for almost four centuries the northern edge of the city of Edinburgh was bounded by the Nor (North) Loch.

The handy body of water was soon put to creative uses, especially in the maintaining of social order and the punishment of

The Old Town in the early nineteenth century, from Princes Street. The drained basin is the former Nor Loch, now the railway and Princes Street Gardens. (From Modern Athens *by Thomas H. Shepherd, 1829)*

41

crime. Both the Presbyterian Church and the Town Council had a dim view of sexual irregularity, and sought to root out 'the filthie vice of fornication'. In 1565 a ducking stool was erected at the east dam of the loch, roughly where North Bridge is now. It was essentially a seesaw, with a rope at one end to raise and lower the stool at the other. 'Persistent fornicators', that is, people who were sexually active outside wedlock, were often ducked in the loch. In 1575, for example, Mary Rose was ducked as a punishment for fornication, while her partner, Thomas Tribe, was thrown into the water with a rope around his waist, and dragged along by mocking crowds on the bank. Adulterers, prostitutes, slanderers, blasphemers, scolding or lazy wives, pickpockets, merchants who gave short measures, and women found drunk in public – all were similarly punished by being placed on the ducking stool. Apart from the public humiliation, there was also a good chance that anyone who swallowed the foul water of the loch would quickly develop severe unpleasantness of the digestive system.

DEATH BY DROWNING

Some crimes, however, attracted more severe penalties. Women convicted of theft or murder were often drowned rather than hanged. In 1599 Grissel Mathew was drowned in the Nor Loch for stealing a strongbox from her master's house. In October 1530, at a time of strict laws designed to limit the spread of plague, two women who had flouted the quarantine were drowned as punishment. And in 1535, in one of the most upmarket townhouses in the city, Katherine Cant murdered her husband

A man having his tongue pierced. (From Bristol Past and Present by J.F. Nicholls, 1882)

TONGUE PIERCING, SEVENTEENTH-CENTURY STYLE

By and large, corporal punishments in earlier centuries rarely went beyond what were regarded as the usual sentences of the time – whipping, branding on the cheek with a hot iron, ducking in the loch, or clipping (cutting) the ears. It was also common for miscreants to be secured to the Mercat Cross or the stocks – sometimes nailed up by their ears – and exposed to public ridicule and volleys of mud and human waste. Occasionally, a more serious crime was rewarded by an even more imaginative and brutal punishment. On 20 February 1650, for example, John Lawson of Leith took part in a dodgy property deal and was found guilty of perjury. As it was his tongue that had offended, his mouth was propped open, pincers extended his tongue to its fullest extent – and it was pierced with a red-hot iron spike.

TORTURE TRAUMA

The use of torture to obtain confessions was legal in medieval Scotland, a situation that continued until at least 1690. The Edinburgh magistrates had at their disposal two appalling devices, each with a disingenuously cute name. The thumbikins was a thumbscrew which, as it was tightened, slowly crushed the bones of the trapped digits. In 1684 a Presbyterian minister, William Carstares, was subjected to the thumbikins for ninety minutes after being suspected of plotting against the government of the day.

The bootikins was a pair of metal 'boots' fitted over the legs between the ankles and knees. Wooden wedges were then hammered into the gaps. As the metal would not give, the wedges crushed first the muscles of the calves, and then the bones. In both cases the agony was so excruciating that the victim would usually confess to any crimes of which they were accused, even if they were innocent.

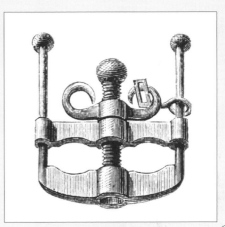

The thumbikins. (From Chambers's Encyclopaedia, *1888-1892)*

Alexander. She was assisted in the crime by her mother, Alison Rough. The argument had been about money and property, as both Alexander and Alison were wealthy merchants. Katherine escaped to England, but Alison was apprehended, taken out into the loch, and her head held below the water until her struggling ceased.

Sometimes men were drowned as well, although only for crimes that were regarded as beyond the pale (mere murderers were usually just hanged). During the 1650s, the time of the occupation of the city by the army of Oliver Cromwell, a high-born man named Low was drowned for confessing to bestiality. As with other sex crimes, the case was heard at night, out of the sight and hearing of ordinary citizens.

THE COFFIN OF DEATH!

None of these unfortunates, however, were the three people whose skeletons were found in the pine coffin. Those bones belonged to George Sinclair and his two sisters. In 1628 all three were convicted of incest. They were placed alive in the coffin and pushed out into the loch. As the water seeped in they drowned, the coffin settling into the muck at the bottom of the Nor Loch. It was a convenient and cheap way of not only executing three people simultaneously, but also of disposing of their corpses (people convicted of incest were forbidden burial in a churchyard).

The Nor Loch was never very deep, rarely reaching 8ft of water. Attempts to drain it started in the 1760s, and took several decades to finally be completed. The skeletons were discovered in 1820, when a drain was being dug through the silted deposits directly below the Castle Rock. The workmen who uncovered the bodies quickly reburied the bones in nearby marshy ground – probably the area where the railway line runs now.

The same excavations revealed other grisly finds, including the complete skeleton of an infant. This was probably one of many newborn babies secretly buried on the margins of the loch or thrown into the water at night. In 1662, for example, Margaret Ramsay was in prison for hiding the corpse of her premature baby in the loch. She was later publicly whipped through the High Street for the additional crime of concealing the pregnancy. Unmarried pregnant women faced not just financial ruin but a host of vicious laws and punishments, and so the killing of neonates was probably the most common (if under-reported) crime of the sixteenth and seventeenth centuries.

Ducking was a popular entertainment, drawing crowds eager for a spectacle of humiliation (especially if a woman was involved). The events were often rowdy affairs. Ducking abruptly ceased as a punishment in 1663, however, as that year Margaret Robb, being ducked for a relatively minor offence, was accidentally drowned in the Nor Loch.

BURN THE WITCH!

Left thumb to right big toe,
right thumb to left big toe ...

Those were the instructions for tying up a suspected witch before ducking them in the Nor Loch. Bound in this manner, the suspect formed a kind of hunched-over St Andrew's Cross or Saltire. A rope was tied around their waist and attached to the ducking stool. If they floated, the belief was that the water had rejected them in the same way that they had rejected their baptism when they joined the Devil; in other words, they were proved guilty by an act of God. And such a divine demonstration of guilt meant a quick trip to the top of Castle Hill, to be tied to a stake, strangled to death, and then burned to ashes.

And if they did not float – well, at least they died innocent.

WRONG RESULT?
TRY AGAIN!

In practice, the 'floating' or 'ducking' of witches was far more common in England than it was in Scotland, even though the latter saw many more witchcraft trials than south of the border. The few Scottish floatings mostly took place in Edinburgh, perhaps because there was a body of water (the Nor Loch) handy, as well as a means of accessing it (the ducking stool). Many authorities rejected floating because, quite frankly, it was both unreliable as a process and subject to great abuse.

In 1629, for example, Isabel Young was put to the ordeal. The first time she entered the water she sank – thus supposedly confirming her innocence – but then managed to crawl out of the loch. As she had neither drowned nor floated this was deemed to be null and void in terms of guilt or innocence, so she was returned to the water. She sank, returned to the surface – and sank again. Once again this was hardly definitive, so Isabel was pulled out, revived, and ducked for the third time. On this occasion she floated, thus giving the result everyone wanted, and so she could finally be burned as a witch.

Isabel Young was unusual in that she saw herself as being on a mission from God. She eagerly confessed to the authorities that the Lord Almighty had told her to use her healing powers to cure all the diseases of mankind, and there were plenty of her clients who claimed she had healed them. Accused witches were a hodgepodge – some were delusional or senile, others charlatans or con-artists, and many were practitioners of folk medicine, although few of the latter claimed their gifts came directly from God himself. A surprising number, however, stated that they had received their powers from the fairies. This was a time when belief in supernatural creatures was still strong, and fairies – Scottish fairies in particular – were regarded not as the twee Tinkerbells of today, but as mercurial, often dangerous beings who could be the size of human adults.

The burning of witches. (Author's collection)

HIS SATANIC MAJESTY

In 1603 James Reid became another victim of the floating mania. A professionally trained doctor, he was accused of having obtained his high degree of medical skill from Satan himself, in whose company he had often been seen. Reid had even been observed strolling with the Devil on Salisbury Crags near Arthur's Seat, with His Satanic Majesty using his red-hot trident as a walking stick. As with Isabel Young, John Reid's first immersion in the Nor Loch was inconclusive – no one could really tell whether he had sunk or floated. On the second attempt he bobbed to the surface, and his fate was sealed.

Ducking witches to determine God-given innocence or guilt lasted a little longer than the use of the ducking stool to punish minor crimes. In 1656 seven Edinburgh residents were accused of witchcraft (although in fact they had been political conspirators pretending to be witches). All were floated: five drowned, and the other two were duly strangled and burned as 'real' witches. Strangulation was thought to release the soul from the body before Satan could catch it; it was thus seen as a 'favour' to witches. Between 1659 and 1670 several other suspects were put to the ordeal by water: one drowned, the others meeting their fiery fate on Castle Hill.

In total, somewhere in the region of 300 people were executed for witchcraft on Castle Hill. A memorial plaque, erected in 1912 in Art Nouveau style, commemorates those so killed, its symbolism and inscription acknowledging that 'special powers' can be used for good or for evil. It can be found at the entrance to the Esplanade in front of Edinburgh Castle.

WITCHES, WITCHES, WITCHES

By the end of the seventeenth century changes in the intellectual climate saw the number of witchcraft trials drop dramatically, and no suspects were tested in the waters of the Nor Loch after 1670. Witchcraft ceased to be a crime in 1735; before that date, being found guilty of practising witchcraft meant execution; after 1735, however, the law stated that witchcraft *did not exist*.

An academic study by Edinburgh University, sifting through all the records of the period, has established that between 1563 and 1727 around 2,500 men and women are known to have been executed for witchcraft in Scotland. This represents about two thirds of all those who were actually accused of the crime. In comparison, England, which had a much larger population, executed about 500 people for witchcraft – a fifth of the Scottish total. In Scotland, the vast majority of those found guilty were strangled to death and then burned, although a small minority were hanged and an even tinier number were burned alive.

1645

PLAGUE!

DESPITE ALL THE wars, battles and massacres down the ages, most people in Edinburgh were not killed by violence. No, the biggest killer throughout the ages has been something far less dramatic but far more deadly – disease.

Bubonic plague – the Black Death – first arrived in Scotland in 1349, just twelve months after it hit southern Europe, having been brought west from Central Asia. Within a year, one third of the population of Scotland was dead. A story has grown up that the Scots brought the plague on themselves – by raiding plague-ridden England. In truth, as long as traders and pilgrims were on the road, and sailors were moving from port to port, the plague would have arrived sooner or later.

The Black Death returned periodically over the next three centuries. Usually the worst of it lasted a few months, but in 1498 the plague persisted for up to fourteen years, moving from an epidemic disease (an outbreak) to an endemic disease (a permanent part of the ecosystem). Another episode commencing in 1602 lasted five years.

From emperors to archbishops and less exalted people, plague (and death) comes to everyone. (Courtesy of the Thomas Fisher Rare Book Library, University of Toronto)

FIGHTING THE PLAGUE

Although we now know that bubonic plague is transmitted by the fleas on black rats, and pneumonic plague passes from person to person by exhalations of the breath, at the time no one understood how the disease was spread. Nevertheless, during a plague year draconian restrictions were put into place, limiting who could travel or enter Edinburgh, where they could stay, and what they could do. Taverns, trading booths, markets and schools were closed. Dogs and pigs running loose were destroyed, and any children not obeying the 'stay at home' rule were placed in the stocks and whipped. Beggars were expelled outside the walls. Goods and clothes brought in from suspected areas were seized and burned. Basically, within the city walls, ordinary life shut down, although grain and food was brought in from plague-free Leith.

The authorities took these anti-plague laws very seriously – anyone attempting to flout any of them would be branded on the cheeks, have their ears cut off and be banished from the town, never to return. Serious wrongdoers – such as those who smuggled in goods or concealed a sick person – could lose a hand or even their life. In 1530, for example, a man who attended church while his infected wife was dying at home was hanged, and Katryne Heriot, who smuggled stolen goods into the city, thus bringing the plague directly into Edinburgh, was drowned. Similar cases of summary justice were handed down during later outbreaks.

QUARANTINE

The plague outbreak of 1529-1530 saw the first use of quarantine. Those who were sick or had been in contact with the infected were relocated to the large open space of the Burgh Muir, south of the city and outside the walls. This became something akin to a refugee camp, with makeshift dwellings,

Death at the plague pits. (Author's collection)

fencing keeping the sick and the 'contacts' apart, and a well-organised range of facilities and supplies laid on – from water and food to places for washing clothing thoroughly. Each fresh outbreak meant the Burgh Muir was once again pressed into service. A gallows on the site reminded everyone of the consequences of breaking the quarantine. The golf course of Bruntsfield Links is the only open space today remaining from the original Burgh Muir, and plague burials took place both here and on The Meadows.

In November 1585, traveller James Melville rode up the Canongate and through the Netherbow Port into the High Street. In the entire city he saw only three people – the rest were hiding indoors or were on the Burgh Muir.

THE GREAT PLAGUE OF 1645

After perhaps a dozen separate outbreaks, Edinburgh suffered its worst attack of plague in 1645. Local government effectively shut down. The streets were deserted. Grass grew in the High Street. Most people remained closed up in their houses, and even the threat of civil war and invasion could not bring out a force of men to defend the city walls (though fortunately, the war swerved elsewhere). In Leith, more than half the population perished – 2,736 people, many of whom

MORE DISEASES

After the apocalypse of the 1640s, the plague did not return to Edinburgh, although in 1799 a Russian ship carrying a form of plague was held in quarantine in the Firth of Forth, and there was an isolated case in 1905. But this did not mean that pestilence was absent from the city. Periodic outbreaks of smallpox, influenza, dysentery, scarlet fever and typhoid culled the population. In 1832 the next big killer arrived – cholera.

Cholera swept across Europe, affecting Moscow in September 1830, and Hamburg in October 1831. Within weeks it had arrived in the north-east of England. In a world linked by passenger steamships and railways, the march of the disease was inexorable. By January 1832 the disease had reached Musselburgh, and quickly leapfrogged into Edinburgh. The contagion wiped out around 600 people within the city, and returned several more times during the nineteenth century.

A European 'Plague Doctor', 1656.
(Author's collection)

were hastily buried on Leith Links, which became another quarantine area. Numerous skeletons have been dug up over the years, and plague burials have also been found as far apart as Craigmillar and Edmonstone (the latter had a large communal grave, while elsewhere bodies were buried individually).

The city also hired 'cleaners' – men who, for a relatively high fee, entered dwellings where the inhabitants were infected, or even dead, and washed and smoked the building in an attempt to drive out the pestilence. Their badge of office was a white wand with a hoop at its end, the sight of which made anyone on the street want to be somewhere else very quickly. Not surprisingly, the cleaners lived apart from everyone else.

1645 saw another innovation – the Plague Doctors. The city hired a physician specifically to treat the infected. The first Plague Doctor, John Paulitius, succumbed to the disease. His replacement, George Rae, was luckier. He walked the streets garbed in a nightmarish costume that looked like something out of a dystopian science-fiction film – an ankle-length leather coat topped by a grotesque beaked mask filled with sweet-smelling herbs. Although he did not know it, Rae's survival of the plague was down not to his mask but to his coat, as it kept the rats and fleas at bay.

1638-1679

A CONCENTRATION CAMP
– in the Middle of Edinburgh

THERE'S NOTHING LIKE a religious war to bring out the worst in people. In the late seventeenth century the conflict was not between Catholics and Protestants, as it had been in earlier years, but between two different kinds of Protestants. On the one side were the Royalists, who favoured an Episcopal church led by bishops who were in turn appointed by the King. On the opposing side were members of the dour (if not extreme) wing of the Presbyterian Church of Scotland, to whom bishops were an anathema. These Puritan-like Presbyterians signed a National Covenant, and hence became known as Covenanters. To sign the Covenant was essentially to oppose the will of the King – in other words, they were committing treason. The Covenanters successively defied Charles I, Charles II and James VII.

The National Covenant was first signed on 28 February 1638, in the church and graveyard of Greyfriars Kirk, off Candlemaker Row. Some of those present drew their own blood with which to sign the document. Many of the signatories subsequently died at the point of a soldier's sword or the hangman's noose. In 1680 two women were hanged in Edinburgh simply for *listening* to a sermon by a prominent Covenanter.

Between 1661 and 1680 perhaps 18,000 Presbyterians were slaughtered for their beliefs – many more than those executed for witchcraft, or killed during the later (and more famous) Jacobite Wars. The era was later dubbed the Killing Times.

The signing of the National Covenant in Greyfriars graveyard, 1638. (From A History of the Scottish People *by Thomas Thomson, 1893)*

Richard Cameron, one of the Covenanter leaders, praying before the Battle of Airds Moss. (From A History of the Scottish People by Thomas Thomson, 1893)

Over the years, many Covenanters were hanged or beheaded in Edinburgh. For example, after their defeat at the Battle of Rullion Green in 1666, some 120 Covenanters were squashed into a part of St Giles' Church called the 'Haddock's Hole'.

As many as ten men at a time were executed on a scaffold erected at the Mercat Cross. The bodies were then dismembered, the heads and limbs being sent to each man's home area to be displayed as a warning to others. In 1680 the head and hands of Richard Cameron, a famous Covenanter fanatic who had been killed at the Battle of Airds Moss, were carried through the streets on the spikes of a two-handed halberd before being fixed on the Netherbow Port, the main gate into the Old Town. Three years later Andrew Gillon was hanged in Edinburgh for the murder of Archbishop Sharp near St Andrews, even though he had had nothing to do with the assassination of the unpopular cleric. Gillon was a Covenanter, and, to a government bent on systematic if unfocused revenge, that was good enough.

LEFT TO DIE

The most shameful episode, however, took place in 1679. Something like 1,200 Covenanters were taken prisoner at the Battle of Bothwell Bridge near Glasgow, and force-marched to Edinburgh. There they were incarcerated within an enclosure of Greyfriars graveyard – the very place where the National Covenant had first been signed. The enclosure had four solid walls and barred gates – but no roof. For five months into the

---

HOLY BLOOD

❦

The brutal persecution and martyrdom of the Covenanters gave rise to several myths. In 1661, for example, when a Covenanter named Guthrie was executed, a rumour went round that as his severed head was fixed to the Netherbow Port some drops of blood fell on the coach of Guthrie's enemy, the Earl of Middleton. The bloodstains could not be washed off, and the leather roof had to be replaced.

Guthrie's small son would often return from playing in the streets to tell his mother that he had been studying his father's decaying head on the city wall.

❦

PRISONS AND POLTERGEISTS

The Covenanters' Prison can be viewed through locked gates in Greyfriars kirkyard. Some of the concentration camp now lies under Forrest Row, while the rows of elaborate monuments you can see were only erected from 1705 onwards, long after the Covenanting period had drawn to a close. There is an elaborate monument to the Covenanter martyrs in the graveyard, erected in 1706, plus a more recent brass plaque.

Greyfriars graveyard also houses the mausoleum of George Mackenzie, the Lord Advocate during the time of the Covenanters. Known as 'Bluidy' Mackenzie, his unsavoury reputation followed him beyond the grave. By the eighteenth century the tomb was widely regarded as haunted, a reputation enhanced when a thief named James Hay escaped from the Tolbooth and hid inside the vault, his noises being interpreted as evidence of the resident ghost. Since the late twentieth century there have been many reports of the 'Mackenzie Poltergeist' apparently attacking visitors on ghost tours.

The gates of the open-air Covenanters' Prison, Greyfriars graveyard. (The Author)

George Mackenzie's mausoleum, Greyfriars graveyard, the home of the alleged 'Mackenzie Poltergeist'. (The Author)

winter the prisoners suffered in the open air, denied adequate food, water and blankets. Their daily allowance was just 4oz of bread a day. Under these concentration-camp conditions, many died of exposure or starvation. Some were executed. A lucky few escaped. Others were released once they had signed oaths of allegiance to the King.

By November 1679 there were 257 men remaining in what by now was called the Covenanters' Prison. Having refused to desert their principles, they were sentenced to transportation to the American colonies to work as slaves. The ship carrying the men sank off the Orkney Islands, drowning all but forty-eight of the prisoners.

1650

THE DISMEMBERED MARQUIS!

THE LEGS AND arms were distributed to Perth, Stirling, Dundee and Aberdeen, to be nailed up in public view. The head was fixed to the highest spike of the Edinburgh Tolbooth. The trunk was buried in the Burgh Muir, in a spot reserved for common criminals. And in the dead of night, a group of men secretly dug up the body and removed the heart ...

Such was the fate of James Graham, the 1st Marquis of Montrose, easily the most celebrated figure of the Covenanting era. An inspiring and brilliant general and military tactician, he was usually called the Great Montrose.

At the start of the religious dispute, in 1638, Montrose declared for the Covenanting party, and won a series of battles. But his skill on the battlefield was not enough in a country riven by inter-clan disputes, where shady dealings and political compromises took place behind closed doors. Alliances shifted constantly. In 1641 Montrose found himself imprisoned in Edinburgh Castle by his own side, largely as a result of a dispute with Archibald Campbell, the powerful Earl of Argyll. He was not granted an open trial because of the danger that inconvenient truths would be aired. After his release on parole, Montrose changed his allegiance and in 1643 allied himself with King Charles I against the Covenanters. For two years he waged a stunningly successful campaign against Covenanting armies in Scotland, but by 1646 the political landscape changed yet again and he was forced into exile.

SEVERED HEADS ON DISPLAY

On any given day in seventeenth-century Edinburgh you were almost guaranteed to come across one or more severed heads fixed to a spike. Usually they were displayed on the Tolbooth or the Netherbow Port, but sometimes they were placed on the gallows themselves. In 1663 two Keppoch men were murdered by their cousins, members of the powerful Highland Macdonald clan. Two years later the killers, Alexander Macdonald and his six sons, were in their turn slaughtered, although this time under a skein of legality. Their heads were separated from their bodies and sent to Edinburgh, where they were 'affixit to the gallowes' on the road between the city walls and Leith.

The execution of James Graham, Marquis of Montrose, in 1650. (Author's collection)

The execution of Charles I in 1649 brought Montrose back into the fray, this time fighting for the King's son, Charles II. But in 1650 Montrose was defeated at the Battle of Carbisdale in Ross-shire. Taking refuge at Ardvreck Castle in Assynt, he was betrayed by the laird, Neil MacLeod (MacLeod was later excoriated for having handed over a man under his protection, a breach of the rules of Highland hospitality). Charles II, negotiating with the Covenanters, cast Montrose adrift as a sacrifice to political compromise. After being put on display in several cities and towns, Montrose was finally delivered to the Covenanters in Edinburgh. Legend has it that, as he was drawn through the High Street on the back of a cart, the crowd that had turned out to mock and abuse him were so taken by his charisma that they just stood in awed silence.

A show trial sealed Montrose's fate. As an aristocrat, he should have been executed by the axe. But his enemies wanted to exact the maximum humiliation. He was hanged like a common criminal, a biography of his military exploits hung round his neck as a final insult. The Marquis addressed the crowd in a moving speech in which he stated he was loyal to the King, and still true to the principles of the Covenant – principles he was convinced his enemies had betrayed. He passed over some gold to the hangman, mounted the ladder, and said his final words: 'God have mercy on this afflicted land.' According to tradition, the hangman had tears in his eyes when he pushed the Marquis off, and the mob was uncharacteristically respectful.

THE TRAVELS OF A HEART

The corpse was dismembered on the platform, and the trunk, barred from consecrated ground, was buried in a pit reserved for ordinary felons. That night Lady Elizabeth Erskine of Mar, the wife of Montrose's nephew, had a team of servants dig up and embalm the heart. It was placed in a steel 'egg' fashioned out of Montrose's sword, and then housed in a box of filigree gold. This relic travelled far and wide. Having passed out of the possession of the Grahams, it turned up in Holland, from where it was taken to India (being damaged en route by a shot fired by a French warship during a sea battle off the Cape Verde Islands). In India the box was stolen and acquired by the local aristocrat, the Nabob of Arcot, who returned it to its rightful owners when a member of the family saved his life during a hunting trip. By 1792 the heart-casket was on its way back to Britain, but went missing during the chaos of the French Revolution, and finally vanished in Boulogne.

Montrose's severed arm and his broken sword. (From The Scots Army 1661-1688 *by Charles Dalton, 1909)*

BODY PARTS

The rest of Montrose's body had an equally strange afterlife. In 1661, now firmly in power, Charles II ordered the scattered remains to be brought together for a grand state funeral at St Giles' Church in Edinburgh. Having betrayed his loyal general in life, Charles was keen to make posthumous amends as apart of his PR campaign. The head, weathered by a decade of exposure to the elements, was taken down off its spike (it was replaced by the severed head of Montrose's arch-enemy, the Earl of Argyll, now himself out of favour). The trunk was exhumed from the Burgh Muir and the legs and arms were recalled from their destinations. But in 1891 a Mr J.W. Morkhill purchased a preserved human arm that was stated to belong to the Marquis – an arm that had been on display in Dundee, and should have been buried in 1661. The gruesome item had holes in the palm and elbow that were consistent with it having been nailed up. Morkhill, an antiquarian, also had documentation, including wills and family papers, showing that the item had been passed down through several generations of well-to-do Yorkshire families, including the Pickerings. Morkill discovered that a Captain Pickering, a Cromwellian soldier, had been on active duty in Scotland before retiring to his native Yorkshire. Several Scottish gentlemen owed Pickering money. It seems likely that the 'Dundee arm' was passed over as part-payment of a debt, and never reburied in Edinburgh.

There is an elaborate memorial to Montrose in St Giles' Church. In the 1880s a search was undertaken of the crypt beneath the Chepman Aisle, where the Marquis's remains were supposed to have been reburied in 1661. No bones were found.

1670

THE WIZARD OF WEST BOW

THE STORY OF Major Weir has it all: sexual perversion, demonology, religious fanaticism, ghosts – and an abiding mystery.

Thomas Weir was a lifelong Presbyterian. Born to a wealthy Lanarkshire family, and having fought bravely in the Covenanting army, he became the commander of the Edinburgh Town Guard around about his fiftieth birthday. He was in charge when the Covenanter-turned-Royalist Marquis of Montrose was brought to Edinburgh for execution in 1650 – and delighted in making the turncoat's last few days as unpleasant as possible. On the way to the scaffold Weir heaped abuse on Montrose, calling him 'dog', 'atheist', 'traitor', 'apostate' and 'excommunicate wretch'.

Eventually Major Weir retired and became the most prominent member of a group of intolerant Covenanting zealots, who were nicknamed the 'Bowhead Saints' as the prayers were usually conducted at Weir's house on the West Bow, the steep dogleg street from the Royal Mile down to the Grassmarket. He was not a minister or a preacher, but his word-perfect recall of Scripture, combined with his austere moral authority, made him a *de facto* leader. He was described by Francis Watt as:

A tall, thin man, with lean and hungry look, big, prominent nose, severe, dark, gloomy countenance, which grew yet more gloomy when one of the conforming ministers crossed his path. Then, with expressive gesture, he would draw his long black coat tighter about him, pull his steeple-hat over wrathful brows, and turn away with audible words of contempt.

SEX CRIMES

In 1670 the major's orderly and pious life collapsed. Out of the blue, he confessed to members of his sect that he had been having an incestuous relationship with his spinster sister Jean since she was ten years old. Further, he had also slept with two female servants, along with Margaret Bourdon, his wife's daughter from her first marriage, whom he had made pregnant. But worse was to come. According to Weir, he regularly had carnal knowledge of horses and cows. Bestiality was regarded as a particularly abhorrent crime. In September 1605, for example, John Jack was executed on Castlehill for the crime, and the poor animal was burned alongside him.

Initially the sect tried to keep a lid on the confession, but word reached the city's provost, Sir Andrew Ramsay, who at first

56

refused to believe the confession, assuming that Major Weir's faculties were slipping away in old age. But then doctors examined Weir and found him *compos mentis*. Eventually the authorities were forced to act, and Thomas and Jean were incarcerated in the Tolbooth. Weir was aged somewhere between seventy and seventy-six at this point, while Jean was ten years younger.

DEMONS AND DEVILS

Major Weir was charged with a catalogue of sexual crimes. Jean, however, raised the bar by confessing to being a witch. She stated she had sold her soul to the Devil, had once been in the service of the Queen of Faery, and on 7 September 1648 she and her brother had made a round trip between Edinburgh and Musselburgh in a fiery horse-drawn coach supplied by the Devil. Satan, according to Jean, had also provided Thomas with up-to-the-minute information about events (such as battles) fought by the Covenanters in England, and gifted him a carved thornwood walking stick that possessed a demonic spirit. According to one rather unreliable account, Major Weir depended on this 'familiar' for errands and messages. When they were jailed, Jean implored the guards to keep her brother away from the walking stick, as he drew his strength and powers from it. Weir did not confess to fraternising with the Foul Fiend, and was not charged with any crimes of witchcraft or sorcery. Within a short period, however, he was nicknamed 'the Wizard of West Bow'.

At the trial there was no evidence presented other than the brother and sister's confessions. Nevertheless, both were found guilty. Major Weir, influenced by the 'Predestination' belief of his gloomy sect, which stated that some people were predestined to go to heaven, while others were bound for hell no matter what they did in this life, refused all religious entreaties.

Major Weir's house on the West Bow, down from Lawnmarket. (From Memorials of Edinburgh in the Olden Time *by Daniel Wilson, 1872)*

'I have lived like a beast, and I shall die like a beast,' were his words. On 11 April 1670, Weir was strangled and burned at the Gallow Lee, a spot off Leith Walk. His stick was thrown into the fire with him, and was said to writhe and contort itself in the flames (earlier, two cloths belonging to Weir had behaved strangely when thrown into a fire). The following day Jean was hanged at the Grassmarket, but not before she attempted to strip off on the scaffold.

A HAUNTED HOUSE

The Weirs' house in Anderson's Close on the West Bow very quickly developed a reputation for being haunted by its most infamous tenant, or at least his demonic friends, with reports of ghostly lights, laughter, human figures, animals (including a headless horse) and a phantom carriage. For perhaps 150 years in overcrowded Edinburgh it remained unoccupied, although the ground floor was used for a succession of shops. It was finally demolished in 1878, and the spot, also known as Stinking Close, has now vanished, replaced by Victoria Street.

At the time of the Weirs' frenzied confessions, few people entertained scepticism towards the reality of witchcraft, pacts with the Devil, demonic familiars and interactions with fairies. Later generations have had different ideas. It is difficult to come to a conclusion about what drove Thomas Weir to make his initial confession. Was he a life-long sexual predator who wished to confess his sins before he died? Was he delusional or suffering from dementia or another mental illness? Or were the gloomy precepts of his religion affecting his mind? And why had Jean confessed to this florid tale of demonology – something not even hinted at in Thomas' first confession? Was she mentally ill as well? Or had Thomas infected his spinster sister with a *folie à deux*, a shared madness? In the end, the bizarre tale of the Wizard of West Bow remains a unique episode in the history of Scottish supernaturalism, and an episode that still has so many unanswered questions.

1682

THE HANGMAN WAS A MURDERER!

ON 16 JANUARY 1682 Alexander Cockburn went to the gallows for murder. What made this execution unusual was that Mr Cockburn was the official hangman.

Cockburn had been convicted of the killing of a beggar called Adamson or Mackenzie, a bedesman or bluegown. 'Bluegowns' were a common sight on the streets of Edinburgh – they held licences to beg and had to display their beggar's badge on the blue gowns they received once a year. In return they were required to pray for the soul of the monarch ('bede' means 'prayer', and a bedesman was one who received alms in exchanged for prayers).

There were no witnesses to the crime, and the evidence against Cockburn was circumstantial – bloody clothes were found in his house, and he lied about Adamson being there on the day of the murder. 'This evidence, too, was chiefly from women,' stated a chronicler, the obvious inference being that women were not reliable witnesses. Their testimony was enough to convict him, however.

Cockburn had hanged many people, from criminals to religious dissidents during the bloody days of the Covenanter wars. For his own execution, the deed was performed by the Stirling hangman – a man named Mackenzie whom Cockburn had previously attempted to have fired. It is not recorded what the two rivals said to each other on the scaffold.

A HANGMAN'S LOT

Other hangmen were also less than model citizens. John High, commonly called Jock Heich, who filled the post of common executioner from 1784, only took the job to escape a punishment for stealing chickens. He lived rent-free in a small house down a lane off Cowgate, passing the time by beating his wife relentlessly. Another executioner came from a well-to-do family near Melrose in the Borders. Having squandered his inheritance on drinking, gambling and other youthful diversions, poverty forced him to take the hangman's salary. The post had a stigma of horror attached to it, and few people wanted to socialise with a licensed killer. But old habits die hard, and the hangman would sometimes, in the words of a historian, 'resume the garb of a gentleman, and mingle in the parties of citizens who played at golf in the evenings on Bruntsfield Links'. One day he was recognised and chased away, accompanied by insults and shouts. Taking the rejection to heart, he threw himself off Salisbury Crags (a favourite suicide spot). The spot was afterwards called the Hangman's Craig.

Social exclusion was definitely the hangman's lot. John Dalgleish, the man in the post in the 1730s, was a pious Christian who always attended church. Even in a crowded church, he always had a pew to himself. The other parishioners also refused to take communion in his company, so he had to wait until everyone else had left before he could be given the act of grace by the minister – and even then he had to use a separate table.

DEATH IN THE AFTERNOON

Executions, by their very nature, attract some strange beliefs. In Edinburgh it was popularly thought that a man could not be hanged later than 4 p.m. In December 1750 forger John Young certainly shared this belief. At 2 p.m, the time scheduled for his appointment to dance the hempen jig, he locked himself in the inner room of his prison cell in the Tolbooth. The authorities had to break through the floor from the room above. Young then faced down a gun pointed at his head, stating that the weapon was not loaded – and anyway, they could not shoot him to death if they wanted to hang him. Eventually a press of guards overpowered him and dragged him down the stairs and out into the street. As he was bundled onto the scaffold Young asked if it had gone 4 p.m., and was told it had not. As it happened, to prevent any outbreak of discontent from the mob, the council kept to the traditional timetable – by secretly stopping the Tolbooth clock. John Young breathed his last around 4.30 p.m.

BOTCHED HANGINGS

A hangman's job was to extinguish life. At times, however, a lack of professional competence meant that death was not the end result. On 18 February 1594 Hercules Stewart was hanged for his alleged part in the political crimes of his kinsman the Earl of Bothwell. Stewart's body was then taken to the Tolbooth to be laid out, 'but within a little space he began to recover,' wrote a historian, 'and moved somewhat, and might by appearance have lived.' It is not clear whether the poor man ever regained consciousness, as he was speedily strangled, this time until he was definitely dead.

Almost 100 years later, in 1688, the execution of Philip Stanfield was bungled so badly that the hangman had to step forward and strangle the man with his bare hands. And in December 1818 condemned thief Robert Johnston suffered excruciating agony as, with his feet still touching the floor of the scaffold, he was slowly strangulated by the too-long rope. Carpenters were summoned and tried to cut away the wood beneath him, but failed. Eventually, after Johnston, still conscious, had been twisting for at least fifteen minutes, the crowd invaded the scaffold and cut him down. Despite the anger at the incompetence of the authorities, there was no attempt made to liberate the prisoner. After recovering in the nearby police office, Johnston was marched out again to the scaffold. This time the rope was the correct length, and he was quickly and efficiently launched into eternity.

HALF-HANGIT MAGGIE

In 1724 Margaret Dickson or Dixon, convicted of killing her newborn child, was hanged in the Grassmarket, and her body placed in a cart for transport to her home parish in Musselburgh. Yet about halfway through the journey she sat upright. As she had already been pronounced dead, the authorities decided they could not return her to the gibbet, and so 'half-hangit Maggie Dixon' went on to live for another thirty years, get married, and have children. She never revealed the circumstances that had enabled her to cheat the hangman's noose.

DEACON BRODIE

Stories such as these appear to have encouraged one of Edinburgh's more famous criminals to believe that he too could survive being hanged. William Brodie was a respectable citizen by day – a cabinet-maker, a deacon in the trades guild of wrights and masons, and a town councillor to boot. By night he was a burglar, using his skills to copy keys that let him into the houses (and safes!) of the wealthy. The money he stole financed his secret second life – his two mistresses (neither of whom knew about the other) and his numerous illegitimate children. After a successful criminal career, Brodie came to grief during a raid on the Excise Office on Canongate. One of his accomplices was captured and fingered the rest of the gang. Brodie fled but was arrested in Amsterdam as he tried to take a ship to America.

On 1 October 1788 Deacon Brodie stepped out onto the scaffold, a structure he had helped fund the year before. He may even have designed part of it. But he was full of good cheer: 'Fare ye well, Bailie! Ye needn't be surprised if ye see me among ye yet, to take my share of the deid-chack!' (After an execution, the provost and council enjoyed a taxpayer-funded dinner known as the 'deid-chack'.) What the cunning deacon had in mind was a subject of great speculation. Had he inserted a silver tube down his throat to

Deacon Brodie's collection of copied keys, and his dark lantern. (From Traditions of Edinburgh *by Robert Chambers, 1868)*

prevent his windpipe being crushed? Was he wearing a steel collar under his clothes? Or sporting a hidden harness whose hooks would hold the noose away from his neck? It may be that any of these was true, or none. In the end, it did not matter. Brodie was hanged, and died, and was buried in an unmarked grave. He had fooled people for decades but he could not cheat death at the end of a rope.

PAGING DOCTOR JEKYLL ...

Brodie's double life inspired Robert Louis Stevenson to write *The Strange Case of Dr Jekyll and Mr Hyde*, the classic split-personality horror story. Deacon Brodie's Tavern can be found on the Royal Mile.

1707

HE ROASTED
THE SERVANT ON A SPIT

– and Then Ate Him!

THE SMELL OF cooked meat welcomed the household when they returned in triumph on 16 January 1707. Their master, Lord Queensberry, despite virulent opposition, had that day seen through the Act of Union between Scotland and England, and the servants had trooped onto the streets to ensure their lordship was not harmed by the hostile mob. Only one member of staff had remained behind, a lad charged with the duty of turning the beef on a spit over a large open fire.

But when they entered the kitchen the servants were not greeted by a standard domestic scene. For roasting on the spit was the young cookboy. And seated on the floor, tucking into a meal of human flesh, was the nine-year-old Earl of Drumlanrig.

The cannibal child was the great dark secret of Queensberry House, the gloomy mansion on Canongate. Described at the time as an 'imbecile', and possessing unusual size and strength, as well as a tendency for tempestuous violence, James Douglas, Earl of Drumlanrig, was clearly mentally handicapped. He was locked up out of sight in a darkened ground-floor room with all the windows boarded up, his only daily contact with the world being the valet who attended to his needs. But on the day in question the guardian had deserted his post, joining the other servants in a show of force

in support of their beleaguered master, who had already suffered death threats because of his politics. The unattended nine-year-old had escaped, killed the scullion, and set about cooking the corpse.

DAY OF JUDGEMENT

For many in Edinburgh, the tragedy was said to be a judgement on Lord Queensberry, the father of the cannibal child. Queensberry had been the chief negotiator in the dubious dealings that saw the Scottish Parliament dissolved and brought Scotland into the new United Kingdom of Great Britain. For this he was handsomely rewarded, not just in cash from the London government, but with titles south of the border – he was elevated to Duke of Dover, Marquess of Beverley and Earl of Ripon, all of which made him a very wealthy man, English estates being more lucrative than Scottish ones. The proceedings prompted Robert Burns' famous lines: 'We're bought and sold for English gold / Such a parcel of rogues in a nation!'

The Act of Union was massively unpopular with the common people, yet it also saved Scotland, because at the time the country's economy was in freefall. A vast proportion of Scotland's money had been lost in the Darien Scheme, an ill-fated attempt to establish a Scottish colony in the tropical jungles of Panama. Union with the rest of Britain helped revitalise both the Scottish and the English economies, eventually leading to the pre-eminence of the British Empire.

FATE OF A CANNIBAL

As for the cannibal killer, there were rumours at the time of the murder that his father had ordered for him to be smothered and disposed of. But this was not the case. James Douglas, the imbecile earl, outlived his father, dying in 1715 at the age of seventeen. His grave is in Calverley in Yorkshire, where he had been under the care of a Mr Richardson – clearly he had been shipped there because his father, as Baron Ripon, owned large properties in northern England. Although he was the eldest son of the 2nd Duke of Queensberry, James Douglas was legally barred from the succession, and the title and estates were inherited by his younger brother, Charles.

Queensberry House was built in 1681. After the family sold it in 1801 it served as a barracks, hospital and home for the destitute. It was renovated from 1999 onwards and is now part of the complex of the new Scottish

Queensberry House today, part of the Scottish Parliament complex. (Kim Trayner, under the Creative Commons Attribution-Share Alike 3.0 Unported license)

Parliament, housing the offices of the presiding officer of the parliament, along with the Donald Dewar Reading Room, a memorial to the late First Minister. Deep within the A-listed structure on Canongate is the Parliament's Allowances Office. Here an original feature is still visible – the very oven where, in 1707, the act of murder took place.

A FAMILY TOUCHED BY DARKNESS

The Queensberry family was no stranger to scandal and tragedy. William, the first Duke, was a notorious land-grabber, bullying and cheating his way to the ownership of large swathes of property. When he died in Edinburgh in 1695, a legend was told that, at the exact moment of his death, his coach was seen driving into the volcano of Mount Etna on Sicily, where he was welcomed by the Devil himself, shouting, 'Make way for the Duke of Drumlanrig!'

Five years later William's daughter, Anne, Countess of Wemyss, accidentally (and fatally) set fire to her nightclothes in bed. Her nose was burnt off and her eyes burnt out. Trying to cry for help, the flames entered her mouth and burnt her tongue and throat.

1736

HE FIRED INTO THE CROWD

– and was Lynched by the Mob!

The mob of Edinburgh, when thoroughly excited, had been at all times one of the fiercest which could be found in Europe.

(Sir Walter Scott, *The Heart of Midlothian*)

The Porteous Riots of 1736 centred around the brutal lynching of a captain in the City Guard, with political consequences that stretched to Westminster and back again. The episode formed the backdrop to Walter Scott's *The Heart of Midlothian*, which was *the* Edinburgh novel of the nineteenth century. It was probably the most momentous event of the epoch in Edinburgh – but what actually happened, and why, is still highly controversial.

The Edinburgh mob – the mass of common people, most of whom lived in the overcrowded tenements of the Old Town, or on the streets themselves – was justly feared. Fickle, volatile, and frequently extremely violent, the mob often rioted against one perceived injustice or another, or simply to show their disdain for authority. Up until the early 1800s, the only force of law and order opposing the mob was the City Guard, a group who were frequently accused of corruption, ineffectiveness, random acts of cruelty, and drunkenness. It was a marriage made in hell.

SMUGGLERS' TALES

Following the 1707 Act of Union, taxes on goods that had been in place in England were now equally imposed in Scotland. Not surprisingly these taxes were universally unpopular north of the border, and served to increase a sense of resentment over the hated Act. Smuggling was widespread, and received popular support from all levels of society. In the fight against the excisemen or 'gaugers', smugglers became minor folk heroes.

In 1736 three such smugglers were caught red-handed in Fife. One, William Hall, turned King's Evidence and was sentenced to transportation for life to Australia. The other two, Andrew Wilson and George Robertson, were destined for the hangman's rope. On 9 April, six days before the execution, Wilson and Robertson executed a cunning plan to escape from the Tolbooth. In concert with a pair of horse thieves in the cell above them, and secretly supplied with saws by friends and sympathisers, the desperados cut through the bars of a window. One thief lowered himself to the ground, but the next would-be escapee, Wilson, was too fat to fit through the hole and became stuck. The breakout was foiled.

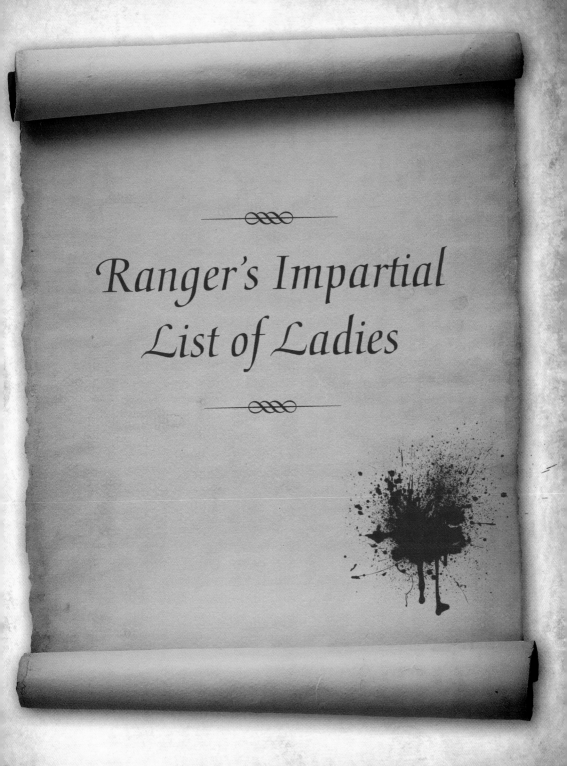

Ranger's Impartial List of Ladies

View of Edinburgh, where Ranger's ladies prowled by night. (LC-DIG-ppmsc-07583)

IN 1775 AN unusual guidebook was published. *Ranger's Impartial List of the Ladies of Pleasure in Edinburgh* was a comprehensive – and candidly detailed – guide to sixty-six higher-class prostitutes and brothel-keepers in the city. The ladies of pleasure were catalogued in terms of the quality of their beauty, figure, skin and hair – with particular attention given to their teeth – and also with regards to their character, social skills (such as conversation or singing), and their abilities in the 'horizontal two-step'. Although stopping just short of obscenity, the descriptions and euphemisms sound remarkably similar to prostitutes' cards of the present day.

The guide has been attributed to a chemist named James Tytler (1747-1805), although this is not certain. Whoever the author was, however, he clearly enjoyed his research – the style is light-hearted and the tone respectful (all the prostitutes are described as 'This Lady ...'), with just the occasional word of disapproval for 'the votaries of the Goddess Venus' who indulge in too much alcohol or have been found helping themselves to the wallets of their gentlemen callers. The introduction to the guide lambasts lawyers, ministers, politicians and military men for taking money for favours, while young women who do the same are unfairly stigmatised.

The sunny, genial attitude found in *Ranger's Impartial List* is a world away from the second major work on Edinburgh prostitution. *Magdalenism: An Inquiry into the Extent, Causes and Consequences of Prostitution in Edinburgh*, written by William Tait in 1840, paints an almost unremittingly grim and dark picture of women forced to sell themselves through poverty, low wages, lack of male support, single motherhood, and other financial woes.

Tait calculated that there were perhaps 800 full-time prostitutes in Edinburgh, or one for every eighty men in the population (the figures were approximate because many Edinburgh sex workers left for Ayr when the rich and idle were attending the races there, while the numbers swelled when the Musselburgh Races brought high society to Edinburgh). There were 203 brothels in the city, of which only three were classified as 'genteel houses of assignation' and ninety-seven were 'very low brothels' which often doubled as low-class eating or lodging houses, licensed taverns, or liquor-free ginger-beer shops. One quarter of all brothels were on the Royal Mile or in the adjacent wynds.

Tait also estimated that around 2,000 women and girls in Edinburgh were 'sly' or secret prostitutes. These were 'dress-makers, sewers, bonnet-makers, book-stitchers, shop-girls, and house-servants' whose low wages and financial and job insecurity drove them to sell sex on an *ad hoc* basis, often on their afternoon off, or when they should have been at church. Perhaps 300 servant-girls regularly brought clients back to the middle-class houses where they worked, which led to a spate of thefts and break-ins as the men pocketed silver cutlery on the way out, or purloined keys for a later visit.

From Tait we learn that brothel clients were called 'cowlies' (from their habit of arriving at the door hooded, so as not to be recognised), and madams were known as 'luckies', while their menfolk were 'fancy men' or 'bullies'. It was a precarious life. Prostitutes who fell ill were usually cast out and abandoned by the madams. Servants and workers caught in the act of 'sly' prostitution would be instantly dismissed. Venereal diseases and casual violence were rife.

An example of the dangers of a prostitute's life can be found in the 1823 trial of Mary McKinnon. McKinnon had been seduced by an army officer at the age of fifteen. Cast out by her disgusted family, she became a streetwalker in Edinburgh, eventually

The pleasures of high society. (LC-USZC4-8764)

A house of ill-repute, eighteenth-century style. (LC-USZC2-544)

graduating to running a house of ill-repute at 82 South Street. One night in February five young men – all very drunk – stumbled into the brothel. Inside were three prostitutes. No sex took place, but after more drink had been consumed, an argument over money erupted into violence, with at least one of the visitors striking one of the women very hard on the head. Further acts of violence took place in the confused, dark house (the tussle had extinguished the candles), with the men desperately trying to leave, and it was claimed that they tried to push one of the women into the open fire.

What really happened is unclear, as most of the witnesses were intoxicated, and many of them perjured themselves in court. Mrs McKinnon herself was out at the time of the incident, visiting friends. When she was urgently summoned, the place was in an uproar, and she charged into the kitchen, shouting, 'Stand back, let me get a knife, and I'll let you see me settle the ****!' There was a further moment of confusion, during which Mary McKinnon was probably assaulted, and then solicitor's clerk Henry Howat was found slumped in a chair with a fatal knife wound.

The **Harlots Nurse**, or Modern **Procuress**.

Behold the practis'd Baud explore,   *Whose lot when she begins to fail*
The Nymph from head to foot all O'er,   *Is Want Diseases and a Jail.*
For Cupers whom shes drefs'd w.th Care   *While it diverts thus Pufsy plays*
(A bait to Catch some Money'd Heir)   *With yonder Mouse, then on it Preys*

Printd for & Sold by the Propriator John Ryall, at Hogarth's Head in Fleet Street, London.

A lady of pleasure is dressed by her procuress. The verse states that the girl is a lure for a 'money'd heir'; but if she fails, disease is her fate. (LC-USZ62-132015)

A more genteel exchange between a lady of pleasure and her gentleman caller.
(LC-USZC4-4741)

The crime was almost certainly culpable homicide (the Scots term for manslaughter), brought on by provocation by a man who had already hurt one of Mary McKinnon's 'girls'. Nevertheless, the madam was hanged for murder at the head of Libberton's Wynd on 16 April 1823, in front of a crowd of 20,000. As was usual at the time, her body was delivered to the surgeons for public dissection.

The distinguished judge Lord Cockburn recorded a tragically romantic moment. On the day before her execution, Mary McKinnon was visited by an unnamed gentleman, clearly of long-term acquaintance. She cut an orange into two, giving one half to him. As she stood on the scaffold, he appeared in a window opposite, and pressed his half of the orange to his lips. She did the same with her half, just before her arms were pinioned and the hood and noose placed over her head. Having thus exchanged a final kiss with her lover, she died, as Cockburn wrote, 'gracefully and bravely'.

RANGER RECOMMENDS ...

———⊶⊷⊷⊷⊶———

Here are some of the Georgian Ladies recommended by 'Ranger':

Miss WATT, at Miss ADAMS'S

This Lady is about 21 years of age, of the middle size, light brown hair, good teeth, but rather surly in her temper, especially after the glass has gone merrily round; notwithstanding of this, she is not a bad companion, as she can sing many very fine songs. It is said, before she would sleep alone, she would rather pay a clever fellow for to do her business, as love is her sole delight.

Miss GILMOR, at Miss WALKER'S

This is a little thick Lady, about 20 years of age, brown hair, good skin and teeth, and pretty good natured. She is also very coy, and amorous to the greatest degree, and has courage enough (although little) not to be afraid of the largest and strongest man that ever drew weapon in the cause of love, upon that account she, for the most part, gives satisfaction.

Mrs KETTY C-------R, *alias* HAMILTON, *alias* YOUNG, and now Mrs P-------, to be found at Mrs YOUNG's

This Lady has had a great propensity for the Gentlemen of the Quill. She was also in keeping with a certain Baronet, but she has left his embraces for one of the former, who goes under the name of her husband. She is very good natured, artful in her amours; and it is said, that was the Devil himself to come in a golden shower, she would as soon meet his embraces as those of Jupiter.

Miss M'CULLOCH, at Mrs YOUNG'S

She is extremely loving, and gives great satisfaction in the Critical Minute, as all those declare, who have had the pleasure of her embraces. She has got fine tempting legs, which she is not a little fond of showing, as she appears very often in men's clothes. Take her all in all she is an agreeable companion.

Miss STEPHENSON, at Miss WALKER'S

This Lady is also tall and thin, black hair, good teeth, bad eyes, but her good nature makes up for that deficiency. She is about 23 years of age; and very fond of that sport which all nature is inclined to. She is very eager in the Critical Minute, and would inspire the dullest mortal with joy and vigour; and if she knows any method to create fresh desire in her lover, she will willingly do it.

———⊶⊷⊷⊷⊶———

A HERO OF THE PEOPLE

On 12 April the handcuffed prisoners were conducted under guard to a church to hear the customary pre-execution sermon. Seizing their chance, they made another bid for freedom. Robertson made it out the door, and eventually fled to Holland, where he spent the rest of his life running a tavern in Rotterdam. Wilson was less lucky. Popular opinion was that, by way of making up for ruining the previous escape, he had deliberately kept the guards occupied (by attacking them with his bulk and his teeth) so that Robertson could get free. In truth, contemporary reports make it clear he had only thought of himself, but, in the imagination of the mob, Andrew Wilson was now not just a smuggler, but a heroic and chivalrous folk hero.

READY ... AIM ... FIRE!

On 14 April Wilson was hanged without apparent incident at the Grassmarket. But what happened next remains a subject of claim and counter-claim. For some reason, a few spectators started throwing stones at the hangman (a not uncommon occurrence). The City Guard, under the command of Captain John Porteous, opened fire. Within a short time at least six people were dead (some reports say as many as nine) and many others were seriously injured. Some of the casualties were standing at the windows and balconies above the Grassmarket, which shows that several of the guardsmen fired above the heads of the crowd.

It was politically expedient to bring John Porteous to trial. He claimed he used legitimate force, and was acting under the orders of the local magistrates, who had authorised the distribution of live ammunition to the Guard that day. Some witnesses claimed Porteous had himself shot into the crowd at point-blank range, something he denied, and he demonstrated

Members of the City Guard. (From Traditions of Edinburgh *by Robert Chambers, 1868)*

that his own pistol had not been fired. Others said he was drunk, or in a foul mood, or incapable of controlling his men. If anything, the trial, which took place in a heated atmosphere, shed even less light on what actually occurred during the disturbance. By a slim majority, Porteous was found guilty of the crimes of murder and mayhem, and sentenced to death.

THE LYNCH MOB

It is rare for a government to let one of its own law enforcement officers suffer for what, in the corridors of power, would be regarded as a justifiable action against a violent mob. It soon became clear that, by royal decree, Porteous' sentence would be quashed. This was not something that the Edinburgh mob could take lying down. On 7 September, the night before the scheduled execution, some 4,000 people took control of central

SPITTING ON THE HEART OF MIDLOTHIAN

The Tolbooth prison has long since been demolished. Where its door once stood in the High Street is a cobblestone pattern in the shape of a heart – the Tolbooth was known as 'the Heart of Midlothian'. The story goes that prisoners used to spit on the door of the hated prison, and these days visitors are encouraged to expectorate on the cobblestones. This may be an invented tradition, but it remains a popular one.

Edinburgh. The city gates were closed, thus shutting out troops stationed in the lower part of the hill. The guards at the Tolbooth were overpowered, and the jail door set alight. In his cell, John Porteous tried to flee up a chimney, but his efforts were in vain. He was carried down from the High Street through the West Bow and into the Grassmarket, where Andrew Wilson had been hanged. It quickly became clear that it would be too difficult to locate and set up the town scaffold, so an impromptu hanging was organised. A shop was broken into and a rope taken (folklore insists the mob politely left a guinea coin in payment on the counter). Dressed only in his nightshirt, Captain John Porteous was lynched from a dyer's pole or street sign. He perished just before midnight.

The traditional version is that it all went quickly and smoothly. In reality Porteous put up a struggle, holding his untied hands between the noose and his neck. He was then hit with an axe, and kicked and punched, and after a drawn-out affray may actually have died from assault rather than asphyxiation.

AFTERMATH

The unexplained aspect of the lynching is that it was clearly well-organised and well-planned, and was followed not by the expected orgy of looting and disorder, but by the crowd simply melting away. At the time it was suspected that 'gentlemen of quality' were involved, with some seeing the hand of the anti-government Jacobites in the action. Another view is that several working men with good organisational skills had orchestrated the proceedings. Whatever the truth, the Westminster government was convinced, possibly with justification, that the Edinburgh magistrates had turned a blind eye to the lynching. Under the speedily introduced Bill of Pains and Penalties, Edinburgh was threatened with the loss of its city status, the demolition of the Netherbow Port, the imprisonment of its provost, and a host of other humiliations. In the end a coalition of Scottish MPs and lords managed to reduce the punishments, but the political fallout was considerable. Many ministers of the Church of Scotland refused to read out a government decree which ordered their parishioners to reveal everything they knew about the identity of the lynch mob, leading to something of a constitutional crisis. The Prime Minister, Sir Robert Walpole, lost sympathy and, a few years later, during another political crisis, this ebbing away of support eventually cost him his job.

No one was ever prosecuted for the murder of Porteous. A commemorative brass plaque stands in the Grassmarket where he was lynched.

JACOBITE CONFLICTS AND THE WAR OF THE CHAMBER POTS

THE JACOBITE REBELLIONS are among the most famous (and roman-ticised) episodes in Scottish history. Compared to the much more complicated Covenanting wars, however, the death toll was comparatively light, and, despite two successive invasions and occupations, they had little overall impact on Edinburgh.

The Jacobites were named after *Jacobus*, the Latin for James. In 1689 the Stuart king, James II of England and VII of Scotland, who was Catholic, had been replaced in a bloodless coup by the Protestant monarchs William of Orange and his wife Mary. Forced into exile in Catholic France, James immediately attempted to regain his throne. His military manoeuvres in Ireland and Scotland resulted in defeat and humiliation. Further Jacobite rebellions against the subsequent Hanoverian kings (George I and II) were led by James' son James Edward Stuart (in 1715) and grandson Charles Edward Stuart (in 1745). The Jacobite adventure came to an end in 1746, when the forces of 'Bonnie Prince Charlie' were defeated at the Battle of Culloden by a Hanoverian government army.

THE SIEGE OF 1689

The 1689 rebellion saw Edinburgh Castle occupied for James II/VII by its Jacobite governor, the Duke of Gordon. His garrison of 120 men contained many supporters of William, so, when they were expelled, the defenders numbered fewer than eighty. A government force blockaded the castle, cutting off all communication, draining the Nor Loch to limit the castle's water supply, and digging trenches and throwing up ramparts and artillery platforms. Gordon had limited ammunition but he did manage to

Death shows himself in favour of war. (From The English Dance of Death, *1815)*

Bonnie Prince Charlie and Cameron of Lochiel. (From A History of the Scottish People *by Thomas Thomson, 1893)*

to take the castle. Pressed by an advancing government army, they retreated and occupied the Citadel at Leith for one night only, decamping during the hours of darkness and marching towards England, taking with them thirty recruits from Leith. Two of these ended up at the end of an executioner's rope. The rebellion later ended in farce and defeat.

A BONNIE PRINCE

Thirty years later Edinburgh was barely better prepared for the advance of the victorious Jacobite forces. Camped just outside the city, Bonnie Prince Charlie sent the following demand to the city council: 'If any opposition be made to us, we cannot answer for the consequences, being firmly resolved at any rate to enter the city; and in that case if any of the inhabitants are found in arms against us, they must not expect to be treated as prisoners of war.' In other words, if the city offered armed resistance, the defenders would be massacred.

In practice, there was little chance of any kind of vigorous defence. There were no effective military units in the city. Lord Provost Drummond rounded up 400 untrained volunteers into a makeshift regiment, but when faced with actually marching out and facing a well-armed foe, this impromptu militia promptly discovered the virtues of reverse gear. As they shuffled back into the Lawnmarket, the volunteers were surrounded by wives, children and parents, urging them not to fight and die meaninglessly. The men who had not already deserted promptly set off to the castle, where they unloaded their arms and melted away into the local population.

As it happened, Provost Drummond had calculated that this would happen. His apparently brave speeches in front of his eighteenth-century equivalent of the Home Guard – 'If you are willing to risk your lives in the defence of the capital of Scotland, and

bombard the government forces, keeping the attackers at bay for many months. As the siege hotted up, cannon fire reduced much of the castle to rubble. The defenders, however, were mostly safe in deep cellars, where they grew so bored that they sent a request out to the enemy for packs of playing cards (the request was refused, which was rather unsporting). After more than three months of on-off fighting, Gordon's troops ran out of water and were forced to surrender. Their casualties were relatively slight, but the besieging troops had lost considerable numbers. Brodie's Close, on the Royal Mile, has a doorstep marked by a deep groove – made by soldiers sharpening their bayonets before going to fight the Jacobites.

1715 AND ALL THAT

In 1715 things were rather different. A Jacobite force entered an entirely undefended city, but they were not equipped

Death signs up another recruit for war. (From The English Dance of Death, *1815)*

the honour of your country, I am ready to lead you to the field' – were just political bravado. He had had no intention of leading his citizens to certain death. An election was due, and, after the rebellion had been defeated, Drummond's heroic posturing ensured his victory.

So Edinburgh offered no resistance to the Jacobites. At 2 a.m. on 17 September 1745 the Netherbow Port was opened to allow a coach out, and the Camerons, one of the key Jacobite clans, sneaked through. By dawn's early light the city had been taken without the shedding of blood (although the small garrison in the castle held out). Charles Edward Stuart installed himself in the Palace of Holyroodhouse. Four days later a government army was roundly and speedily defeated at the Battle of Prestonpans, 8 miles east of Edinburgh. The Jacobites were triumphant, but their subsequent invasion of England and retreat to the Highlands proved to be disastrous.

AN IRRELEVANT WAR

The Rebellion of 1745-46 convulsed the Highlands, threatened London, and has generated hundreds of books on Bonnie Prince Charlie and his romantic Jacobites. Yet in the Scottish Lowlands events proceeded differently. The citizens of mercantile Glasgow viewed the whole affair as bad for business, and declined to get involved. In Enlightenment Edinburgh, filled with the intellectual debate of new thinking and new ideas in economics, politics, science and philosophy, the great rebellion was largely treated as an inconvenience. Those who could afford it moved out to their country houses until the fuss blew over. For ordinary people, there was little to choose between the Stuarts (who had persecuted the Covenanters mercilessly) and the marginally less unattractive Hanoverians. Both were bad news. There was no armed resistance, no urban warfare, no mob attacks, and no enthusiasm for joining up either. Charles Edward Stuart may have temporarily entranced some of the local aristos with his glamour, but when all was said and done, Edinburgh thought the entire Jacobite episode was a bit of a nonsense.

Commenting on the city's actions during 1745, David Hume, one of the greatest of the Enlightenment intellectuals, thought that Edinburgh had only one defence against invaders: chamber pots. The skyscraper-like tenements of the Old Town were notorious for cries of 'Gardy-loo!' (from the French, *garde de l'eau*, 'watch out for the water'). Within a second of the shout, anyone unlucky (or slow) enough to be in the street below would be showered with a chamber-pot's worth of urine and faeces.

1811

RIOT!

RIOTING SEEMS TO have almost been a way of life for some of Edinburgh's citizens. Public executions, economic woes, perceived injustices, too much whisky – all could set off a riot. Sometimes the purpose was political – in 1792, for example, agitators for long-overdue parliamentary reform rioted violently outside the George Square home of Robert Dundas, the Lord Advocate and the most powerful man in Scotland. The Riot Act was read (which authorised lethal force unless the crowd dispersed), and then soldiers of the 53rd Regiment, brought down from the castle, opened fire. At least one protester was shot dead. The following day the riot continued, the target this time being the house of Provost Stirling. The crowds were dispersed (without fatalities) by troops from Leith.

PRESS GANGS AND STREET THEATRE

In 1682 a riot was sparked by the press-ganging of a group of young apprentices. The military escort were stoned and assaulted, first by tradesmen, and then by a general mob. The major ordered his men to open fire, and between ten and twelve people were killed. The riot continued on the following day, with the mob stoning political targets. And in 1561, craftsmen and apprentices met to stage the play *Robin Hood*, a rough-and-tumble piece of street theatre that had been performed for hundreds of years. But the Reformers of the new Protestant religion had banned such displays of frivolity, so the authorities broke up the gathering, and arrested one of the 'ringleaders'. When this token criminal was condemned to death on a trumped-up charge, the mob smashed the gallows, stormed the Tolbooth, released the prisoner, and kept the magistrates and council imprisoned overnight.

SECTARIAN RIOTS

Sometimes, however, the rioting was religious in nature. In 1779 an anti-Catholic riot saw looting and the burning of a chapel, with the authorities refusing to stop the rioters or help put the fire out. The Town Guard even accepted bribes to open the doors of Catholic houses so they could be plundered. Anti-Catholic violence remained Edinburgh's shame for centuries to come. The last riot took place in 1935 under the influence of the virulently sectarian group Protestant Action, which had a hardcore of zealots. Their leader later founded Kormack's Kaledonian Klan, organised on the lines of the Ku Klux Klan.

The fatal blow. (From Scribner's Monthly, *1879)*

THE NEW YEAR RIOT

Other riots, however, lacked any kind of ideological basis. They were just violent for violence's sake. Both the 1792 and 1561 riots had occurred during holidays or special days, and these were usually the touchpoints. In the first decade of the nineteenth century, alcohol-fuelled disturbances at New Year became commonplace. But on the night of 31 December 1811 things became far uglier. Gangs of what were described as 'rough young artisans and idlers' took over the streets, bludgeoning passers-by with heavy sticks. Many people were attacked and robbed of watches, penknives, keys, money and hats. Seventy public lamps were smashed. A member of the City Watch, Dugald Campbell, waded in and was struck a fatal blow, later dying in the Royal Infirmary. Another 'have-a-go hero', James Campbell, also died from blunt-force trauma. The violence continued until two in the morning.

Edinburgh was moving away from the systematic horrors of its earlier years and was attempting to become (relatively)

A STONE'S THROW

In 1705 Daniel Defoe (author of *Robinson Crusoe*, and a political spy for the London government) was in Edinburgh gathering intelligence on the situation regarding the forth-coming Act of Union between England and Scotland. He discovered first hand why no one in an upper tenement apartment looked out into the street during an Edinburgh riot – because a stone went whizzing past his head. Throwing stones at windows was standard practice during a riot, as it reduced the chance of unwanted witnesses being able to later identify the rioters.

respectable. The riots galvanised public opinion and two huge rewards of 100 guineas apiece were offered for information leading to the identity of the rioters. Six men aged between sixteen and nineteen were arrested. One managed to escape, and another two were sentenced to fourteen years' transportation to Australia. Of those arrested, Hugh McDonald, Hugh McIntosh and Neil Sutherland bore the brunt of the punishment. Convicted of being 'art and part' of both robbery and the murders of the two victims, they were condemned to be hanged on 22 April 1812.

Ideas about execution protocols moved in and out of fashion. At the time there was a move to hang criminals, where possible, at the scene of the crime (if this was not practical, the body, after the execution, was often hung in chains at the site of the murder). The rioting had occurred near the heads of several lanes off the High Street, so the scaffold was erected opposite Stamp Office Close; the last view the three youths would have had was of the spot where the police watchman was murdered. The triple hanging was planned as a dramatic and dreadful warning to the rioters, and commenced with a slow and solemn procession from the Tolbooth down to the scaffold, which loomed high above the condemned youths as they shuffled forward. No one could estimate the size of the crowd that gathered on the day, which was said to be the largest ever seen in Edinburgh. The very rooftops were overflowing with people. Order was maintained by 400 troops of the Perth and Renfrewshire Militia.

Of the three youths, Hugh McIntosh was convicted of delivering the fatal blow to the police officer. As the *de facto* murderer, he alone had his body given to the surgeons for dissection practice.

1821

PIRACY AND MURDER ON THE HIGH SEAS!

THOMAS JOHNSON, THE captain of the *Jane of Gibraltar*, was struck with the butt of a musket, weighted down with stones and an anchor, and thrown overboard alive. James Paterson, a seaman, suffered a similar fate. Two Scottish members of the crew were locked in the forecastle and suffered smoke being wafted under the door: on the point of suffocation, they agreed to surrender. Andrew Camelier, a cabin-boy from Malta, was also threatened with death unless he co-operated. It was 19 June 1821. The ship, carrying 38,180 Spanish dollars from Gibraltar to Brazil, was now in the hands of pirates.

The pirates were two of the crew: thirty-six-year-old Peter Heaman from Sweden, and a twenty-four-year-old Frenchman, François Gautiez. They steered the *Jane* up the west coast of Scotland to the Isle of Lewis, where they scuttled the vessel. Unfortunately for them, the island's Excise Officers were on the ball, and the pirates were arrested and brought to Edinburgh for trial. Heaman and Gautiez were found guilty of piracy and murder on the high seas, and, on 9 January 1822, in front of perhaps 40,000 to 50,000 spectators, they were hanged within the low-water mark on the Sands of Leith, while the great bell of South Leith Church tolled its note of doom every sixty seconds. The duo were the last convicted pirates executed in Edinburgh.

A SEA VIEW

Most of those found guilty of piracy were hanged on the Sands of Leith, overlooking the sea (although in 1554 two pirates were executed on the Burgh Muir in the city). In 1551, for example, John Davidson was not merely executed on the Sands, but his body was also hung in chains from the gibbet for many months until the flesh fell off the bones. This was the first time hanging in chains was used as a post-mortem punishment in Scotland. It was clearly designed as a lesson to others, particularly the sailors who passed the rotting corpse on their way to and from Leith Docks.

In 1609 two English pirate captains, Perkins and Randall, along with twenty-five of their crew, were hanged in batches on the Sands. Their vessel, *The Iron Prize*, had terrorised shipping from the Firth of Forth to the Orkney Islands – which was where they were captured, after a bitter and bloody fight, by three ships sent from Leith. The following year a further eight pirates – Captain Peter Love and his English, Welsh and Irish crew from the ship *Priam* – were all hanged in Leith for numerous acts of piracy off the north-west of Scotland; they had been betrayed by their collaborator, the Hebridean outlaw Neil MacLeod.

PIRATES OF THE CARIBBEAN

The Leith Sands also provided the last moments of life for some of the pirates of the Caribbean. On 17 December 1720 and 11 January 1721 respectively, John Clark and Richard Luntly met their ends overlooking the Firth of Forth. Both had been associated with the notorious pirate of the Spanish Main, Bartholomew Roberts, or 'Black Bart'. Clark's vessel had had the misfortune to founder off the Mull of Kintyre, thus coming within Scottish jurisdiction, while Luntly, having been forced into piracy at gunpoint, had later rebelled against Roberts and then, in classic pirate fashion, had been marooned on a deserted island. He was rescued by a ship bound for Britain, and charged with piracy. Both men may have been unlucky rather than wicked; in Clark's case, for example, another seventeen of his crew were reprieved on the grounds that they were not 'true pirates' and had been coerced into their actions.

Any romanticised view of pirates as lovable rogues should be discarded. Anyone unfortunate enough to be on board a ship

Pirates at work. (From The Boy's Own Annual, *1905)*

taken by pirates, and not instantly murdered, would end up as a slave – Peter Love, for example, kept several of his Scottish captives in truly vile conditions. Rape and torture were also common.

PIRACY OR WARFARE?

In many cases, such as with Perkins and Randall, the crime of piracy was quite straightforward: these men were basically sea-borne thieves, preying on whatever shipping sailed within their ken. Similarly, Heaman and Gautiez had murdered their way to the takeover of their ship. But in other instances the very word 'pirate' was a political term, especially when a state of hostility (whether declared or otherwise) existed between seafaring nations. One nation's pirate was another country's privateer or even patriot. And Scotland's age-old, on-off, off-on conflict with England was the perfect breeding ground for political piracy.

From the Middle Ages onwards, privately owned ships were used as an arm's-length military tool by kings and governments. As long as the captains of these privateers attacked vessels belonging to the enemy, there was no question of 'piracy' – unless you were caught by the other side, that is. In 1489, for example, Andrew Wood, a Leith shipowner, fought and won a two-day battle against English ships in the Firth of Forth. There is still some dispute as to whether the English ships were simply bounty-seeking pirates, or privateers quietly engaged by Henry VII of England as part of his foreign policy. In Scottish eyes they were definitely pirates, and Wood was allowed to 'press' (enslave) the captured English sailors and force them to build his castle in Fife. Ironically, the triumphant Wood was himself a form of legalised part-time pirate, operating against shipping belonging to Scotland's enemies.

In 1555, when a state of 'cold war' existed between England and Scotland, the English

A MOVABLE GALLOWS

There was no permanent gallows at Leith, and the rope was erected on any convenient stretch of sand, or even the pier. It was generally stated as being 'within the floodmark', because piracy was dealt with by the High Court of Admiralty, whose jurisdiction covered the seas as far as the limit of the tides on the shores of Britain. The general area of the executions was north of the present-day Constitution Street, in what is now the complex of basins and developments of Leith Docks.

Leith Docks in the early nineteenth century. (From Modern Athens *by Thomas H. Shepherd, 1829)*

vessel *Kait of Lynne* captured several supply ships bound for the French army in Scotland. The *Kait*'s captain, Hilbert Stalfurde, and two of his crew were subsequently hanged in Leith as pirates, although it could be argued that the capture was an act of war, not piracy.

SACRIFICES MUST BE MADE

Something much nastier took place in 1705, which saw the fallout of larger political events claim a number of unrelated (and innocent) victims. The financial catastrophe of the Darien Scheme in Central America meant that Scottish assets worldwide were seized in lieu of payment of debts. The *Annandale* was one of those assets, and the ship was seized in the Thames Estuary and subsequently sold by the East India Company. With anti-English sentiment running high because of this kind of thing, the East India ship *Worcester* had the misfortune to put in to a Fife port in search of repairs. In reprisal for the events in the Thames, the *Worcester*

8

PIRATICAL HANGOVERS

Although capital punishment for murder was abolished in the UK in 1969, in theory the sentence of hanging could still be handed down for two crimes: treason, and piracy with violence. In 1998 these ceased to be capital offences for civilians, but it was not until 2004 that hanging was taken off the statute book for members of the armed forces found guilty of treason or piracy.

was seized by the Scottish authorities. Some of her crew intimated that the *Worcester* had attacked a ship, the *Speedy Return*, belonging to the Scottish India Trading Company. The event supposedly took place off the Malabar coast of India, and all those on board were alleged to have been slaughtered, the cargo plundered and the ship sold. Captain Green and thirteen of his crew were immediately indicted on charges of piracy and murder on the high seas.

The trial was a farce, with flimsy or fabricated evidence. All the accused were found guilty, and sentenced to hang. The executions were delayed due to political pressure from both England and Scotland, as the prospective Act of Union between the two countries was under discussion, and it was feared that the obvious miscarriage of justice would jeopardise the negotiations. In addition, Captain Drummond, who had supposedly been murdered on board the

Speedy Return, was known to be alive, and other members of the ship's crew had arrived back in England. It seemed as if the story of the attack was completely false.

A move was made to pardon all of Green's crew, but the Edinburgh mob was having none of it. On the day of the scheduled executions, a crowd tens of thousands strong attacked senior figures of the Privy Council on the streets, including the Lord Chancellor. In a desperate attempt to appease the fury of the mob, a compromise was quickly put into place: Green, the first mate John Madder, and gunner James Simpson were the sacrificial pawns. They were hanged at Leith on 11 April 1705. After enough time had elapsed for people to forget their passions, the rest of the crew were quietly released. Green was remembered in the ballads of the time as a bloody and ruthless pirate, when almost certainly he was innocent of the charge.

1822

DUEL!

ONE OF THE last duels in Britain was fought on 26 March 1822, when James Stuart of Dunearn shot and killed Sir Alexander Boswell. It was a classic case of upper-class pigheadedness resulting in a needless death.

The early nineteenth century was characterised by vicious party politics between supporters of the Whigs and Tories. Newspapers and journals, covertly funded by one side or the other, often carried barbed personal attacks that edged into outright slander. In 1821 an Edinburgh Tory paper, *The Beacon*, said a great many rude things about James Stuart, a prominent Whig lawyer and landowner. Stuart responded in robust fashion, charging into the paper's offices in Parliament Square and horsewhipping the printer, Duncan Stevenson. Stevenson challenged Stuart to a duel, but the Whig grandee refused to respond, as Stevenson was not a 'gentleman', and only gentlemen fought duels.

The row escalated, with several Tories, including Sir Walter Scott, now publicly funding *The Beacon*. When the paper started libelling Whig grandee James Gibson of Ingliston, Gibson threatened to challenge Scott to a duel. Scott had no desire to be looking down the business end of a pistol, and so was forced to withdraw his support. Starved of funds, *The Beacon* folded. The story did not end there, however, as another Tory publication, the Glasgow-based *Sentinel*, kept up the attacks on Stuart. In the course of an unrelated court case, Stuart acquired some handwritten documents that revealed the author of the most scurrilous pieces to be Sir Alexander Boswell, hitherto unsuspected in the calumny. Boswell, the son of James Boswell, the famous biographer of Dr Johnson, had been a successful MP and had purchased a

IS THERE A DOCTOR IN THE HOUSE?

In 1802 two medical students fought a duel at Duddingston. The first two shots appeared to have missed. Each man reloaded and fired again. Once more, no damage seemed to have been done, so Mr Leckie came over to shake the hand of his opponent, Mr Romney. Only then did he realise he had been hit in the groin. Leckie died four days later.

baronetcy. Stuart asked Boswell to either deny he was the author of the offending pieces, or to apologise. Boswell refused. As the *Sentinel* pieces had accused Stuart of cowardice, it became a matter of honour. With neither side backing down, a duel was inevitable.

Recognising that trouble was brewing, the sheriff ordered both men to keep the peace within Edinburgh and the county of Midlothian. The duellists simply relocated to Auchtertoul, in Fife. At noon on 26 March 1822 a piece of ground was solemnly chosen by the two seconds, the Honourable John Douglas and the Earl of Rosslyn. The latter described what happened:

There were but two pistols, of which Mr Douglas took one, and I took the other. The ground was measured first, immediately after loading the pistols, at 12 very long paces. The distance was intimated to the two parties by Mr Douglas, and by me, and it was agreed that they should fire together by our word. They both fired, and Sir Alexander fell.

A how-to guide for duellists and swordsmen. (Author's collection)

Of all the reasons for violent death, duelling was one of the most stupid. The act itself was for many years a capital crime, being legally regarded as little more than formalised murder (or assault, if no one actually died). The trial of James Stuart lasted eighteen hours (in those days court cases went on without a break until a conclusion was reached). After consulting for just a few minutes, the jury declared him not guilty of murder.

WORKING-CLASS DUELLISTS

Edinburgh had its fair share of duellists, and not all of them had titles to their names. On 2 April 1600, for example, Robert Auchmuty, a barber, killed James Wauchope during a duel on St Leonard's Hill (the records do not tell us what they argued about). Locked up in the Tolbooth, Auchmuty pretended to be sick and blocked off the light from the windows with his cloak. Now unsupervised, he poured *aqua fortis*, a solution of nitric acid in water, on the bars. When the iron was eaten through, he readied an escape rope and arranged for his apprentice to give a signal when the guards went off duty. Unfortunately for him, however, the waving of the handkerchief was spotted, and his cunning plan was foiled. Ten days later Auchmuty lost his head to the Maiden.

Other executed duellists included: William Douglas (killed a man in Leith after a dispute in a tavern, 1667); tailor William Mackay (killed a soldier during a swordfight in the King's Park, 1670); and James Gray (killed a man outside a tavern, 1678). In 1708 a young man named Baird of Saughtonhall was lucky to escape punishment after a dispute in a tavern in Leith, and a shared coach ride to the Netherbow, resulted in Robert Oswald being on the receiving end of a fatal sword thrust. In each of these cases, alcohol had been a key factor in the argument.

Death takes a duellist. (From The English Dance of Death, *1815)*

'YOU ARE A SCOUNDREL, SIR'

Much more refined (but equally pointless) was an aristocratic dispute from 1790. Captain James Macrae of Marionville in Restalrig felt himself insulted by a footman during a visit to the theatre, and beat him severely. The servant was in the employ of Lady Ramsay, and on the following day Macrae apologised to both her ladyship, and her husband, Sir George Ramsay. Sir George answered that the servant had indeed been insolent, and as far as he was concerned that was the end of the matter.

The following week, Monday 12 April, the footman, James Merry, brought an action against Macrae for assault. At 2 p.m. on Tuesday Macrae wrote to Sir George asking him to either instruct Merry to drop the prosecution, or to dismiss him from his service. At 3.30 p.m. Sir George wrote back stating that he saw no reason to interfere. By the evening Macrae had responded via a hand-delivered note:

I must now once more insist on your servant being turned off; and have in consequence sent my friend Mr Amory, to know your final determination. In case you refuse to comply with what I have demanded of you, he will inform you of the opinion I entertain of your conduct. I am, Sir, your hum. Servant.

Sir George repeated to Mr Amory that he had been given no good reason to intervene in a matter that rested solely between the footman and Captain Macrae. At which point Amory gave Macrae's pre-prepared response – that Mr Macrae looked upon him not as a gentleman but the contrary, as a scoundrel. In the coded language of polite society, that was the equivalent of a spit in the face.

At noon on Wednesday 14 April, Sir George and Captain Macrae, accompanied by their seconds, met on the sands at Musselburgh. For two hours the seconds shuttled back and forth between the two grim-faced opponents, attempting to find a form of words that both could agree to. It was all in vain. Standing 14 yards apart, each man took aim and, at the drop of a handkerchief, fired simultaneously. Macrae was wounded on the cheek, but Ramsay suffered a wound that killed him two days later. Macrae and his second fled abroad.

1824

FIRE!

I can conceive no sight more grand or terrible than to see those lofty buildings on fire from top to bottom, vomiting out flames like a volcano from every aperture, and finally crashing down one after another into an abyss of fire, which resembled nothing but hell; for there were vaults of wine and spirits, which sent up huge jets of flames wherever they were called into activity by the fall of these massive fragments!

(Sir Walter Scott, 18 November 1824)

The Great Fire of 1824 destroyed much of the Old Town, annihilating tenements that stretched, skyscraper-like, up to fourteen storeys high. It raged for three days and killed thirteen people, including two firefighters. It also led to a sea change in the way fires were fought around the country.

THE FIRST DAY OF FIRE

The fire started on the evening of 15 November at Kirkwood's Workshop, a copperplate printers engaged in the engraving of maps and Scottish banknotes. An employee apparently forgot to blow out a candle at the end of his shift. The printhouse was located on the second floor of a seven-

storey building in Old Assembly Close, one of the many narrow lanes running off the High Street part of the Royal Mile – it is between St Giles' Cathedral and Cockburn Street. This part of the Old Town was vastly overcrowded,

The Tron Kirk, as rebuilt after the fire of 1824. (From Modern Athens by Thomas H. Shepherd, 1829)

and within an hour the flames had reached the roof and had spread to the neighbouring tenements. These included the offices of the *Edinburgh Courant* newspaper, as well as a bookbinder's. The flammable paper stocks in these businesses helped the fire rage unchecked.

As it happened, the Edinburgh Fire Establishment had been formed just a few months earlier, the first municipal fire brigade in Britain. Although lacking training and equipment, the force responded quickly, pulling their hand-hauled fire engines through the streets from their station on the Royal Mile. Ladders 45ft high were rushed down from the castle through the High Street by hand. Unfortunately, Old Assembly Close, Borthwick's Close and Old Fishmarket Close were too narrow for the vehicles, and there was also a problem raising sufficient water pressure. The townspeople formed bucket lines, bringing water from the wells on the Royal Mile to the firefighters, but confusion reigned because every petty official present insisted on giving orders – which often contradicted what someone else had said a

few minutes' earlier. By 11 p.m. the original building was an inferno, and spreading. Sparks drifted down the sloping wind tunnels of the narrow closes, setting fire to dwellings in the Cowgate below.

THE SECOND DAY OF FIRE

By the morning the main fire seemed to have burned itself out; but around midday the flames had engulfed the seventeenth-century Tron Kirk (now the Visitor Information Centre at the corner of High Street and South Bridge). The great bell fused and crashed to the ground, the spire was destroyed, and molten lead from the roof ran through the streets. With immense bravery the firemen tackled the blaze, and eventually brought in under control. That was to the east of the original fire; now, after an apparent pause of a few hours, windborne sparks spread west up the High Street and ignited an eleven-storey tenement in Parliament Square. Once again the fire engines had great difficulty reaching this location, with the result that,

Parliament House, Parliament Square. (From Modern Athens *by Thomas H. Shepherd, 1829)*

BLAZE UPON BLAZE

⬥⬥⬥

Edinburgh's timber buildings and overpopulated urban density was always an accident waiting to happen. After several fires in the seventeenth century, a great blaze in 1700 destroyed several tall tenements around Parliament Square – on the very spot which saw the worst destruction during the 1824 fire. On 7 December 2002 a tall building on Cowgate that reached as high as South Bridge caught on fire, and it took three days for the fire to be finally controlled.

⬥⬥⬥

as on the previous day, adjoining structures were caught up in the conflagration, including part of the court buildings. The overcrowding of the Old Town, combined with the narrowness of many closes and the height of the buildings, not only gave further fuel to the fire, but also prevented its effective containment.

THE THIRD DAY OF FIRE

On the third day, 17 November, the majority of the fires were extinguished, largely through a fortuitous fall of rain and sleet. When the smoke finally cleared, the extent of the destruction was clear. Much of the heart of the Royal Mile was a wasteland, with a trail of collapsed and burned-out buildings stretching for almost 200 yards, the damage extending down the slope to Cowgate. Two people had been killed by falling masonry, while another eleven, including two firefighters, had perished in smoke or flames. Over 1,000 people were homeless, and were given temporary shelter in Queensberry House on Canongate. Damage was estimated at £200,000 (over £8 million in today's terms). Despite the best efforts of the nascent fire brigade, the fire control measures had only been partially successful, and the blaze could well have continued for longer had nature not intervened. It was clear that changes needed to be made.

The brigade was headed by the energetic and far-sighted James Braidwood, Edinburgh's 'master of fire engines'. He reorganised the force, bringing in new equipment and putting an emphasis on intensive training. He also wrote what became the definitive manual on firefighting. Crucially, he insisted that in all future emergencies, the fire master had absolute authority on the scene, giving a clear and straightforward chain of command. After a decade in Edinburgh, Braidwood moved south to found the London Fire Brigade. A statue to this 'father of modern firefighting' stands in Parliament Square on the Royal Mile, close to the location of the fiercest inferno of the Great Fire of 1824. The Museum of Fire on Lauriston Place – a fascinating visit – has one of the original hand-hauled fire engines that was used to tackle the Great Fire.

BURKE AND HARE

– Serial Killers!

BURKE AND HARE are the world's most famous bodysnatchers. Which is strange, considering they never snatched a body in their lives.

No, what Burke and Hare were were murderers. Bodysnatchers, also known as resurrection-men, entered graveyards and dug up corpses for sale to the anatomists. This was dangerous work, as there was always the chance of being arrested or coming to the notice of an angry mob. Burke and Hare cut out this aspect of the trade, and simply sold the fresh corpses of those they had just murdered. Between November 1827 and October 1828 they slaughtered sixteen people in cold blood, a toll which makes them the most prolific serial-killing duo in British history. Killing people for profit was easy, as Hare ran a cheap lodging house where the guests were at the very bottom of the social heap. Such destitutes could vanish without anyone noticing. Even today we do not know the names of six of the victims, and another two are only recorded by their first names.

BODYSNATCHERS AND THE LAW

Bodysnatching had first started in the mid-eighteenth century. Edinburgh had the largest and most highly regarded medical school in Scotland. To pass his degree, every student had to dissect a corpse. But the only bodies available for medical education came from those who had been executed for murder. People hanged for other crimes, from theft to incest, were simply buried, whereas murderers were granted the additional punishment of being cut up *post mortem*. With a huge deficit in the number of bodies available, medical students were forced to dig up graves, break open coffins and extract the required corpses. By around 1815 to 1820 the demand for cadavers was so high that the trade was overtaken by career criminals, who recognised a nice little earner

Burke and Hare removing the body of Hare's lodger from its coffin – their first sale. (Courtesy of Cate Ludlow)

The first murder by Burke and Hare, using their standard suffocation method, which left an unmarked (and therefore more valuable) corpse. (Courtesy of Cate Ludlow)

when they saw one. To give you an indication of the character of these criminals, one, 'Merry' Andrew, dug up the body of his own sister and sold it for a tidy sum.

BURKE AND HARE, AT YOUR SERVICE

Burke and Hare weren't part of this criminal fraternity. They entered the world of corpse-supply by accident. One of Hare's elderly tenants died, leaving an unpaid debt for rent. Struck by an idea, the two men removed the body before it could be buried, and, rather amateurishly, managed to sell it to a well-to-do anatomist in Surgeons' Square. In exchange they received £7 10s, wealth beyond imagining for two Irish immigrants

down on their luck; when they had worked as labourers on the Forth and Clyde, they had received just 2s a day. Over the next twelve months they suffocated sixteen men, women and youths, and usually received around £10 per corpse, depending on the 'quality'. Most of the money they spent on drink.

The two men were aided and abetted by their partners, Margaret Logue and Helen McDougal. Both women participated in at least one murder. Margaret was the actual owner of the lodging house run by Hare, and she always made sure she got a £1 'landlady's fee' for every murder Burke and Hare committed on her premises.

Eventually the killers became careless – targeting well-known street characters who would be missed – and were caught. The problem for the prosecution was that, with the bodies dissected and disposed of, there was no solid evidence. So William

Burke and Hare's female partners participating in one of the murders. (Courtesy of Cate Ludlow)

MORE MEDICAL MURDERERS

Burke and Hare may have been the most efficient murderers-for-money during the anatomists' era, but they had a small number of less effective predecessors. In December 1751 nurses Helen Torrence and Jean Waldie killed nine-year-old John Dallas. They successfully sold the body to an anatomist, but the boy's alcoholic mother raised the alarm, and the partially dissected corpse was later found dumped on the street. As the murder itself could not be proven, Torrence and Waldie were charged with kidnapping the boy and selling the body, and both were hanged in the Grassmarket in February 1752. Then in 1826 a poor Irishwoman offered to sell a surgeon both her two-month-old baby and her thirteen-year-old son, 'whom he could kill or boil or do what he liked with.' She was arrested, and the children continued in life, unmolested by scalpels.

Hare was persuaded to turn King's Evidence in exchange for his freedom. As part of the deal, Margaret Logue was also released. Burke's common-law wife Helen McDougal was prosecuted but not convicted. The only person found guilty of the crimes was William Burke.

BURKE'S BLOOD, SKIN AND BONES

On 28 January 1829 a vast crowd turned out to watch Burke hang. Window seats in the overlooking buildings were rented out at £1 5s each, or 16 per cent of the average value of a fresh corpse. Burke's body was then handed over to Professor Alexander Munro of Edinburgh University, and publicly dissected in a packed-to-the-rafters anatomy theatre. Thousands of people filed past the corpse before the anatomy class began. The Surgeons' Hall Museum on Nicolson Street, home of the Royal College of Surgeons, has William Burke's death mask, plus a pocketbook fashioned out of Burke's skin. The Anatomy Resource Centre of the University Medical School on Teviot Place (not usually open to the public) has Burke's actual articulated skeleton on display. After the dissection, Munro picked up his quill and scribbled a note: 'This is written with the blood of Wm Burke, who was hanged at Edinburgh on 28th Jan. 1829 for the Murder of Mrs Campbell or Docherty. The blood was taken from his head on the 1st of Fe. 1829.'

Following the trial, the word 'burking', meaning to kill by suffocation or strangulation, entered the English language. Bodysnatching ceased after the Anatomy Act of 1832 changed the way corpses could be procured legally.

1850

EDINBURGH'S DEADLIEST RESIDENTS!

OF ALL THE means of committing murder, poison attracts a particular horror. There is something about the insidious, invisible nature of the crime that strikes a certain chord within us. The use of poison also typically suggests a domestic context, with family members quietly trying to bump each other off and remain undetected. Who knows what dark secrets lurk behind the respectable façades of Edinburgh's households?

Marriages rarely go well if one partner is a secret bigamist. William Bennison married Jane Hamilton in Paisley in 1839, neglecting to mention that he had already wed Mary Mullen in Portadown, in his native Ireland. But that didn't really cause any problems, as Mary later mysteriously disappeared on her way to join William in Airdrie. According to William, she had become fatally ill on the voyage over to Scotland, and he, lacking funds for a proper funeral, had buried her in a pauper's grave. By 1850 William was working in an Edinburgh iron foundry and he, Jane and their daughter were living in a tenement on Leith Walk. Meanwhile, William was assiduously but subtly courting another woman, Margaret Robertson, a fellow member of his Methodist Church. (Margaret later stated that she had had no idea her fellow worshipper was even interested in her.) William obviously thought it was a good idea for his wife to conveniently die, so he purchased twopence worth of arsenic from the local chemists' – 'for the rats,' he said. That evening he made Jane some porridge. She was stricken with stomach cramps, lingering for three days. During her agonising illness, William seemed unconcerned, and made no efforts to call a doctor.

Jane was buried without a post-mortem, and from William's point of view, all seemed well. But then a dog that had eaten the remains of the porridge was found dead. The neighbours voiced their suspicions to the police, and eventually Jane's body was exhumed. Tests showed a high concentration of arsenic in her stomach. After just a short consultation, the jury unanimously declared William guilty of her murder. Twenty thousand spectators gathered for the hanging on 16 August 1850. A street ballad of the time described the scene:

Great was the throng to see him hung
For crimes that were so vile.
To Edinburgh upon that day
They tramped for many a mile.
They led him out all clad in black –
Black coat and vest so white –
A mocking smile was on his lips,
He wore a nosegay bright.

It seems likely that William Bennison had murdered his first wife as well.

THE ARSENIC KILLER

John Hutchinson had problems. He was massively in debt, and everything, including his car, had been repossessed. His parents, however, were well off. John saw a solution. On 3 February 1911 his parents held a party in Dalkeith to celebrate their fiftieth wedding anniversary. During the celebration the finest fresh coffee was handed round, John himself being in charge of the cups. Within minutes the party turned into a nightmare, with fifteen people struck with severe vomiting and stomach pains. Two – John's father, Charles, and a grocer named Clapperton – died. Tests showed that the coffee was laced with arsenic. John was a chemist, with easy access to the poison. As the law closed in around him, he fled, first to London, and then to the Channel Isles. In Guernsey he was recognised, and, rather than face arrest, he himself swallowed a fatal dose of arsenic.

POISON CHEESE

William Laurie King was a dedicated amateur chemist. In May 1924 he was conducting yet another experiment in the laboratory outhouse at his parents' home in Wester Coates Terrace. The extraction of magenta dye from coal tar required a considerable quantity of arsenious oxide: arsenic. Realising he could not obtain enough of the controlled substance just by going to the local pharmacy, William found a simple solution to the problem: he forged an invoice from the garage where he worked part time, and was swiftly in possession of 1lb of the substance.

Four days later William's father, a chartered accountant, complained that some home-made cheese he had just eaten was burning his mouth. His wife, possibly miffed at the implied criticism of her cooking, determinedly ate a second slice. William had a small piece, while his brother Alexis had none. Later that night the whole family, with the exception of Alexis, was violently ill. By two in the morning Mrs King was dead. The verdict: arsenic poisoning.

William was put on trial for murder. His case was not helped by his attempt to obscure his possession of the arsenic, but then the truth came out. His mother had confiscated the bag of arsenious oxide as being dangerous. It lay on a shelf in the pantry, with one damaged corner leaking minute quantities. The arsenic had probably trickled into the cheese as it was setting. The jury considered that if William had intended to murder his parents, then keeping the murder weapon in an easily discovered place was just plain stupid. He was acquitted of the charge.

DATE-RAPE DRUGS, SEVENTEENTH-CENTURY STYLE

In 1682 Janet Stewart, a servant attending an Edinburgh dinner party, was induced to swallow a 'sweet' by a gentlewoman named Mistress Elizabeth Edmondstoun. The young girl fell into a fever that lasted for twenty days. This was not the intended effect – the apothecary who had created the tablet, James Aikenhead, had told Mistress Edmondstoun that it would produce 'strange wanton affections and humours in the bodies of women'. In other words, it was an involuntary aphrodisiac. We can imagine what intentions Mistress Edmondstoun's guests had for the servant girl. As it was, it seemed the resulting fever left her permanently unwell.

1864

HANGED BY THE NECK
UNTIL YE BE DEAD

He rushed in, went straight to the nursery and leaped on Jane Seaton like a wild beast. He dashed her to the ground, and would have strangled her had not her mistress come to the rescue. Bewildered for a moment by the shower of blows which this lady rained on his head with an umbrella, the murderer relaxed his hold. The girl started to her feet, and fled like a frightened deer from the house. Bryce pursued her like a staghound whose quarry had wrenched itself with lacerated flank from his blood-dripping fangs. Just as she raised her hand to the latch of a cottage in which she would have been safe, the villain once more seized her, and before any one could interpose, he had cut her throat from ear to ear.

This sensational account from the New Zealand paper *The Otago Daily Times* (20 August 1864) indicates how the case of 'the Ratho Murderer' attracted international attention. The killer, George Bryce, had become convinced that Jane Seaton had influenced Isabella Brown's decision to end her relationship with him. After stalking the young nursemaid for two weeks, he killed her in March 1864, in the village of Ratho, which is now just west of Edinburgh Airport. Bryce had attempted suicide several times and was

probably mentally ill; his plea of temporary insanity was disregarded and he was found guilty by a unanimous vote of the jury. He became the last person to be executed in public in Edinburgh.

Thirty-year-old Bryce met his doom at 8.20 a.m. on Midsummer's Day, 21 June 1864. Many people still regarded an execution as entertainment, so more than 26,000 congregated around the scaffold at the top of Libberton's Wynd, on the Lawnmarket, just below Castlehill. The *Edinburgh Evening Courant* described the scene:

The black timbers of the gallows presented a horrible aspect in the twilight hours – for there was no darkness – and in the strong light of the full moon, which, excepting when occasionally veiled by murky clouds, shone upon the dismal scene. As daylight advanced the crowd increased, every road leading to the High Street contributing its almost continuous stream. The body of the crowd nearest the scene consisted chiefly of the roughest portion of the community. Some of the women had children in their arms, and others had their little ones with them, whom they occasionally held up. Shop lads and shop girls were present in large numbers just before the hour of going to business.

A crowd enjoying a public execution on the Royal Mile. (Courtesy of Cate Ludlow)

When Bryce appeared, the crowd erupted in a frenzy of catcalls, insults and missiles (mostly rotten vegetables). Despite the enjoyment of the crowd, many people in the upper echelons of Victorian society were changing the way they felt about public executions: suffering was no longer regarded as a fit public spectacle. As a result, the lower part of the scaffold was now obscured by a black screen: once the condemned man was dropped through the trap door, no one could witness his death struggles. As it turned out, this was a good thing, since the executioner, James Askern, bungled the job and Bryce slowly strangled to death over several minutes.

THE PRIVATISATION OF DEATH

Four years later the Capital Punishment Amendment Act made public executions illegal; from now on, all condemned criminals were to breathe their last in private, within the walls of prisons. Diagonally opposite Deacon Brodie's Tavern on the Royal Mile,

a brass plaque commemorates Bryce's execution, as being the last public hanging in Edinburgh.

The first execution under the new regime took place on 31 May 1878. Eugene Marie Chantrelle, a French teacher, was hanged for the murder of his wife Elizabeth. Chantrelle was a violent man who frequently abused his much younger spouse. Having insured her life for £1,000 (£45-50,000 in today's currency), Chantrelle poisoned Elizabeth with an opiate and broke a gas main in the bedroom: if it appeared that his wife had died of an accidental inhalation of gas, Chantrelle could collect the insurance.

Initially it seemed as if he had got away with it, as the post-mortem suggested death by coal-gas poisoning. But traces of opium were then found in the dead woman's vomit, and Chantrelle was arrested. Found guilty after a four-day trial, he proceeded to lecture the court on the chemistry of opium and morphia before finally being told to hold his peace.

One of the curiosities of the Chantrelle case is that the prosecution was unofficially

The new jail on Calton Hill, site of all executions after 1868. (From Modern Athens *by Thomas H. Shepherd, 1829)*

assisted by Dr Joseph Bell, the man widely regarded as both 'the father of forensic science' and the model for Sherlock Holmes. Holmes' creator, Arthur Conan Doyle, had been Bell's clerk.

Chantrelle was launched into eternity within the walls of Calton Jail. Thousands of people took up positions on Calton Hill overlooking the prison, but their view was thwarted by the erection of screens. The executioner was William Marwood of Lincolnshire, who despatched the wife-killer while the Lord's Prayer was still being read.

MURDERERS UNDER THE CAR PARK

Calton Jail was demolished in the 1930s, and the site is now home to the massive edifice of St Andrew's House, the home of the Scottish Government (not the Scottish Parliament, which is on Canongate). In 1878 Eugene Marie Chantrelle was buried in the prison yard, as were seven other murderers over the following fifty years:

Robert Flockhart Vickers and William Innes (31 March 1884). The poachers had murdered gamekeeper James Grosset on a Midlothian estate.

Jessie King, the 'Stockbridge Baby Farmer' (11 March 1889). King was paid to look after unwanted children, and murdered at least two of them.

John Herdman (12 May 1898), executed for the astonishingly brutal murder of his common-law wife Jane Calder at their home in Milne's Close. 'She suffered the worst human injuries I have ever seen,' the police surgeon told the court.

Patrick Higgins (2 October 1913), hanged for throwing his sons, aged four and seven, into the waters of the disused quarry at Niddry Mains Farm. He was

MURDER IN THE FAMILY

George Bryce was not the first person in his family to face the hangman's drop. On 3 April 1844 George's uncle, James Bryce, was executed in front of a crowd of 30,000 for the murder of his brother-in-law, John Geddes. Geddes had refused to advance the impecunious labourer another loan, and so James beat and strangled him to death, and ran off with £6 in silver. Twenty years later, his nephew made the same last walk to the gallows.

arrested when, having been underwater for eighteen months, their tethered bodies finally rose to the surface.

John Henry Savage (11 June 1923), found guilty of cutting the throat of Jemima Nicholson in a house in Bridge Street, Leith; both Savage and Nicholson were alcoholics.

Philip Murray (30 October 1923). Murray lived off the earnings of prostitute Catherine Donoghue. One night, very drunk, he argued with one of Donoghue's 'johns' in her house on Jamaica Street, and pushed William Ronald Cree out of the window to his death. Murray was the last person to hang in Edinburgh.

Visitors to St Andrew's House may unwittingly park their cars over the graves of these murderers – because their last resting place is now under the car park.

1916

THE NIGHT OF THE ZEPPELINS

THIRTEEN PEOPLE KILLED. Twenty-four injured. Property damage (in today's terms) in excess of £11 million. And all in forty-five minutes of floursack-sized bombs being dropped by hand from a lumbering bag of gas.

The night of Sunday 2 April 1916 saw the only air raid on Edinburgh during the First World War. Four Zeppelins had set out on the moonlit night to attack the naval base of Rosyth and Royal Navy warships at anchor in the Firth of Forth. But aerial navigation was in its infancy – the crews had to try to work out where they were by following landmarks, and the lighter-than-air vessels were easily blown off course – and so one Zeppelin simply got lost, while a second unloaded its bombs harmlessly over Northumberland. A third, *L22*, just made it to Edinburgh but only caused superficial damage. It was left to the Imperial German Navy Zeppelin *L14*, commanded by Kapitänleutnant Aloys Böcker, to drop death and fire from the skies over the city.

WHISKY GALORE

The principal target was never spotted by the Zeppelin, which probably mistook Leith Docks on the south shore of the Firth of Forth for the naval base of Rosyth on the north shore. The battle cruisers lying at anchor below the Forth Bridge were also untroubled. Fortunately for Kapitänleutnant Böcker, many merchant and small ships lying up alongside Leith were fully lit up, providing a perfect marker. After failing to make a major impact on the docks, around ten to midnight the raider scored a direct hit on the bonded whisky warehouse of Messrs Innes & Grieve. The inferno lit up the surrounding area, making both navigation and the selection of targets that much easier. The exploding casks flooded the streets with whisky, prompting men, women and children to rush out armed with bottles and jugs to collect the 'stagger juice'. What could not be saved was drunk out of cupped hands on the spot, and soon Leith was awash with not just whisky, but whisky-sozzled citizens and sailors.

Several more bombs were dropped on Leith, and the *L14* followed the moonlight reflecting off the Water of Leith towards the Old Town, and then ranged as far south as Prestonfield and Causewayside, before changing course to hit the West End. In total, twenty-four bombs were dropped, six of which were incendiary and the rest high-explosive. The National Museum of Flight at East Fortune, 20 miles east of Edinburgh, has one of the unexploded bombs from that night. It still has the metal handles on the top – these bombs were dropped by a crewmember hanging over the side of the gondola holding on to the looped handles, and just letting go. It was hardly precision bombardment.

CIVILIAN CASUALTIES

Not surprisingly, this extremely basic form of aerial warfare meant that bombs intended for strategic targets such as railways often hit civilian targets. In Bonnington a one-year-old boy died in his crib when a bomb exploded on a railway siding. A sixty-six-year-old man was killed in his bed at Commercial Street in Leith. At 183 Causewayside four tenement dwellers were hurt, and a seventy-one-year-old woman later died from her injuries. One man was killed and three injured outside the White Hart Hotel on the Grassmarket. A four-year-old child perished at a tenement at 69 St Leonard's Hill. The occupants of 39 Lauriston Place survived a direct hit but a man standing in Graham Street (now Keir Street), some 80 yards away, was killed by shrapnel. And at 16 Marshall Street a number of people who had taken refuge in the open doorway of a tenement entrance were showered with blast debris when a high-explosive bomb landed on the pavement. Seven died, while six were injured. Among

the total number of victims on the night were a tramway inspector and a magistrate.

Several of the bombs landed on the open spaces of King's Park and the Meadows, doing little damage. An incendiary bomb failed to set fire to the Royal Infirmary. A bomb aimed at the castle missed and

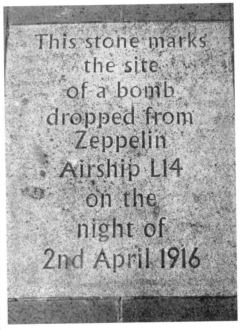

A flagstone in the Grassmarket commemorating the Zeppelin raid. (Kim Trayner, under the Creative Commons Attribution-Share Alike 3.0 Unported license)

THE BIRTH OF THE ZEPPELINS

The first Zeppelin flight took place in 1900, at Lake Constance in Germany, the brainchild of Count Ferdinand Graf von Zeppelin. By 1910 Zeppelins were taking passengers on scheduled commercial flights between Berlin and Lake Constance. When the First World War broke out four years later, the Zeppelins were adapted to a new form of warfare – aerial bombing. In the first few months of the war, as part of the psychology of 'war fever', hundreds of false Zeppelin sightings were reported from all over the UK, including many places where it was impossible for the airships to reach. It was only from 1916 onwards that Zeppelin technology improved enough to reach areas further than the south-east of England.

LUFTWAFFE OVER EDINBURGH

Compared to other British cities, Edinburgh got off quite lightly during the Second World War. Between 1940 and 1942 a small number of air raids killed eighteen people and injured more than 200. The largest loss of life occurred on 22 July 1940, when eight fatalities were reported. On 5 November the same year, Edinburgh Zoo was hit, killing several animals and releasing other occupants into the streets.

The first shots of the air war were fired above the Firth of Forth on 16 October 1939, when Spitfires from Drem and Turnhouse airfields shot down two Junkers Ju 88 bombers that were attempting to attack warships moored in the Firth.

In 1941 two Spitfires on a training exercise collided above Edinburgh. One of the aircraft plummeted to earth, the pilot's parachute failing to open. In September 2010 the remains of the crashed fighter plane were unearthed in Edinburgh's Royal Botanic Gardens.

glanced off Castle Rock, the stone shards annihilating all the windows on Castle Terrace. There was extensive damage to the County Hotel on Lothian Road, George Watson's College on Archibald Place in Lauriston, the School for Children with Skin Disease, the Royal Infirmary Jubilee Wing, the Corn Exchange on Grassmarket, and a nursing home on Chalmers Street. Elsewhere dozens of houses and shops were hit, some to the point of total destruction. Many of the properties, including the whisky warehouse, were not insured against enemy action.

It must have been an eerie sight for the citizens, who were out in the streets in their hundreds, drawn by the tumult. The huge, elongated gasbag of the Zeppelin was clearly visible above them, and the throb of the engines filled the night sky. When there were no bombs falling, it must have been a compelling vision. For most people it would have been the first time they had seen an airship. And it was certainly the first time that the people of Edinburgh had been bombarded from the sky.

FIRING BLANKS AT THE BOMBERS

With just a few exceptions – such as the halting of the trams and the lowering of the electric streetlights – Edinburgh was almost entirely unprepared for such an attack. There were no anti-aircraft defences. The only resistance the city could offer was some occasional small-arms fire from the southern slopes of Arthur's Seat – which could never reach the height of the Zeppelin – and the firing of the celebrated One O'Clock Gun into the air. As the latter was a purely ceremonial field gun that was loaded with blank ammunition, this was hardly an effective response. A lone fighter did take off from East Fortune airfield, but the Avro 504 biplane was entirely unequipped for night flying, and after failing to find the Zeppelins, Flight Lieutenant G.A. Cox of the Royal Flying Corps crash-landed on his return, suffering severe injuries.

As a direct consequence of the raid, three airfields for fighter planes were set up around Edinburgh. One, Turnhouse, survives to this day – as Edinburgh International Airport.

BIBLIOGRAPHY

BOOKS

Alison, Archibald, *Principles of the Criminal Law of Scotland* (W. Blackwood; Edinburgh, 1832)

Arnot, Hugo (ed.), *A Collection and Abridgement of Celebrated Criminal Trials in Scotland, from AD 1536 to 1784* (A. Napier; Glasgow, 1812)

Buchan, John, *The Marquis of Montrose* (Thomas Nelson; London & Edinburgh, 1913)

Chambers, Robert, *Domestic Annals of Scotland, from the Reformation to the Revolution* (W. & R. Chambers; Edinburgh & London, 1859)

Chambers, Robert, *Traditions of Edinburgh* (W. & R. Chambers; Edinburgh, 1868)

Daniel, William S., *History of the Abbey and Palace of Holyrood* (Duncan Anderson; Edinburgh, 1852)

Fife, Malcolm, *The Nor Loch – Scotland's Lost Loch* (Scotforth Books; Lancaster, 2004)

Gillies, J.B., *Edinburgh Past and Present* (Oliphant, Anderson & Ferrier; Edinburgh, 1886)

Grant, James, *Cassell's Old and New Edinburgh: Its history, its people and its places* (Cassell; London, 1887)

Henderson, Jan-Andrew, *Edinburgh: City of the Dead* (Black & White Publishing; Edinburgh, 2004)

Howell, T.B., *A Complete Collection of State Trials and Proceedings for High Treason and Other Crimes and Misdemeanors from the Earliest Period to the Year 1783* (Longman, Hurst, Rees, Orme & Brown; London, 1816)

Hume Brown, Peter, *History of Scotland from the Revolution of 1689 to the Disruption, 1843* (Cambridge University Press; Cambridge, 1911)

Linklater, Eric, *Edinburgh* (Newnes; London, 1960)

MacClure, Victor, *She Stands Accused* (Harrap; London, 1935)

Massie, Allan, *Edinburgh* (Sinclair-Stevenson; London, 1994)

Merriman, Marcus, *The Rough Wooings: Mary Queen of Scots, 1542-1551* (Tuckwell; East Linton, 2000)

Roughead, William, *Twelve Scots Trials* (William Green; Edinburgh & London, 1913)

Russell, John, *The Story of Leith* (Thomas Nelson; London & Edinburgh, 1922)

Scott, Sir Walter, *The Heart of Midlothian* (Oxford University Press; Oxford, 2008 – first published 1818)

Scott, Sir Walter, *Letters on Demonology and Witchcraft* (Wordsworth/The Folklore Society; Ware & London, 2001 – first published 1830)

Sharp, Alan, *A Grim Almanac of Edinburgh & the Lothians* (The History Press; Stroud, 2009)

Shepherd, Thomas H., *Modern Athens, Displayed in a Series of Views, or Edinburgh in the Nineteenth Century* (Jones & Co.; London, 1829)

Smith, A. Duncan, *Trial of Eugene Marie Chantrelle* (William Hodge; Glasgow & Edinburgh, 1906)

Stevenson, David, *The Scottish Revolution 1637-44* (John Donald; Edinburgh, 2006)

Stevenson, David, *Revolution and Counter-Revolution in Scotland, 1644-51* (John Donald; Edinburgh, 2003)

Thomson, James U., *Edinburgh Curiosities 2* (John Donald; Edinburgh, 1997)

Turnbull, Michael T.R.B., *The Edinburgh Book of Days* (The History Press; Stroud, 2011)

Tytler, Patrick Fraser, *History of Scotland*, Vol. 4 (William Tait; Edinburgh, 1842)

Warrand, Duncan (ed.), *More Culloden Papers* (Robert Carruthers; Inverness, 1927)

Watt, Francis, *Edinburgh and the Lothians* (Methuen; London, 1912)

Watt, Francis, *The Book of Edinburgh Anecdote* (T.N. Foulis; London & Edinburgh, 1913)

Williamson, M.G., *Edinburgh: A Historical and Topographical Account of the City* (Methuen; London, 1906)

Wilson, Daniel, *Memorials of Edinburgh in the Olden Time* (Thomas C. Jack; Edinburgh, 1886)

Young, Alex F., *The Encyclopaedia of Scottish Executions, 1750 to 1963* (Eric Dobby; Orpington, 1998)

JOURNALS

Edinburgh Medical & Surgical Journal, Vol. 49 (1838)

The Gentleman's Magazine, Vol. 75 (1805)

MacLennan, W.J., 'The Eleven Plagues of Edinburgh' in *Proceedings of the Royal College of Physicians of Edinburgh* Vol. 31, No. 3 (2001)

The Scots Magazine & Edinburgh Literary Miscellany, Vol. 67 (1810)

Stevenson, David, 'Major Weir: A Justified Sinner?' in *Scottish Studies*, No. 16 (1972)

King Death contemplates his dominion.
(From The English Dance of Death, *1815)*